Tao to Earth

Michael's Guide

to Relationships and Growth

by Jose Stevens, Ph.D.

"This system of knowledge is a way of living your life that makes perfect sense and is fun. It is a way of knowing the truth and the reasons for existence."

-Michael

Tao to Earth

Michael's Guide
to Relationships and Growth

Copyright © 1988 Jose Luis Stevens
First Printing

Published by:

Affinity Press
19 Muth Drive
Orinda, California 94563

I am interested in your views and any further information. Write to the above address.

Printed and bound in the United States.
Cover design by Nina Bookbinder.

LCCN:817-091980
ISBN 0-942663-02-0

Dedication

To Sasha, my loyal friend, and all her fellow creatures.

Acknowledgements

I want to sincerely thank everyone who supported me in the process of getting this book into your hands.

Special thanks are due to a few folks I will mention here.

I want to acknowledge J.P. Van Hulle and Aaron Christeaan for their invaluable assistance in channeling important parts of this book.

I am fortunate in having editorial support from Lonnie McAllister who also assisted me in formatting and preparing the book for printing.

I am thankful to Lenore Schuh for her sense of humor and for her many creative illustrations; Nina Bookbinder for her wonderful cover design; Janet Reed for proofreading.

I am grateful to my wife Lena who gave much helpful advice and supported me in the making of this book.

Thanks are due to Simon Warwick-Smith for writing assistance and for motivating me to get this book out solo. Thanks are also due to Kate Warwick-Smith for her valuable suggestions in the preliminary stages of the book.

Acknowledgements are due to the books *Messages from Michael* and *More Messages from Michael* by Chelsea Quinn Yarbro (Berkeley Books, 1983 and 1986) for introducing the Michael material.

Finally, I wish to thank Michael for his free and unconditional generosity in providing this system of knowledge to whoever is interested.

A Brief Overview

The goal of this body of knowledge is to promote unconditional acceptance of self and others. Of course should you find this a challenge, mild tolerance will suffice to start with.

This knowledge is being re-introduced, as it has been historically during times of great change, to help with the current planetary shift toward the mature soul stage. The people of Earth have been dominated for thousands of years by young soul lessons and play. They have amassed power, wealth, influence, and learned the lessons of competition and personal glory. Now, the majority are ready to grow to a new level of perception. The new mature level of perception focuses on the value of relationships and growth through self understanding.

Accelerated growth is greatly assisted by an understanding of each step in the evolutionary process on the earth and especially a fuller knowledge of the true nature of relationships. Here then is a book about those relationships and each individual's part in the grand scheme.

Although this teaching is not associated with any known philosophy, psychology, or religion, readers will recognize elements of many systems of thought, both Eastern and Western. Perhaps the most recognizable are the works of Gurdjieff and his students, Ouspensky and Rodney Collin, pioneers who began disseminating this knowledge earlier in this century.

More recently, this system of knowledge has been channeled by a variety of competent students who are dedicated to the twin values of self-understanding and unconditional acceptance of others.

Michael, the non-physical source of this information, gives it freely and unconditionally to anyone who is interested. Michael is simply a convenient name for an experienced entity who once lived many lifetimes upon the earth. Michael completed the lessons and games of the physical plane and now compassionately teaches from experience.

Contents

List of Illustrations

Preface

The source of the material in this book is Michael as well as the psyches of the various channels who worked together to access this body of knowledge. A channel is a person who is able to access wisdom from a non-physical source and deliver it accurately through speech, automatic writing, or other technique.

Nevertheless, any channeled information is subject to distortion by the personality of the channel, the time of day, weather factors, and a great number of other variables. By using more than one channel I was able to cross-check and keep the information consistent throughout. Since most channeled information is a one man or woman operation this is not usually possible. Michael is unique in that he is glad to come through a great variety of talented channels. This keeps the teaching fresh, consistent, and non-exclusive.

Michael has always insisted that you validate all channeled information for yourself. This is the only way to truly learn and grow. Therefore do not believe anything you read here. Simply check it out for yourself.

One of my tasks as the author was to organize, edit, and transcribe a vast number of tapes and notes; years' worth of channeled material. My other principal task was to channel information to fill the gaps in the material and create bridges between parts that were isolated from one another. Therefore I wrote much of this book in a light trance state.

The book is divided into six parts so that you can readily find major subject areas. If you wish you can read the book from cover to cover, or you can use it as a reference, looking up areas of interest as you will.

Introduction

This book builds upon the foundation set down in *Essence and Personality: A Michael Handbook.* That book detailed the fascinating relationship between essence and personality and described at length all the facets that make up personality, lifetime after lifetime. It covered soul age development and described the current and coming global transformation in terms of essence development planet-wide.

Here in this book you will forge ahead into the world of relationships, an exciting journey revealing the inner processes and reincarnational meaning of your connections with friends, lovers, and enemies. Here you will discover the workings of karma and maya, the foundation stones of the earth game.

You will gain insight into the deeper meaning of relationships and you will learn about the types of alliances that bring you joy and suffering on your evolutionary path. You will learn about monads, essence twins, cadres, quadrants, septants, families, sex, communication, imprinting, and the power of your position within groups of different size.

Here you will gain the tools to understand the larger context of your relationships and discover how to be more accepting of them or effective at completing them.

Then read on to learn about the tools for personal as well as spiritual growth. Discover how your relationship to the planet itself can accelerate your evolution and bring more satisfaction into your daily life.

Read these pages and enjoy the expansive view that gives you a whole new understanding of all your relationships.

For those of you who may wish to refresh your memory or become acquainted with the Michael system for the first time, I have included a brief review of the basic teachings in Appendix A. Reading this section will help tremendously in understanding the concepts upon which this book is based.

PART ONE

GETTING DOWN TO EARTH

Chapter One

Arrival

The Tao (or God) thinking aloud.

I am pure light, speeding toward my chosen goal, physical reality and earth life. As I travel, I explode into thousands of fragments and "I" becomes "We." We gradually feel ourselves slowing down to accomodate physical form. Now we have arrived and we're ready to play.

Will we like it here on this watery planet called earth? Well, after all we created it! Nevertheless we'll spend some time finding out whether we want to evolve here or pursue another line of experience. After being perfectly whole and "One" for so long, we're looking for diversity, uniqueness, and individuality. Yet we must begin with a global experience and gradually move toward separateness in order to get used to it. Let's see. Where do we start? That's it. We'll combine with the planet itself, experience its myriad forms, and re-create as we go. We'll travel through the mineral, plant and animal kingdoms

*and get to know them by living out a variety of their lives. We'll
prepare long and well for our first human lives. As we begin those
infant lives, we'll pretend to be separate and alone. Gradually
we'll learn from one another what we forgot. That we're all one.
Our relationships will enable us. The law of karma will teach us.
Our challenges will focus us. Love will remind us. Let's play.*

ARRIVAL

What is the order of this gradual preparation for human
form? How do you set up each individual lifetime? What are the
key relationships that enable you to progress in your evolution
toward self understanding? Here we will reveal to you that order
so that you may know the vastness of the life you have chosen.
We will reveal the way you play with the other fragments that
you arrived here with. In this book you will find the
relationships and configurations that underlie the incredible
play of consciousness. Have fun and learn what you already once
knew and are about to remember.

YOUR RELATIONSHIP TO THE PLANET

You have seen how you sprang from the Tao as sparks of light
to become fragments of an entity or family of consciousness. As a
fragment you have taken multiple human lives progressing in the
difficult and fast-learning school of earth through the infant to
old soul stages in order to contribute to your entity's overall
experience.

Let's return to the time before you became human. Who and
what were you before you took the human form? How did you
prepare for your human lives? In this section you will learn in
more detail how you chose to leave the womb of the Tao to
develop your relationship with the physical plane.

You arrive on the earth not yet as infant souls ready for
human life but as pure abstract energy wishing to experience the
very foundations of the planet itself. You choose to experience

mountain and sea, cloud and river, plant and insect, fish and mammal, on the road to human life.

In spirit form you use these primary experiences to make choices about whether you wish to continue toward sentience and if so, what path you will pursue. At any juncture you may choose to opt for a different line of creativity, a different developmental arena of experience that does not necessarily lead to human form. Yet all of you in human form have chosen this option because of your personal interest and curiosity about the experience of intelligent, binocular bipeds, that you inhabit and live through. How's that for a detached look at yourselves?

Exactly what is your developmental course like and what is the structure of it? Exactly how do you prepare for that first infant soul life?

Not surprisingly, inorganic and organic matter on earth is divided into seven kingdoms of ascending order of diversity and complexity. As primordial units of consciousness and energy you begin to live through each of these kingdoms according to a specific order. Here is an outline that shows you the progressive steps from your birth as a fragment to your first infant soul lifetime.

ESSENCE BIRTH

1. You leave the Tao as a vast mass of intense energy, one fragment among 100,000 or more, with the intention to experience all of life. The Tao gives you birth through a great outpouring of love. The love becomes light, light becomes energy, and energy becomes matter.

2. As an intense ball of energy you explore the universe, sightseeing, visiting and experimenting with the various options for play and learning. You are looking for the best opportunity for you to explore separateness and uniqueness. You want to explore this separateness so fully that it eventually leads you back to unity with the Tao once again.

SEVEN LEVELS OF ESSENCE DEVELOPMENT

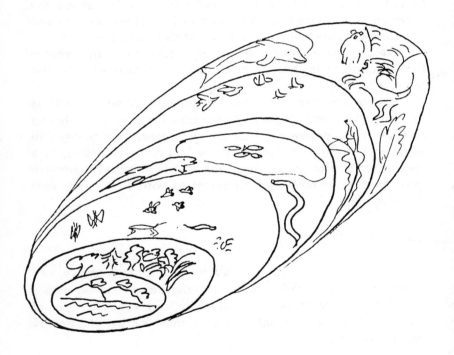

3. There are many planets and dimensions to explore. You contemplate many others before you choose Earth for its special qualities that you now know so well.

ESSENCE DEVELOPMENT ON EARTH

FIRST LEVEL: You approach this planet sensing it and its energy only energetically; you have only the broadest sense of what it is. You are sensing the planet as a whole, not as its parts. This is the point to which you will return afterward having experienced every single detail that is possible on the planet from all perspectives.

•You waft gently with the wind in spirit form, a timeless zephyr, caressing the grasses, the rock faces, and the peoples, as you gradually become more familiar with the planet. You, with your family of fragments, your entity, begin to take a hand in creatively molding the face of the planet, changing its surface features gradually according to a larger overall plan. You have become a deva, a spirit who is caretaker of some segment of the physical plane.

•After centuries some entities have chosen to move on to another planet, not finding their exact needs met here. You decide however to proceed, to move closer to this planet. Gradually you pursue even greater separateness and individuality. You become an ocean with boundaries that wash the shores of continents. You experience a relationship with the moon and feel the tides that move you ever so lightly. You experience many living forms within you, and you, with thousands of other entities, have a hand in shaping those forms and the landmasses that contain you.

•Some entities withdraw...this planet is not for them. They seek a different path. You choose to continue, intermingling your energy with a mountain range where you experience the profound solidity of rock mass. Now you are even more defined, more separate. You have become a deva of the mineral kingdom.

•You pursue more and more individuality, specializing in specific minerals and strata of earth at definite locations on the planet. You experience the molten interior as well as the cooling of surface gemstones and metals. Again, as before, you help to shape and create new forms as you experience them for eons. Later in human form you will find affinity for those locations that you experienced in your essence form.

SECOND LEVEL: You move on to the plant kingdom after thoroughly experiencing the mineral kingdom. You become a deva that attends the grasses and simple plant forms that have a mass character such as moss. Gradually you specialize into specific individual plants of greater complexity such as a fruit tree. You assist in their evolution, helping to develop new strains and hybrids. You favor your experiences with some kinds of plants while moving away from types that you cannot relate to as well. Later as a human you will sense an affinity with some plants and may subconsciouly know their unique characteristics and uses because you have been them.

THIRD LEVEL: You evolve to attend to more complex lifeforms now and begin with the simple bacterias, microbes, and amoebas. Gradually you move on to the more complex crustaceans and insect forms such as bees, finding in these an opportunity for rapid acceleration of creative adaptation.

FOURTH LEVEL: Following the insect kingdom you proceed in Devic form to coexist with fish and reptiles of the land and water. Here, as in the insect kingdom, you develop the rudiments of the instinctive center that you will use as a human for basic survival. As a helping spirit you attend to these animals but do not interfere with their natural lifestyles. You may however assist them with their evolution through mutation.

Recall that at any juncture in Devic development you may decide to leave the planet in favor of other planetary experiences.

FIFTH LEVEL: When you have spent as much time as you wished with the reptiles and fish, you move along to the birds and mammals who represent a quantum leap in your evolutionary movement toward individuality. You begin to attend to simple, warm blooded, less intelligent mammal forms such as antelopes, hippos, and mice. You accompany birds who derive most of their identity from the flocks they belong to. As an animal Deva you assist and accompany the animal through seven reincarnational cycles. Here in the fifth level you begin to develop the moving center that you will use as a human being. Here also, in the latter part of the fifth level, you begin to accompany and assist a single animal rather than the entire herd.

SIXTH LEVEL: After completing the fifth level you proceed to highly intelligent animals such as tigers, wolves, boars, and horses. Eventually you will seek companionship with men because you are preparing for your first infant soul life as a human being. You may be the Deva of a faithful dog or cat living in the company of humans for many years.

Here at the sixth level you also attend in Devic form to the highly intelligent, more independent birds of prey.

Sixth level experiences begin to develop inspiration and the emotional center that will be evolved in the human cycle.

SEVENTH LEVEL: Here you experience the lives of higher primates, river dolphins and the like who, although highly intelligent have not yet made the leap to sentience. Here you are tool and symbol users who enjoy experimentation and risk-taking. You may fraternize with men in hopes of becoming familiar with the abilities and possibilities of humanness. At the seventh level you begin to develop intellectual powers that you will need for your first infant soul life.

•You are ready for your first infant soul lifetime. Once you begin this evolutionary cycle you are committed to completion. You no longer have the option of moving on to another planet. The reason for this is that, as a human, you form karma immediately and this requires balancing. You are off on your exciting series of lifetimes from infant through the old soul cycle.

YOUR COMPANIONS ALONG THE WAY

The first thing to remember is that you do not travel alone. You are one fragment in an entity of over a thousand fragments, all experiencing life just like you. You are also a member of a larger family called a cadre consisting of seven entities. You tend to know the fragments in this cadre intimately throughout your lifetimes. You also have an essence twin and task companions that assist you in your evolution.

The second thing to remember is that you have specific relationships to experience and work out before you can cycle off.

You must experience being both the parent and the child of the same person over several lifetimes. Likewise you must be someone's teacher as well as their student, a leader and a follower, a jailer and a prisoner, and so on.

You have special groupings that help you to accomplish tasks and meet your goals. Triads, quadrants, sextants, and so on, all create an opportunity for essence growth each lifetime.

You have agreements to keep and special sources of support to help you keep those agreements that you make. Why do you make agreements? Because you want to play the game and you want to learn, and those are the ground rules.

THE UNDERLYING PROCESS

The next thing to remember is that you have special processes that assist you to play out your relationships. These processes that are presented in detail later in this book, help you to create and then resolve your karmic ribbons. They are the universal forces of three and seven.

The triad or force of three governs the nature of all human experiences. All events have a positive component, a negative component, and a neutral component that represents resolution. Each position tends to automatically bring about another position into play. So the play of life continues on and on until you are ready to cycle off. All the overleaves that make up your personality are made up of these triads.

As you shall see shortly the triad is the basic force that supports the law of karma.

The septant is the other universal process that governs all developmental growth. All growth is composed of seven steps leading to the next octave, just as in musical notes, the final step being the first step of the next set of seven.

That is why this teaching is a system of sevens.

THE BASIC RULE

Now let's look at the basic rule that makes the earth game work. This rule is of course the law of karma already mentioned. The law of karma dictates that every imbalance that you create must be redressed so that balance is once again restored. If you take a life then you owe a life. If you steal money then you must pay back the money you took. If you do not redress the imbalance in this life then it must be done in the next one or the next.

This law of karma follows the triadic law. First you create karma or imbalance with yourself or another. Secondly you redress the imbalance. Third you experience neutrality about the issue. Then you are ready for a new karma and so it goes.

Why have such a law?

Simply speaking, karma allows the earth game to work. It ensures that you will stick around to learn and find your way back to the Tao. You learn by doing. You learn what the consequences of your actions are. This is how all small children learn and is the basis for all learning on the physical plane. When you have completed all karma and your balance sheet is even, you are an old soul ready to cycle off the physical plane.

PLANNING AND LIVING A LIFETIME

You know the players, you know the process, and you know the basic rule. Now you are ready to begin a lifetime in your long journey back home. How do you do it?

First you choose the set of overleaves that you want to work with in your next life. You choose these overleaves because they will help you create conditions and experiences that you will grow from. Secondly you choose the proper culture and the family set-up that will allow you to fulfill your life plan. This plan includes your life goal, your life task, your agreements, and the karma you wish to create, experience, and resolve.

Next you choose the proper moment of birth that will give you the exact astrological configuration you will need to have your unique personality and a general life pattern.

After your birth you begin to maneuver yourself and those around you so that you can obtain just the right imprinting or conditioning that you wish to experience.

You have embarked on your life and in the process of a complete life you experience the seven internal monads that lead to completion at death.

THE SEVEN INTERNAL MONADS OR RITES OF PASSAGE

These are the seven major rites of passage that constitute a complete lifetime. In order for you to evolve from one level to the next you must have experienced all seven rites of passage. Therefore if you die young and fail to complete all of them, you return for a complete lifetime before transiting to the next level. You may already have already completed the seven monads however, and return briefly as an infant to complete an unfinished lesson.

The seven internal monads are:

1.   Birth.

2.   The experience of developing autonomy at age two.

3.   Puberty-adolescence.

4.   The mid-thirties, or age thirty-five, when essence can manifest.

5.   Retirement or early sixties when you feel that your life task has been mostly accomplished.

6.   The realization that death is imminent.

7.   Death itself.

Each of these steps is an intense rite of passage that marks a major transition from one state of awareness to another. Each monad is a time of great energy as well as a time of vulnerability. Events surrounding the transition can have a major influence on the outcome. For example the trauma surrounding birth or the lack thereof can have lifelong repercussions. It is important to remember that these variables are chosen to produce specific results.

The monads usually have a quality of tension to them and can be experienced by you and those close to you as times of great difficulty. They can nevertheless be experienced joyfully on occasion. A good example of this is death, the seventh monad.

1. Birth.

Essence uses the gestation period as an opportunity to get used to the new body you will inhabit. There is no standard pattern to this process. Sometimes essence occupies the developing body

SEVEN INTERNAL MONADS

from conception onward. In other situations essence does not actually enter the new body until the moment of birth. Mostly esssence gets used to the new body by degrees and focuses into the body more at birth. The birth of course marks the beginning of life outside the protection of mother's body.

2. Autonomy: approximately age two.

The second internal monad is not transited in a few minutes or hours as is the birth monad. It may take place over a period of days, weeks, or even months. The monad is complete when the child fully recognizes himself as functioning independently of mother. Generally this monad occurs between two and two and one half years of age.

3. Puberty-adolescence.

As with autonomy, the onset of puberty is not an overnight event but is a gradual process marked by massive hormonal releases. The discharge of hormones signals the onset of adult sexual activity and thrusts you into a time of intense karma. The physical changes in your body facilitate the forming of karmic ribbons and their resolution. Valuable lessons in the art of living can be the result. This is the time when all chief negative features are sampled and one is finally chosen. The monad is over when the hormonal activity has achieved homeostasis and you have identified yourself as having left childhood behind.

4. Essence manifestation (approximately age thirty-five).

The fourth monad occurs much later in life and is usually complete by age forty. Age thirty-five is the most probable year for older souls to manifest their soul age. When this monad is accomplished you look and act like your true soul age as opposed to manifesting your imprinting or conditioning. In order for this to be accomplished you must drop enough parental and cultural conditioning so that your true overleaves can manifest. Until you do this your overleaves are overshadowed by those of your parents, relatives, and so on.

This personal housekeeping can be facilitated by counseling or intensive work on the self under the guidance of a teacher. Sometimes the work can be assisted by an abrupt life change such as a divorce or a life-threatening illness that gets you to reconsider who you are.

The more personal growth work you have done prior to the shift, the less traumatic is the actual monad. Like many of these life passages, the fourth internal monad can take weeks or months to negotiate.

Not everyone successfully accomplishes this monad and some delay it for many years so that a person might be in their sixties before they truly manifest if at all.

5. The realization that your life task is mostly accomplished.

There is no set year when this fifth internal monad is normally completed: however it usually occurs after age fifty-six. To accomplish this monad you must review your life's work, what you consider to be your successes and failures, and make peace with yourself. You evaluate the relative success you have had in completing your life task and you develop a strategy for the rest of your life. That is, you decide for yourself what you have left to do, and you decide how you are going to do it. In addition, you begin to shift into a state of being rather than the intense doing state that you have used most of your adult life. For many people who have been driven to accomplish all their lives, this can be a difficult task. In general the older the soul, the easier this transition is to make.

6. The realization that death is imminent.

You begin this monad the moment you know for sure that you are about to die. During this monad you must come to terms with your death and how to handle whatever fear you have about it. Now this can take place only a few seconds, minutes, hours, or days before your death, or on the other hand up to a year before the event. Sometimes you select lingering, disabling illnesses such as AIDs, that give you plenty of time to accomplish this. In other lives you pass through this monad rapidly, for example after you have been mortally wounded in an accident or on the battlefield. In some lives you die so suddenly that you have no experience of this monad at all.

7. Death itself.

The seventh internal monad is like the first (birth) in reverse. It is the actual transition from physical reality to the astral plane and the life review that accompanies this shift.

Your essence leaves the body either by degrees or all at once depending on the circumstances of your death. Your experience of the moment of death is reflective of the life you have led. If you have confronted your fears in life and have gained a measure of detachment about death, the transition can be ecstatic. If your fears have run you and you have resisted death, the event can be terrifying.

In general older souls have an easier time with death than the younger souls for two reasons. First they tend to be more detached about such matters. Secondly they are old hands at death, having lived many lives before, and they know what to expect.

When you have accomplished all seven internal monads in one lifetime or in several, you are ready to go on to the next level within your soul age.

During each life you attempt to complete your internal monads as well as those with others. You attempt to fulfill your agreements, seek to accomplish your life task, and without fail, you take some important experience back to your entity.

Eventually you custom-design your death to facilitate as much karma as possible.

As mentioned, following your death and transition processes, you evaluate your just completed life in terms of lessons learned and opportunities passed by. You begin to plan the next lifetime in light of what you have not yet mastered or completed.

THE TOOLS OF THE TRADE

Your major tools each lifetime are your physical and energetic bodies, the vehicles through which all life is experienced. Through trial, error, and experience you gradually learn to use these bodies to full advantage each lifetime. You learn to handle stress, to care for the balance and health of both bodies, and to refine the powerful energetic properties of each. You learn how to harness the powers of the physical body to fulfill essence goals.

You gradually learn how to use the tools of the planet as well. Eventually you learn to use your relationship to the mineral, plant, and animal kingdoms to assist you in your spiritual awakening.

You learn the major processes that encourage essence growth such as meditation, concentration, study, and conservation of energy. You learn to recognize and receive help from teachers both physical and non-physical. You learn how to communicate from an essence level rather than solely from false personality. And finally you learn how to stay awake enough to recognize the illusion of maya that threatens to send you back to sleep.

In the following chapters we go into much detail about everything that has been introduced in these opening pages. We would say that a complete understanding of the basic rule of karma is essential to your evolution and growth. Therefore we will begin with a thorough discussion of karma and self-karma before moving on to other sections. You will find that topics are grouped into parts that reflect common themes. Nevertheless the material can be organized many ways because it is all interrelated.

Chapter Two

Karma: The Rule of the Game

What is Karma? Where does it come from? What is its purpose? How do you create it and how do you resolve it? When you know the answers to these questions you gain an advantage in learning to handle karma. The more you know about karma, the greater your ability to complete it and reduce its control over your life.

In your culture you frequently confuse karma with fate or the notion that the future is written indelibly in ink. You may even believe that you are a victim of karma and that no matter what you do you can not escape its tentacles. Most of you have had lives where you despaired and gave up all hope because you felt that karma would inevitably deal you a terrible blow. You might even think that karma is a punishment for misdeeds meted out from a cosmic parent that harshly judges and disciplines you.

Another error you can fall into is the belief that karma is good or bad. You might subscribe to the notion that good karma is like good luck while bad karma is bad luck. These beliefs, while hinting at the truth, are misleading and confusing at best. In this chapter we will help you to clear up the confusion surrounding karma. First we will discuss the law of karma as it relates to your involvement with others. In the next section we will look at the self-karma that involves your own personal issues only.

Karma is the universal law of consequences. Any experience of a certain basic intensity will record and generate the necessity for a balance of that intensity. Let us go into to this a bit more specifically. Intensity is the medium through which thoughts, deeds, and emotional experiences are recorded in the Akashic records. The Akashic records are a complete record of all events and experiences that occur on every plane of existence.

Remember that the Tao created the game of life to experience as much of itself as it is able. The law of karma is what makes this possible.

Let us look at it this way. Any thought, action, or emotional event is like a pebble thrown onto the calm surface of a pond. The pebble creates ripples that have consequences as they spread out on the pond's surface and interact with floating objects and the shoreline. The greater the size of the pebble and the stronger the intensity with which it is thrown, the greater the size of the ripples. This of course creates an experience for the pond, so to speak , and this is what the Tao is looking for, experiences. Throwing the pebble in the pond ensures that there will be consequences leading to more consequences and so on. The game of life then is in process.

The Akashic Records, the Tao's memory bank, keeps track of events according to certain blocks or ribbons of experience. Think of it this way. With each event an imbalance is recorded in an open file on the imbalance column. The imbalance generates an impetus for immediate or eventual balance of the sheet. When the event has been experienced in reverse the balance column is checked and the file is then considered closed. This is the law of

KARMA

karma, sometimes called the law of debt. The Akashic records are kept perfectly and no file is ever lost or forgotten.

Let us look at some examples of the law of debt regarding emotional experiences.

> *If a thief steals a person's life's savings, that person will probably feel intense emotions as a consequence. The thief will also probably have intense feelings during and after the course of the theft—perhaps excitement, fear, guilt and so on. These intense emotional experiences are recorded and generate the necessity for both the thief and the victim to experience the opposite emotion. So the victim will then become the thief who steals the former thief's savings. If John shoots Mary in one life, karma is recorded. An imbalance remains on the books waiting for another lifetime when comparable circumstances exist for repayment. Mary will then cause John's death and the balance sheet is complete.*

You may ask at this point, "Is that the only way karma can be repaid, a tooth for a tooth and an eye for an eye?" The answer of course is no, not necessarily. If John shoots Mary when he is a baby soul and does not meet up with her again until they are both old souls, Mary is not likely to repay the Karma by wanting to shoot Tom. A number of alternatives exist for them. John could save Mary's life and lose his own life in the process and the debt would be satisfied. On the other hand Mary might inadvertently kill John in a traffic accident and again the debt would be repaid.

The creation of karma has everything to do with choice. You choose all your karmic lessons no matter how disagreeable you might feel they are. However, whether you judge karma good or bad has to do with your impact on other people's choices. When you interfere with the free choices of others you create what looks like negative karma. When you promote and create the opportunity for greater choices for others you create what appears to be positive karma.

Karma however is neither good nor bad. It is your judgement which makes it appear positive or negative. You may generate what you may call positive karma by donating a large sum of money to a needy individual. In another incident you may generate what you call negative karma by stealing a large some of money from your neighbor. Both are important lessons in living that ultimately lead toward greater human understanding and love. The one judged negative simply is the longer path.

Remember that karma is necessary in order to play the game of the physical universe. Karma makes it possible for lessons to be learned and development to take place.

KARMA CREATION AND SOUL AGES

Infant souls and baby souls are on the lookout for intense situations and experiences to create because their essence knows that this is the only way to learn their lessons.

The infant, baby and young soul stages are karma-ridden. Karma is predominantly "sown" in these stages. Theft, assault, murder—those things which are intensely painful—are especially experienced in these earlier cycles. These experiences ensure younger souls that they will have ongoing developmental lessons and a wide variety of situations to interact with other people. This is akin to the young child's experiments with breaking things and torturing insects to find out about them.

In the mature and old soul cycles the theme switches to karma repayment. Karma is generated in these older cycles but it lacks the primitiveness of karma of the younger cycles. Older souls often avoid potentially karmic situations because they recognize them as being lessons they have already learned.

Whereas a younger soul might relish the opportunity to participate in the intensity of battle, the older soul *might seek conscientious objector status instead. The younger soul of course cannot understand why anyone would want to avoid battle (especially for a cause) and might accuse the older soul of cowardice. The older soul is simply desiring to avoid the creation of more karma. This is not to say however that old souls do not participate in wars because they do. But they will try to find positions where they can avoid creating new karma. The people they might kill will be old karmic debts. These agreements of course are carefully orchestrated. The right person will be in the right place at the right time.*

During the earlier cycles, when you are a younger soul, you usually do not have a clue that you are creating karma or repaying it. You have not yet learned about the law of karma and are busy finding out, just as a child finds out about a hot stove by playing near it.

When you are an older soul on the other hand, you begin to be conscious of creating karma and you are often aware of your karmic debts. This greatly enhances your ability to weather karmic situations and to balance the karmic records.

The sixth level of any soul level is devoted to repaying the bulk of the karma that has been incurred throughout all the earlier levels of that stage. So a sixth level baby soul will attempt to complete most of the karma sown in earlier levels. This is what makes the sixth level so busy and such an intense experience. Therefore, it may take a number of lifetimes to complete. It would not be uncommon for a sixth level old soul to have five to ten lifetimes at the sixth level.

Sixth and seventh level old souls create little or no karma with others because they are finishing up their cycle and will not be returning to repay the karma.

KARMA AND THE LIFE CYCLE

The early years of your life tend to be the most karma-filled. Adolescence is often the most intense time of all in a life. The hormonal and developmental changes tend to accentuate the difficulties of that period and facilitate a climate wherein much karma can be played out. This is also the time when you experiment with the different chief negative features: self-destruction, greed, self-deprecation, arrogance, martyrdom, impatience, and stubbornness. Generally by about the age of 21 you select one of them to settle down with. After the age of 30, karmic intensity is greatly reduced. There are exceptions to this, as is the case with those people experiencing lifetimes at the sixth level of any stage (heavy karma balancing), and those with a goal of growth.

HOW KARMA REPAYMENT WORKS

Karma is supervised and organized by essence. Often the personality knows nothing of the purpose and impending unfoldment of the karma. There is good reason for this. False personality often operates out of fear. If your conscious personality knew that an intensely painful karma were about to occur with someone, it would run as fast as possible in the opposite direction, thus avoiding the repayment or the lesson that essence had in mind. Your personality usually feels like a victim in karmic situations. Essence planned the karma repayment without flinching. Even when you are an old soul you need this benevolent amnesia to meet your more difficult karma.

As mentioned earlier, karma usually comes with no warning even though it is essence directed. It frequently comes like a freight train rounding the bend and coming down the tracks with inexorable speed. The train is upon you before you can run away. When you are in the midst of a karmic situation you feel foggy and unclear, and you may feel strangely unable to get out of the situation. You often wonder how this happened to you all of a sudden.

> You may walk innocently into a meeting and within minutes are insulted and humiliated by the new director on your job. You are instantly plunged into painful emotions and wonder what you did to deserve it. The answer is often that you didn't do anything this lifetime to deserve it. You simply showed up to balance the record sheet.
>
> Likewise you may be penniless and lost in a foriegn country and a complete stranger suddenly appears on the scene and takes you in, cares for you and gives you an airplane ticket home.

When karma has been completed a feeling of freedom and relief ensues. The fog clears and you gain insight into the preceding events. You become neutral about the issue that had so recently carried such intensity for you. You don't care anymore. You may even wonder how you could have been so upset about the issue. The purpose of karma completion is to get you neutral on the issue so that you can move on to new and more interesting lessons. You have reached the neutral position on the triadic experience and you are ready for something new.

Remember again that karma is not fate. Fate is a notion of predestination. You choose karma specifically with the purpose of undergoing an emotional or learning experience.

Think of karma as ribbons that draw together experiences and weave a distinct pattern that is the product of many lifetimes. Remember also that those ribbons cause you to be in specific places and to meet certain people, sometimes to your great surprise. If you have a karmic debt with another individual living in a foreign country you will suddenly find yourself drawn, sometimes almost magically, to travel to that other country where the debt can be repaid. Occasionally the obstacles in the path of meeting are too great and the karma must be deferred to another lifetime.

For example you may decide that this lifetime you will complete ten major karma, seventy-five medium karma, and one hundred and fifty minor karma. Typically you tend to bite off more than you can chew, so that if you complete most of these karma the lifetime will feel successful to you no matter how uncomfortable for your personality. Some karma will be judged too difficult to complete for now. There is always free choice about when to complete a karma. The choice to complete it is made by essence at the time of initiation of the karma. It will always be completed.

> _Let us say that you have karma with a Mr. Chang who resides in China, and you live in Brazil. On an essence level you feel an urge to return the good deeds he has done for you in the past that will take a full year to repay. You however have not been able to travel to China and are heavily involved in completing and creating karma in your locality. Mr. Chang is able to visit Brazil for one week and you feel a pull to attend a lecture he is giving in a nearby city. You go out of your way to see him even though the topic is not of interest to you. You realize that although you are strongly attracted to him you will not be able to complete the karma in this life because of his short stay._

Such flirting with karma is a common experience and happens all the time. On the other hand if Mr. Chang announced that he would be in the vicinity for several years, the pull to complete the karma would be almost irresistible.

Sexual attraction is one of the greatest facilitators of karma. When an imbalance exists between two people there is a strong essence-driven impetus to balance the record sheet. However, personality may sense a possible danger and wish to avoid the situation. Strong sexual attraction will make this avoidance less likely.

> For example if you embezzled a large sum of money from Marsha in an earlier lifetime and you suddenly run into Marsha in this lifetime you may want to run and hide. You sense that she has come to collect. However if you are distracted by the fact that Marsha is now a beautiful blonde, your very type, then your lust will lead you directly into the karma. How convenient. You may later wonder how you ever could have gotten involved with her after she has divorced you and taken your house and car in repayment.

KARMA AND TIME

How long does karma last? Is there a time limit or a way to speed it up? The answer is not a simple one.

Sometimes karma lasts only for a few seconds, such as a short intense pain; other times karma can last a whole lifetime, such as having a benevolent aunt who constantly looks out for you for many years. In another vein a foe can cause you the loss of your arm early in life, a handicap that can last for decades. The length of the karmic experience is directly in proportion to the length of the first incident. If you deprive someone of the use of their legs for twenty years then this becomes a twenty-year karma. If you cut short someone's life by one year then your own life will be cut short by one year in a later life. If you raise an orphan with kindness and generosity for twelve years then you will be repaid with a twelve-year kindness. Balance then, is the name of the game.

However, you can drag karma on, escalate it or creatively manipulate it according to the experiences and lessons desired by all parties involved. In order for karma to be truly complete everyone involved must acknowledge the completion of it at an essence level. Karma can be such a delicious source of growth and lessons that often all parties would rather refuse to recognize the repayment and generate more karma instead. The karma builds and becomes more intense lifetime after lifetime until ultimately the lesson of forgiveness is learned. Sometimes a person will feel an intense tug to repay a karmic debt that they owe you. You may recoil at their appearance and try to avoid them based on past painful experience. This is like saying "Oh no! Not you again! I'm getting out of here!" So the chase is on until the debt is repaid.

However, people are not always successful at repaying the karma.

> For example Tom may owe Susan for abandonment one lifetime. When they meet again the intention is to repay the debt. Nevertheless Tom may get cold feet at the prospect of being abandoned and instead repeat the original offense by abandoning Susan all over again. The karma then has just escalated. Small wonder then that some people get skittish when they see their old enemy show up. The question arises "Am I about to be repaid or am I about to be burned again?" The game of cat and mouse can go on for centuries. Again, in the end, all is forgiven, balanced and completed.

Occasionally you play the game of "Who can be the most generous?" lifetime after lifetime, by building karma of a positive nature with someone.

On the other hand old souls wishing to cycle off the planet become adept at completing karma efficiently and creatively, sometimes accomplishing several at the same time.

KARMA AND THE SEVEN PLANES

Karma may be played out on various levels of experience. Physical karma, such as the giving or taking of large sums of money, must be balanced on the physical plane. If, as a doctor you save a person's life, your own life will be saved in such a fashion.

However, karma is not always a physical act, but rather may be purely emotional. For example you may be instrumental in making someone feel wonderful emotionally. On the other hand, you may hurt someone's feelings intensely. Since no completely physical transaction has occurred, this karma may be repaid in the dream state or on the astral plane. In fact a great deal of emotional karma is both created and resolved on the astral plane.

The law of karma or balance operates throughout all the planes of existence. However the karma of the higher planes is inconceivably different from the karma of the physical plane.

KARMA AND OVERLEAVES

You incur karma each lifetime through your personality and this is a function of the poles of the overleaves you choose each lifetime. The karmic experience is incorporated by your essence at your death, adding to its richness, experience and growth.

You choose specific overleaves to facilitate the payment or development of certain karma. Ordinal overleaves such as stoicism or caution mode are tilted toward self-karma, and exalted overleaves such as dominance or passion facilitate karma in the world.

For example the ordinal chief feature of martyrdom relates to internal suffering and feeling a victim. Its opposite in the pair, the exalted chief feature of impatience, often causes you to act out impatiently toward others.

This inward/outward character of the ordinal/exalted overleaves is true for most of the overleaves.

Often the negative pole of any overleaf facilitates what you judge as negative karma and the positive pole may be experienced as helping to complete karma or to be karma-free.

For example, in the negative pole of passion mode (identification) you are well set up to experience suffering in a karmic situation such as a divorce. However on the completion of that karma you would then slide to self actualization, the positive pole, and feel expansive and free.

Selected Action Overleaves

Ordinal	Exalted
Goals	
+Devotion	+Leadership
SUBMISSION	DOMINANCE
-Exploited	-Dictatorship
Modes	
+Persistence	+Dynamism
PERSEVERANCE	AGGRESSION
-Immutability	-Belligerence
Chief Features	
+Selflessness	+Daring
MARTYRDOM	IMPATIENCE
-Victimization	-Intolerance

KARMA AND RELATIONSHIPS

In upcoming sections we will examine in detail agreements and monads between individuals. Here we will simply say that a monad is a specific agreed-upon relationship between two people such as mother-daughter or leader-follower. These relationships are played out reciprocally and usually involve a great deal of karma. The monad itself is not the karma. It is the way these monads are played and the choices that are made that determine the nature of the karma. For example if a mother is cruel to her daughter, karma is created requiring balance. If the mother is generous and kind with her daughter karma is again created that is reciprocated. Theoretically it would be possible to conduct such a monad without the creation of any karma whatsoever. However this would be pointless since karma carries the lessons and experiences you are all looking for during development.

HOW TO HANDLE KARMA IN GENERAL

An excellent technique to complete karma is the following. Before going to sleep, postulate that you want to get more neutral about a specific issue or person. This sets up the intention to work through the karma and creates positive communication channels between you and the other person with whom you want resolution. It will also bring up from the subconscious or instinctive center memory banks the issues to be resolved. These may be revealed symbolically in dream form or come to your awareness spontaneously the following day.

Another excellent tool is to do the obvious. Sit down and talk to the person about the matter. See if you can both agree to work on the issue as the situation probably isn't comfortable for either of you. Perhaps you can reach some communicative agreement and look at the current issues. You will find that often you have deliberately miscommunicated to keep the karma going.

If the person has died or is otherwise unavailable, you can still communicate with them in a meditation. You can simply imagine them and communicate to them what you wished to tell them. With practice you can even hear their responses and carry out a complete discussion. Your intention knows no boundaries or physical obstacles. Time and space are not a barrier to your wish for karma or self-karma resolution.

A word of warning is in order here. Work on one issue at a time. You often bite off more than you can chew and the result is confusion and more karma.

That which you judge to be negative karma usually needs deliberate work to complete, because of your resistance to it.

That which you judge to be negative karma usually needs deliberate work to complete, because of your resistance to it. Positive karma on the other hand tends to work on itself. You enjoy them and work on them every minute of the day. You want to spend every minute with the other person. As a result the karma tends to be completed very quickly.

Similarly you could complete a negative karma if you worked on it night and day and were around that person constantly.

Because karma is a foundation stone that keeps you progressing, everything in life is somehow related to it. Therefore each issue we will discuss in this volume will relate to this central theme of karma.

In this section we have explained how karma works in relation to others. In this next section we will show how you produce and resolve what we call "self-karma," those life lessons and experiences for which you alone are responsible.

PART TWO

SETTING UP A LIFETIME

Chapter Three

Setting Tasks and Challenges

PART II

This section focuses on those processes that contribute to the makeup of a single lifetime on earth. We continue our discussion on karma focusing instead on "self-karma," the lessons you set up for your own learning each lifetime. Here you will discover how you set up your own personal astrology to determine your overleaves, your life plan and tasks. You will learn how imprinting affects you and how patterns are carried from one lifetime to the next. You will see also how you select your family for the best karmic lessons and for that specialized imprinting you were hoping for. Finally you will learn the significance of your death each lifetime and discover how you can make it work for you.

SELF-KARMA (Completing cycles)

What is self-karma and how does it differ from karma with others? How is it created and how is it resolved or balanced? What is its purpose? Here we will focus more specifically on karmic experiences that you orchestrate for purposes of internal balance. Self-karma, then, does not directly involve anyone else to be experienced and resolved.

For example, you may wish to experience the extreme pinnacle of success followed by losing everything and plunging into poverty and failure. Within this self-karma, you experience two extremes. You may wish to experience these extremes within the same lifetime or experience the opposites in back-to-back lifetimes, one of wealth and success and the other of poverty and failure. Of course a more interesting twist would be a life of wealth and failure and another life of poverty and success.

Remember that we defined karma as an experience of emotional intensity. If Judy makes five thousand dollars in an investment and it means nothing to her, there is no self-karma. If William makes ten dollars and is exuberant, self-karma is generated.

Much of your life experience is self-karmic by nature because this is where you learn some of your most valuable lessons.

There are levels upon levels of self-karma. Everything that you judge to be good about yourself is a self-karma as well as all that you feel is bad. Feelings about personal success or failure are the most self-karmic experiences. Self-karma then, concerns how you relate to yourself and how you manage yourself out in the world.

On an essence level you have no bias toward positive or negative self-karma. There is a tendency however, to use up or

SELF KARMA

pass over the good-feeling ones quickly and to try to avoid the bad-feeling ones. This resistance causes the bad-feeling ones to drag on.

You might get nine good evaluations from the board of trustees about a job well done, but the one negative evaluation will tend to grab your attention. You speed over the positive ones but linger over the negative evaluation because that is the one you resist.

You tend to become neutral about some wonderful talents after a time and simply acknowledge that that is what you are good at. You are often neutral about some amazing skills you have.

Suppose you were a talented pianist, to the admiration of friends and colleagues. However, you may feel fairly flat about this talent after a time and get much more worked up about your new-found ability to say a few words in French.

Self-karma is never bad, but simply a challenge you have set up so as to learn all about something. You choose what you want to work on each life and give yourself the experience.

SELF-KARMA AND SOUL AGES

The most self-karma is experienced in the older soul ages while the most interpersonal karma is experienced during the younger soul ages.

Mature and old souls tend to be deluged with self-karma. This is why their lifetimes can appear so extreme at times. They like to run the full gamut of experience. To some extent self-karma is all they have left. The self-karma at these ages tends to be more pervasive.

THE FOCUS OF SELF-KARMA

Self-karma tends to concentrate in certain main categories of experience. These areas are: body image; health; wealth or lack thereof; sexual preference and behavior; and family membership. These areas traditionally provide the most intense experiences in life.

Let us examine how this happens and then look into each of these areas individually.

First of all, as you know, you select experiences for yourself that you want to learn about. For example, it is no coincidence to have five consecutive relationships with unfaithful partners. Often the case is that for your own self-karmic purposes your essence brings these similar relationships into your life until you learn what you wanted to learn from them.

Let's say you want to learn about alcoholism. This may be because you are challenged with being in relationship to alcoholics or perhaps you did not relate to alcoholism in the past and had very little compassion for those experiencing it. Maybe you decided to spend a life as an alcoholic and now you wish to learn about it by living with alcoholics. You end up marrying a string of alcoholics and have intense experiences with them. You may in fact develop or resolve karma with them but you are also working on your own self-karma. You wish to have the experience from both sides so that you can develop understanding and compassion. Then you will feel good enough about your experience to let go of it and form a relationship with someone who is not an alcoholic.

Often these self-karmic experiences evolve from resistance to the situation in the first place. Maybe you resisted submissive people and decided to give yourself the experience of being submissive for a life. Let's say that instead of developing compassion you spend the entire life hating yourself for being submissive and you resist it even more. The greater the resistance the greater the self-karma created. Essence then chooses a lifetime of even greater submissiveness until you can relate to it and become neutral about it.

SELF-KARMA AND BODY IMAGE

The most common form of self-karma is about body image. The body is the easiest form to identify with on the physical plane. Because you live inside of it and through it, your body experiences the most karma-forming emotional intensity. Stature, girth, coloring, bone-structure, and shape can all contribute to intense feelings of worthlessness, vanity, well-being, satisfaction and so on. Culture and fashion, both great producers of maya, can determine the relative acceptableness or unacceptableness of your looks and body type.

In addition your physical body can be a great source of pleasure and pain, both highly self-karma-producing. Your body then, is a perfect object to experience intense lessons through.

Seldom do you actually like all your body parts as well as your general appearance. You may like your own eyes or mouth but hate your teeth or hair. You might like your legs and feet but feel your hands are ugly and misshapen. Scars and disabilities all contribute to the mayhem of feelings about the body. When you choose to have a physical disability through accident or birth, you give yourself the opportunity for intense self-karmic experiences. Your task is to eventually achieve acceptance and neutrality about your physical conditions.

Let's say for example, that you don't like your nose and you never did. Maybe you have never had it fixed surgically but spent years worrying about it. Maybe you did have it altered and you don't like the result so you still don't like your nose. Or you like your new nose but soon after your operation it gets broken and looks dreadful again. This is a self-karma that will stay with

you lifetime after lifetime until you become neutral about
your nose no matter how it looks.

Basically weight works the same way. The more you resist it
the fatter you get. On the other hand indulging doesn't work
either. Neutrality is the only thing that produces results in terms
of being the weight that you want to be.

SELF-KARMA AND SEX

Sexual preference, habits, and relationships is the second
most self-karma producing arena. This is usually related to your
imprinting, your parents and culture, and sexual experiences in
past lives. You may have been born male and are expected to be
dominant sexually but if you have submission as a goal you will
feel out of step with this expectation. As you can see this could
become a rich source of self-torture and self-deprecation until you
develop acceptance regarding your own style. The same would be
true for a woman with a goal of dominance expected by culture to
be submissive in sexual play. Commonly, sexual feelings and
outlets such as masturbation and fantasy are associated with
shame and feelings of guilt. Again these feelings are products of
parental and cultural imprinting and can become years-long
sources of intense self-karma.

Since sexual feelings are so closely related to body image,
these two self-karmic areas go hand in hand. You may feel you
are not attractive enough to the preferred sex and avoid sexual
contact for this reason. On the other hand you may have a
beautiful body that attracts others in droves. If you feel uncertain
about how to handle yourself you may run and hide or become
involved in a long series of apparently inappropriate relationships that cause you much distress. Much of your upset here
would be self-karmic.

A common self-karma occurs involving the choice of a
mate. Let's say you are a blue-eyed blond and everyone
around you sees you as terrifically attractive.

Interestingly you choose a mate that prefers brown eyed brunettes and is not attracted to you at all. Here you get to have intense feelings of rejection and feel unattractive despite your beautiful looks.

Past lives are frequently the source of much intense sexual self-karma. For example if you are a warrior who has had a string of male lives and you are female this lifetime you may feel out of place. Your culture or family expect you to act and respond in highly feminine ways but you feel like a male trapped in a female body. You find yourself preferring male oriented tasks and can't relate to female oriented ones. You may be labeled a tomboy early in your life and suffer many self doubts about your sexual identity. If you have retained your sexual preference for females then you will be homosexually oriented, thus creating more intense self-karmic feelings.

This same scenario would be true in reverse for a male with a recent string of female lifetimes. He may have difficulty with the expected macho behavior of his culture leading him to withdraw or discover a homosexual lifestyle in which he feels more comfortable. Sometimes the man overcompensates in trying to fit in by becoming an ultra stereotype of the male image such as a Hell's Angel or weightlifter. Behind this macho male parody the man may experience intense self doubts regarding his gender identity.

SELF-KARMA AND PROSPERITY

The next most popular self-karma arena is that having to do with prosperity and the ability to have more of whatever you wish. The issue becomes how much you can have. This most often relates to money in this society (that is, all levels except young souls, who generally have wealth handled well). Culturally speaking how much you can have is related to how much you are worth. Self-esteem is at the root of this issue and of course is excellent territory for self-karma.

Very few people are satisfied with what they have.
You either feel you have too much money and give
yourself trouble about it or you feel you have too little
and feel badly about the lack. You experience envy,
jealousy, admiration, hate, and love all related to what
you can have, what you cannot have, and what others
have, or have not.

Prosperity relates to how much you can have in every area of life such as talents, skills, qualities, time, rest, pleasure, and almost anything else you can think of. These are the things you give yourself the most trouble about.

In fact prosperity is such a major issue that it will be covered in depth in a subsequent chapter.

SELF-KARMA AND THE FAMILY

The next favorite arena for self-karma concerns family relationships. The question raised here is, "How can I have good relationships in my family and feel good as a member of the family?" Although family is usually a focus for karma between people, it is just as suitable as a setting for self-karma. How you feel about your family membership is a foundation for most other intense experiences throughout life. Upon this is based self-esteem and much of the activity of the chief negative features that provide so many personal lessons.

If you feel intensely close to your family of origin you may in fact have trouble becoming independent to form a new family. You may always run back to Mama or Papa when trouble strikes and feel dependent on them for answers well into your twenties, thirties, and even forties. If you feel alienated from your original family you will perhaps experience isolation and rejection or you could react by being motivated to form a new close family.

Your position in the family will also determine what kinds of self-karmic experiences you will have. If you are the firstborn you will perhaps have to feel more responsible for younger siblings or maybe feel poorly about your lack of leadership and responsibility. If you are middle born you may feel squeezed by other siblings and react by feeling neglected and passed over. If last born, you might feel like the baby all your life or on the other hand you might feel unfettered and free to express yourself after the older siblings have worn your parents down over the years.

Your new family is also an excellent arena for the play of self-karma. You can have lessons regarding how you feel about mothering or fathering. You can experience isolation and rejection with one child and closeness and rapport with another. You can feel like a good provider or you can berate yourself for being a lousy one. These are all powerful personal or self-karmic lessons having to do with family.

THE SELF-KARMA MOANS

How often have you heard yourself or others pose the question, "I have a lousy job (or relationships or health etc)—how on earth does that serve me? How can that possibly do me any good? Did I ask for this?"

Let's discuss this. If you are at a job you dislike you can be asleep most of the time. By asleep we mean you don't have to be conscious, you don't have to think. You don't have to do anything that would make you wake up, pay attention and be an adult at any part of the day or night. It serves false personality to stay in self-karmic situations because then it has something to complain about. It serves essence to have self-karma because it will eventually lead you to learn the lesson associated with it.

Let's say you feel quite safe and secure. You know that you are going to receive $325 per week and that's exactly what your pay check will be. You know exactly what time you start work, what hour you come home, so you clock in and clock out, comforted by the structure and not having to take responsibility. You feel totally secure. The rest of the time you go around moaning about your job,

complaining to your cronies and resisting actually doing
your job. You play around in the evenings and weekends
and the rest of the time you go back to work and put in
your hours again. You are busy learning that resisting a
bad situation doesn't make it better.

However this pattern also effectively keeps you a child, and
leaves you with no personal responsibility. This keeps you from
being aware and awake about your life which can be painful and
difficult at times. This also gives you many hours at work that
you can in reality be asleep about your true nature. This encour-
ages you to be asleep the rest of the time too. You can stay numbed
and lulled into a false sense of security. You are provided with
minimal survival and your body will get by fine. You can buy a
little apartment and live like that forever. You can stay asleep
and not look at anything too closely.

This is how you can cushion yourself with incredible quanti-
ties of down pillows of asleepness. There is no need to wake up.

The truth of the game of the physical plane is to handle all
spheres. To be emotionally open without being walked on, and
without being too closed off; to be in the knowledge of what is
true, working with what is true and still know that with human
fallibility you are not going to do what is true every moment; this
means you can be in forgiveness about yourself so that you can be
back on the path of walking the line between truth and false-
hood as well as you can.

HOW TO HANDLE SELF-KARMA

Self-karma also conforms to the law of triads, a subject that
will be covered in detail in a subsequent chapter. Here we will
mention it briefly because the triadic relationship is the most
karmic one and knowledge of it can greatly facilitate the
completion of self-karma.

The three positions of the triad are 1. affirming; 2. denying;
and 3. neutralizing. The intensity of self-karma comes from

either the affirming position or the denying position. You do not get intense about the neutral position.

For example when essence sets up a self-karma, it sets up the following situation; "I am going to have a desire within myself which may or may not involve other people. Then there will be some kind of denying force that prevents me from getting what I want. The self-karma is that I want something and I can't have it."

The neutral position is already available but usually you have not realized it or you have overlooked it. That position says, "Although I don't have what I want I am O.K. the way I am right now. Things can change and that's O.K. too."

When you look inside yourself and seek the neutral position the problem disappears and the situation becomes much easier. The challenge then doesn't have to be overcome, because you can learn how to find neutrality. This does not mean that you have to give up everything you desire to find happiness. It does mean that when the pressure is off, you are much more likely to discover and have what you wanted.

> *Let us take the example of losing weight. The affirming position is that you want to lose weight. You feel that it is important. You truly want to do it.*
>
> *This elicits the negative response. You think, "I can't lose weight. I can't lose weight because I like to eat too much or because I have big bones or because I have high stress at work. Every time I diet my weight goes up. I get nervous and that makes me eat. I feel very bad about all this and so I feel like giving up. I guess I am not worthwhile as long as I am fat."*
>
> *The neutral position is, "I acknowledge my weight and I am O.K. regardless of my body weight. I am not defined by my weight."*

Easier said than done! How does a person reach the neutral position? This is not simply an intellectual exercise. Let us examine how this can be accomplished.

Self-karma is usually related to past history. As mentioned earlier, self-karma has often been going on for a long time and may be related to past life sequences or to childhood imprinting. Often there is a cause that triggered it all in very early life. This can be dug out by regression either through hypnosis or light trance work. In this manner you can also examine past lives and see what it was that made essence say that this would be an interesting self-karma for this life.

> _For example maybe you didn't like being heavy in a past life. All right, next lifetime you shall be even heavier and so on until you get neutral around being heavy. You may get heavier and heavier until that happens._
>
> _You might have starved to death for a few lifetimes and decided to go for big bodyweight and experience what that is like._
>
> _Perhaps as an infant in this life you associated eating with being accepted or loved by your mother. Or you developed the fear that if you change then people won't accept you._

There can be layer upon layer of negative blocks from the present, from earlier this lifetime, and from experiences in previous lifetimes. This gives you a massive amount to become aware of consciously. When the issue becomes conscious you can then have a choice about whether it will continue to control you or whether you wish to release it. Releasing it makes the neutral position possible.

Therefore it is of utmost importance to look at the essence issues. You may discover that the issue on an essence level gets far removed from the fact that you cannot stay on a diet.

You can complete self-karma by embracing the neutral position and letting go of intensity around the issue. The basic bottom line fear is that you cannot love yourself or cannot be loved by others just the way you are. The underlying issue on an essence level is always unconditional acceptance of yourself and others.

Now that you have seen how the basic law of karma provides an opportunity to learn lessons by experience, you can get a sense of how the game of life on earth is run. Let us now take a look at how you set up the conditions at birth for the specific karmic influences that you wish to deal with. Let's take a simple look at astrology from the reference of this teaching.

ASTROLOGY

The study of astrology has been with you thousands of years, a constant if ephemeral thread running through all major civilizations. Why is this so? What is astrology and how does it influence you?

This section explains how astrology works to give you a blueprint for karma. Astrology is simply a map of how you bring in your karma, and as such it facilitates different sorts of experiences in your life.

Your personal astrological chart is chosen by essence to provide a series of influences on the personality you want.

When you were born all the planets in the solar system were in a particular configuration in relation to the earth; the earth is taken as the central point because that's where you are.

Some planets and stars are further away, some are closer and so on. Astrologers have studied for many centuries exactly what this means. They have mastered the finer points and set these down in great complexity.

At the time you were born there was a particular configuration of houses and planets. Houses are a means of slicing up the sky above you like a large pie. The sky is notionally divided up into twelve segments or slices so there are twelve houses. When you were born the planets were in certain houses. If you were born in July the heavens look different from the way it would look if you were born in January.

ASTROLOGICAL INFLUENCES AROUND KARMA

The Houses

1ST	PHYSICAL BODY, PUBLIC PERSONA, HEALTH
2ND	MONEY, POSSESSIONS
3RD	DAY-TO-DAY INTERACTIONS, SHORT JOURNEYS, SIBLINGS, SCHOOLING.
4TH	HOME, FAMILY, ROOTS.
5TH	CREATIVITY, SHORT TERM SEX KARMA, YOUR CHILDREN
6TH	WORK KARMA, EMPLOYEES, EMPLOYERS, MAJOR ILLNESS
7TH	PARTNERSHIP, MARRIAGE, LONG TERM SEX KARMA
8TH	DEATH, REGENERATION
9TH	PHILOSOPHY, HIGHER EDUCATION, OTHER CULTURES,LONG JOURNEYS
10TH	CAREER, REPUTATION, AUTHORITY IN COMMUNITY
11TH	FRIENDS, ACQUAINTANCES, SOCIAL CIRCLE
12TH	INSTINCTIVE, THE UNCONSCIOUS, FEARS, RE-EVALUATION

Each person has all of the twelve houses listed here and you have all of the qualities of all the houses in your life. You have a body, you have money, you have possessions, you have a family and so on. These twelve houses specialize in those different areas of your life.

This gives you the picture of what the twelve houses are. They are always the same—the first house is always to do with your body, etc.

What is different is that when you are born you will have the planets in one or another of those houses and they won't be the same as anyone else's.

For instance if you were born when the sun was in your fourth house you are going to be different from your next door neighbor who may have the sun in their sixth house.

That is the basic information that you need to know. The qualities attributed to each planet are as follows. Note that they are only the qualities relating to karma and self-karma, so the qualities give a narrow interpretation for the purposes of this discussion.

The Planets

SUN	SELF-KARMA, MOVING CENTER (MOVEMENT/PRODUCTIVITY) KARMA, HOW YOU USE YOUR OVERLEAVES
MOON	EMOTIONAL SELF-KARMA, MOOD SWINGS
MERCURY	COMMUNICATION KARMA, KARMA WITH MECHANICAL DEVICES
VENUS	LOVE KARMA, KARMA WITH WOMEN
MARS	SEX-KARMA, KARMA WITH MEN
JUPITER	SUPPORT KARMA, EXPANSIVE KARMA, GROWTH KARMA

SATURN   STRUCTURED AND DIFFICULT KARMA

URANUS   ECCENTRIC KARMA

NEPTUNE   SPIRITUAL & CONCEPTUAL BELIEF
            SYSTEM KARMA; MENTORS AND
            MUSES

PLUTO   TRANSFORMATION AND DEATH

(There are two additional planets, very far away, yet to be discovered and of minimal influence, giving a total of twelve influences.)

The question is, "What do the planets do for you?." What they do for you is to put you in touch with your karma. Remember that karma is intensity in your life. It leads you to be able to experience a person who walks in the door as an intensity—a positive intensity or a negative intensity. You decide this.

All that the planetary influence does for you is that it puts a little bit of a charge, a magnetic charge, on the fact that you are going to be paying attention to this particular issue today, or this week or this month.

This happens because of the fact that a particular planet is sweeping through a specific house right now.

The solar system comprises all the planets spinning around the sun like a gigantic wheel. All the orbiting planets act like a huge electric generator; the sun is the magnet and the planets are the coil. The gravitational and magnetic fields they generate create an energetic effect that influences us in daily life.

Take Mars, which relates to karma about sexual matters. Mars comes sweeping into one of your houses, let us say careers. What you will find is that out in your career place you are running into sexual karma. It is as simple as that. So out there in your career people will come up and you will have the opportunity of participating in sexual karma with them. You may choose to pick up that sexual karma or let it rest. You can go ahead and play in that arena or say no, I don't want to. You also can have the sex karma as positive or you can bring in one that is negative.

Now the planets are continually moving. So what happens is that you get a chance to have Mars for instance visit each of your houses over and over again. When Mars visits your second house you find that you have your sex karma coming up around financial matters, so you encounter them while you are out cutting a business deal.

The principles are as simple as that and the basic notions are really very easy. If you want to find out what house Mars is running through right now, you can ask your local astrologer to tell you, and you can say Aha! Mars is here.

Again, you can look at Venus and see where all your love karma is. Venus also has to do with hate. You can see where you might run into people you particularly dislike. This will happen if you decide you want the karma to be negative.

THE SUN AND THE MOON

The Sun is a little more specialized because it is not strictly a planet. The Sun is not influential in what may happen to you but is focused on your self-karma, such as the challenges you set up for yourself. The Sun governs who you are on a day-to-day basis out there in the world for people to see.

You can notice where your Sun is moving with respect to your houses. For example if you are Gemini, near your birthday, the Sun comes back to where it was when you were born, emphasizing the house of communication. The issue of communication becomes doubly re-emphasized. You will have communication karma all around you. Because the Sun does its circuit annually and your birthday is annual, this particular phenomenon will be a regularly occurring event.

The Moon is related to karma that is going on for you internally and emotionally in a more hidden fashion within yourself. Like the Sun, you can also notice it with respect to your houses.

Let us examine the astrological influence of the Moon and see how it works. It pulls on the water and the oceans on this planet and creates tides. A human body is 90% water. When the moon is relatively close, it pulls on a person in a certain direction since he is a body of water. Because the Moon is the closest celestial body to earth and its pull is so strong, it crowds out the other influences at that time. The influence then is quite visible.

Statistically this has been recorded in the upsurge of hospitalizations, reported crimes, and other indicators of social intensity at   the full moon, the time of the moon's peak influence.

The Moon will then affect a person emotionally and the nature of that affect will be determined by what the affect was at the time of birth. Before that, it influenced the mother and related to her astrology. So a person's own private astrological setup started at the moment of birth. The person's emotional susceptibility was determined at that moment. The magnetism influences a person to be more in touch with emotion than usual.

THE NATAL CHART

Now if you look at what your astrologer calls your natal chart, it will tell you what karma you are going to have this entire lifetime over and over again. The natal chart shows what houses the planets were in at the time of your birth.

Let's say when you were born, Saturn was in your Fourth House. Saturn has mainly to do with obstacles and the Fourth House has mainly to do with your family.

That means your family will introduce you to most of your obstacles, and that will be a general tendency for your whole lifetime.

For example, your mother or father becomes a nemesis to you and your brothers and sisters introduce various difficulties into your life and so on. That sounds simplistic but you will notice that around your family you will always have opportunities this lifetime to have obstacles to work through.

Whether or not that happens depends on how you have your karma set up around a particular issue. Your birth chart will indicate what the themes are for you this entire lifetime.

For instance suppose you were born with the Sun in your First House. For your entire lifetime you will have self-karma about your body; like it or not you will feel intense about your body most of the time.

However you may resolve your issues about your body after a number of years during which it is a source of problems. Perhaps you are able to complete all the karma you set up for yourself regarding your body. Even though you are complete on this issue, your astrology will cause opportunities to continue to arise.

Someone will come up and say "Gee you're looking exeptionally ugly today." You get a chance to say to yourself - "I could get into self-karma about my body right now" or to say "No, I won't let that happen. He's not going to get a rise out of me. That's just his opinion. My body's just fine."

So the most important chart you can look at is your birth chart. The planets are always moving and their influences are constantly changing, whereas your birth chart is fixed and the influences apply to your whole life.

As a result, when the planets indicate a certain emphasis and the emphasis is already in a person's birth chart, the effect of the influence is doubled; a double whammy effect. So if the Sun is in your First House today and it is also in the First House in your natal chart, then you are doubly likely to feel the intensity of your feelings about your body. A person in this situation really finds himself tested as to whether he has this self-karma handled and is truly neutral.

Now you can have two or more planets in the same place more or less at the same time—say the house of careers. This would result in your having self-karma about your career, communication karma with your career, sex karma in the career, people that you are falling in love with in your career and so on. One could assume that there wasn't much more to your life than what was happening in your career.

One house that this is particularly noticeable in is the house concerning money.

> _When you have multiple planets there at one time, you might experience an unfortunate divorce case where your spouse is regrettably successful at making off with the family assets; your favourite child has an appendix operation with complications costing thousands; your grandmother dies and the funeral and legal expenses are astronomical and so on; in other words issues with women; issues with family; issues with money; all contributing to the experience of major self-karma._

A point to be highlighted here is that astrologically speaking, whatever karma you have lined up for this lifetime, a guide is provided as to when it may occur and in what setting. Astrology is only an indication as to the time and setting. The karma must be already in your plan for the lifetime or it will not occur. Therefore two people born at the same moment and with the exact same astrological configuration may have quite different experiences depending on the karma they have agreed to experience.

In summary all you need is a basic natal chart so you can see what you are dealing with, as to how you have set up experiences for your whole life.

In looking at the chart you can recognize themes as they are displayed. This then crystallizes issues and enables you to investigate and work on the goal of neutrality, if that is what you want. You can examine the themes of your life and the karma that you have decided upon.

Most old soul karma tends to be more subtle than the younger soul levels and they can be viewed as growing and learning experiences. The planetary influences can be examined and you can be more aware of the kinds of opportunities that may arise for learning and growth.

Remember that this section is solely oriented to how you can use astrology to determine what karma is likely to be coming into your life. There are a myriad of other facets to astrology, such as many other qualities that surround each planet, and this is beyond the scope of this introduction.

SOME HIGHLIGHTED POINTS

1. People's signs are not all that accurate as a guide. When astrological influences first began, the planets' locations and patterns were different. Those influences now are relatively minor. They still exist to some degree however. What matters is the house that different planets are transiting. So being a Leo is less relevant than knowing what house your Sun is in.

2. There are two additional planets not listed here and they are far enough away for their influence not to be significant. When they become discovered the gaps in astrological charts will probably not be deemed to be important.

3. Biorhythms are not related to astrology at all, but instead to the magnetic patterns of this planet and how they affect you.

4. Relationship charts are not about adding two charts together and getting twice the number of planets. One person relates to his own karma and the other relates to theirs. Midpoint astrology is valid and may show up stress points in a relationship.

5. Astro-cartography validly shows where your karma is on the planet. You can calculate the different locations and travel to places where you might be seeking certain sorts of karma. Money karma for example would be related to where you might either go bankrupt or strike it rich.

6. Each seventh year birthday is a major milestone for you astrologically speaking.

To summarize, karma puts a charge on experiences and relationships so that you are anything but neutral about many of your daily encounters. Astrology is a probable map of those experiences derived from your birth chart, the planets and the houses. From your natal chart you can see how the deck is stacked for your whole life.

You have seen how you set up the conditions for creating and resolving karmic ribbons in your life. Now let's take a look at your life task and how you go about achieving it.

THE LIFE TASK

What is your life task? How is it different from your goal in life? How do you accomplish your life task and how do you identify it?

Your life task is that principle activity in life that you have set out to accomplish. Essence has programmed your cells from conception with particular talents, skills, and abilities that eventually move you toward this life task. By nature then you

come adequately equipped to be good at whatever your life task
is. Now it is important to realize that your life task is not
necessarily synonymous with your career even though it might be.

> *You may find that you have an exceptional talent for*
> *archery when you are in high school. Now because of*
> *your family's economic situation you decide not to go to*
> *college but to become a fireman instead. You work for*
> *years as a fireman and are able to support your family*
> *with the salary you receive from this work. Yet your*
> *interest in archery grows and you enter local competitions*
> *where you gain a reputation as a hotshot. Eventually you*
> *are singled out for your country's Olympic team and you*
> *win gold medals at the Olympic competitions. You*
> *continue to work as a fireman but you spend every spare*
> *moment at archery, your heart's delight. Eventually you*
> *train others in your unique method and leave your mark*
> *on the entire field. Inspiring people through archery*
> *then is your life task.*

Even if the circumstances of your life limit you greatly, you
can still accomplish a major life task. A good example is the
Birdman of Alcatraz who, although imprisoned for life in the
federal penitentiary, managed to become an expert healer of
birds.

Most people do not embark upon their life task until they are
at least twenty-eight years old. Some people do not discover it
until they are in their early forties. The reason for this is that
your life task demands concentration and dedication, both
difficult when you are busy being imprinted and working out
karma. When you have sorted out your conditioning and dumped
unwanted programming you are in a much better position to focus
on your life task. Let us give you another example.

> *You are raised in a chaotic household that causes you*
> *to feel intensely insecure and alienated during your ado-*
> *lescent years. You spend your twenties doing clerical work*

LIFE TASK

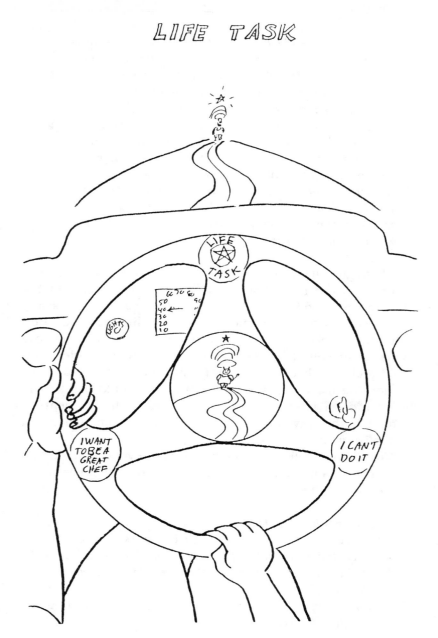

and embark on several short-lived painful marriages. You begin to work on yourself and for a number of years you dedicate yourself to becoming a more stable and secure human being. Eventually you marry a man with whom you have a successful relationship. You give birth to several children among whom is an exceptionally gifted child. Because of what you have learned you are able to provide a stable, secure, and inspirational environment for your children. Because of your love and your dedication you are able to support your gifted child in her development as a world leader. Your life task then has been to raise, imprint, and inspire this daughter for major world influence.

Although your life task is different from your goal, it is most certainly assisted by it. You would never choose a goal that is contradictory to your life task. For example, you would probably not choose a goal of discrimination if your life task had to do with public relations. You would not be likely to choose stagnation if your life task was to be a military leader. You would probably choose dominance if your life task was to be the founder of a major educational system. You would be likely to choose growth if your task was to work with the mentally retarded. In this way you get to proceed toward your goal as you accomplish your life task.

Not all your skills and talents lead you to your life task. You may carry certain abilities forward from former lifetimes where you developed these skills.

Having been a doctor for several lifetimes you may have a particular talent for this kind of work. You can do it easily and it provides you with a good income, yet it doesn't excite you anymore. What excites you now is politics and since you are a good public speaker you gradually move in this direction. Your life task is politics and not doctoring.

You can see then that your life task has to do with what excites you and what you love to do. Just because you are good at something does not mean it is your life task.

When you have decided what you are talented at and what you enjoy doing as well, you can then proceed directly toward fulfilling your life task. However even the most enjoyable tasks have parts that you may find distasteful or unpleasant. While you may be a master musician who loves to perform, you may find that booking your engagements is a tedious and stressful task.

You are more effective in accomplishing your task when you delegate what you do not enjoy doing to someone who does enjoy it. For someone, booking engagements for other people is a special talent that they love to do. This is their life task. The more you employ people and surround yourself with people who are doing their life task, the easier it is for you to accomplish your own.

You truly accomplish your life task when you spend the majority of your time and energy doing the part of it that you enjoy the most. The rest you must seek support for. If your life task is writing, you may need an editor, an agent, and a publisher. If your life task is managing a zoo, you may need fundraisers, veterinarians, suppliers, and keepers. You cannot accomplish your life task in a vacuum.

In order to meet your life task, you need to get rid of imprinting that blocks you. This requires that you know how you are imprinted in the first place. In the next chapter we will explore everything you want to know about imprinting.

OVERLEAF CHART

| | EXPRESSION | | INSPIRATION | | ACTION | | ASSIMILATION |
	Ordinal	Exalted	Ordinal	Exalted	Ordinal	Exalted	Neutral
ROLE	+Creation ARTISAN -Self-Deception	+Dissemination SAGE -Verbosity	+Service SERVER -Bondage	+Compassion PRIEST -Zeal	+Persuasion WARRIOR -Coercion	+Mastery KING -Tyranny	+Knowledge SCHOLAR -Theory
GOAL	+Sophistication DISCRIMINATION -Rejection	+Agape ACCEPTANCE -Ingratiation	+Simplicity RE-EVALUATION -Withdrawal	+Evolution GROWTH -Confusion	+Devotion SUBMISSION -Exploited	+Leadership DOMINANCE -Dictatorship	+Free-Flowing STAGNATION -Inertia
ATTITUDE	+Investigation SKEPTIC -Suspicion	+Coalescence IDEALIST -Naivety	+Tranquility STOIC -Resignation	+Verification SPIRITUALIST -Beliefs	+Contradiction CYNIC -Denigration	+Objective REALIST -Subjective	+Practical PRAGMATIST -Dogmatic
CHIEF FEATURE	+Sacrifice SELF-DESTRUCTION -Suicidal	+Appetite GREED Voracity	+Humility SELF-DEPRECATION -Abasement	+Pride ARROGANCE -Vanity	+Selflessness MARTYRDOM -Victimization	+Daring IMPATIENCE -Intolerance	+Determination STUBBORNNESS -Obstinacy
MODE	+Deliberation CAUTION -Phobia	+Authority POWER -Oppression	+Restraint RESERVED -Inhibition	+Self-Actualization PASSION -Identification	+Persistence PERSEVERANCE -Unchanging	+Dynamism AGGRESSION -Belligerence	+Clarity OBSERVATION -Surveillance
CENTER	+Insight INTELLECTUAL -Reasoning	+Truth HIGHER INTELLECTUAL -Telepathy	+Perception EMOTIONAL -Sentimentality	+Love HIGHER EMOTIONAL -Intuition	+Productive MOVING -Frenetic	+Integration HIGHER MOVING -Desire	+Aware INSTINCTIVE -Mechanical
BODY TYPES	+Grandeur JUPITER -Overwhelming	+Agile MERCURY -Nervous	+Luminous LUNAR -Pallid	+Rugged SATURN -Gaunt	+Voluptuous VENUS -Sloppy	+Wiry MARS -Impulsive	+Radiant SOLAR -Ethereal

Chapter Four

Basic Learning

IMPRINTING

Imprinting is one of the major processes that shapes your personality during the beginning of each lifetime. Although you have chosen a set of overleaves to be born with, your personality and the way you use your overleaves is influenced by early childhood experiences. Imprinting is, in part, another word for behavioral conditioning or programming. On the other hand imprinting includes cellular memories of all relevant past life experience.

Some imprinting is essential for survival and basic orientation in life. Problems arise when you are over or under-imprinted.

Imprinting therefore is a complex issue. Let us here unravel its inter-woven parts.

Each lifetime you are born with a predetermined yet chosen set of overleaves that you want to experience and experiment with. Your body comes well equipped for learning the set of beliefs and behaviors necessary to carry out this task. Each cell of your body comes equipped with a complete memory of all past life experience that relates to the overleaves you have chosen.

If you have chosen the attitude of pragmatist, your cells will contain all past life information that relates to pragmatist. It will provide you with a detailed set of information relating to the successes and failures you have had as a pragmatist. Therefore you need not start all over again every lifetime you choose pragmatist as an attitude. You arrive well informed and well armed. Each decision you make as a pragmatist is based on a wealth of experience. You will automatically allow imprinting that helps you to use it the way you wish this lifetime and disallow any programming that you do not desire.

Now some of your imprinting will directly influence how you use your own overleaves. However much of your imprinting will be about behavior unrelated to your personal overleaves. You may be a pragmatist but your parents might both be cynics. You will be imprinted with a cynical point of view that may over-shadow your own pragmatic viewpoint for many years, possibly always. It is important to realize that you select your imprinting, no matter how undesirable it might appear to be. The essence has chosen it to enable lessons to be learned and certain karma completed. Many of these karmic lessons take place in the first half of life so that some specific imprinting is necessary to carry them out.

For example it may be necessary for you to act like a cynic during your high school years in order to get through this rough period. When you have completed this karma you can cast out the cynicism and manifest your true pragmatist attitude.

Your job in each life then, is to toss out all programming that is no longer desired or relevant to the ways that you wish to use your own overleaves. We will say more on removing imprinting later. For now let us examine the process of becoming imprinted.

HOW YOU BECOME IMPRINTED

Imprinting is best described as a set of belief systems and reinforced behaviour that is learned predominantly in the first years of life.

The most intense imprinting comes from family members; secondarily, you are imprinted by school and society—peers, teachers and friends. Because each lifetime is a unique experiment with a host of free choices, you can never predict ahead of time exactly what influences you are going to meet up with.

You might choose parents who have power mode so that you can be imprinted by this influential style. However you cannot predict exactly how they will use their power mode because they have free choice. If they abuse it or are constantly in the negative pole of it you might be imprinted in ways you had not planned on. You then have to make decisions based on this spontaneous pattern. You may choose to move away from them much earlier than planned or accept a certain amount of oppression and make the most of the challenge in getting rid of it.

THE ROLES AND IMPRINTING

Your role affects your ability to imprint or be imprinted. In general the solid roles tend to be better at imprinting children than the more fluid roles, and likewise become more strongly imprinted.

Warriors and kings

Warriors and kings make the strongest imprinters and they of course are the most solid roles. They know the most about having a physical body, how it functions, and how to use it. In addition they are the most organized and action oriented. This makes them excellent at providing an educational environment for children and conditioning them with necessary survival skills. In addition they are the most receptive to conditioning themselves. As children they actively seek guidance in how to do things and how to order their world.

Whereas warriors make the strongest immediate imprinters, kings are the most influential imprinters of all. The presence of a king in a family or group situation is enough to establish lines of imprinting that last for generations.

> *The perfectionism of a king is enough to make children, grandchildren, and great grandchildren perfectionistic no matter what their roles are.*
>
> *Kings are able to set the tone for an entire organization or even a country John F. Kennedy is a good example of a king who imprinted an entire nation with the values of physical fitness and striving for excellence.*

Servers and priests

Servers are good at sticking around the immediate family, serving and inspiring and imprinting their children to do the same. They imprint more by example than by direct teaching as a warrior might. In countries like the United States where servers are at a minimum, they are often so taxed by serving many people that they do not have the time to spend imprinting a single child. In countries like India and China however where there are an abundance of servers, the entire nation becomes imprinted with strong server traits.

Often, rather than imprinting their children to serve, servers produce a different result in their children. They can do too much for their children, undermining their ability to become self-sufficient and independent. Their children can then become imprinted with the belief that they will always have someone to do things for them, or develop the belief that they cannot do anything for themselves.

Servers are quite easily imprintable.

Whereas servers are apt to spend time imprinting their families, priests are usually so active in the world that they are not around enough to imprint strongly. Their extremely high frequency makes them good at trouble-shooting and inspiring larger groups into action, not imprinting a few.

Priests are not as imprintable as the more solid roles because they are rapid processers and not as identified with their bodies. The body and the personality are the ones imprinted and not the essence. As a result priests are not as good at surviving as the more solid roles.

Artisans and sages

The artisan is a high frequency, fluid role and as such is the least programmable of all roles. They are highly creative by definition and resist all attempts to program or condition them. They often go their own way to the chagrin of dutiful warrior parents who wanted to give them a sound foundation by imprinting them with solid and grounded traits. If the artisan chooses more solid overleaves such as dominance or power mode they may leave themselves open for more imprinting. Kings are perhaps the only truly effective imprinters of artisans other than other artisans who act as a reference and model for them.

Artisans are usually too high frequency, creative, and chaotic to be strong imprinters of children. Children of artisans often have to fend for themselves because their artisan parents tend to be inconsistent in their patterns of behavior. This is not to say that artisans cannot provide a loving environment or consistent support. However artisans do not provide the order and organized home base that warriors do.

On the other hand artisans see others as canvases upon which to paint their creative ideas. The artisan is interested in recreating others and this can have its lasting effects.

For example an artisan mother may wish that she had had a daughter rather than a son. In her attempt to recreate him to her fantasy she may discourage his assertiveness and encourage him to act in more feminine ways.

Sages likewise do not often make good imprinters of children unless they have chosen more solid overleaves. Because they tend to mature late and are fun-loving by nature they tend to be more playmate to their children than imprinter. Sages are built for communication with large groups and are often not satisfied with the sometimes tedious work of imprinting children. Nevertheless because they are such good communicators they are good at imprinting others with these skills.

Sages are more imprintable than artisans because their creativity is more focused and they do not see imprinting as a threat to their very being. However they will strongly resist any attempts to program their style of communication.

Scholars

Scholars, true to their nature, vary in their ability to imprint others. As a solid role they are firmly embedded in their bodies and as such they know well the basic survival lessons. They are good at imparting this knowledge to others. However because of their neutrality they are not as strong at imprinting as the other solid roles, warrior and king. They may see others more as objects of study than as clay for the molding.

Scholars, like all the solid roles, are easily imprinted. In fact they are more so because of their assimilative nature. They draw in conditioning like a sponge and may spend a good deal of time dumping unnecessary imprinting later in life. Scholars are more prone to physical ailments because they are so vulnerable to conditioning. They store all this information in their bodies where it sometimes plays havoc with their health.

IMPRINTING AND THE LIFE CYCLE

Imprinting follows a seven year cycle. The first seven years achieves 80% of all imprinting. Here you are conditioned by your parents, guardians, and siblings regarding your major belief systems and habit patterns. Here you make the most important decisions about how you will run your life. You may decide that in order to be loved by mom you must repress your own creativity; or you may decide that in order to win dad's love you must turn away from mom (and all women) and so on.

In the nine months of fetal life there is heavy imprinting, mainly by the mother. There is secondary imprinting by the father and those who spend time around the pregnant mother. During this time you, as a fetus, are imprinted with the foundations of language and a basic orientation to the world based on trust or the lack thereof. You learn whether you are wanted or not and you sense the nature of the environment that you are about to experience.

The most powerful imprinting has to do with survival lessons. This type of imprinting is the deepest and in some ways the most difficult to change later in life. These are the decisions you feel forced to make out of a fear you will be annihilated or maimed. To an infant or young child loss of love is considered catastrophic.

You might decide that to assert yourself in the face of dominant parents would endanger your safety and survival, causing you to strengthen your chosen caution mode.

Children are powerful at manipulating the environment so that they can have precisely the experiences their essence is

IMPRINTING

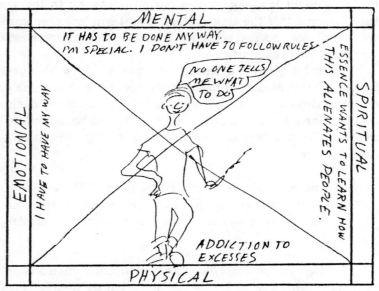

seeking. In divorce situations it is often the case that a child will manuever to be with a particular parent.

Sometimes a child in a family will influence one parent to leave the family. This persuasion may be done on an essence level in the dream state. Perhaps the child didn't want that particular parent's imprinting, only their genetic contribution.

Adoptions, foster homes, and step-parents all provide alternate imprinting patterns. Even though these often produce apparent hardship and suffering they provide the necessary ingredients to challenge personality in its spiritual development. Although such chaotic childhoods often lead to lives of criminal activity or mental instability in younger souls, they just as often contribute to the spiritual challenges of older souls.

The ages 7 to 14 years account for the secondary imprinting. This less powerful imprinting governs such things as personal habits, how the role and overleaves are expressed, what it means to be male or female within the culture, values, religious beliefs, a sense of right and wrong and so forth.

From 14 years of age onward, imprinters are usually chosen for selective learning. You may gravitate toward a certain teacher or model so that you can learn something very specific from them, such as how to succeed in the real estate business, or how to look after a young child. More abstract examples would be how to be more spiritual or how to be more macho.

The major period of imprinting is complete by the late teens but you continue to be imprinted for the duration of your life. You are imprinted by your mate, colleagues, children, boss and by your political, social, and religious affiliations. Perhaps most of all you are imprinted by the culture you choose to live within.

PROCESSING IMPRINTING

Between the ages of twenty-one and twenty-eight you begin to process your imprinting, discriminating about which to keep and which to let go. You make further decisions about what other imprinting to seek. This is characterized by a period of self evaluation. The review reaches its peak about the age of twenty-eight. Those years can be intensely uncomfortable.

From ages twenty-eight to thirty-five are major dumping years. Here you usually cast out all imprinting that is obscuring your chosen set of overleaves and any imprinting that obscures your true soul level.

> *If you are actually a mature soul who has baby soul parents there is a good chance that you will act somewhat like a baby soul until you are in your late twenties. Here, if you have not done so already, you make a special effort to cast off the programming that keeps you from manifesting as a mature soul. Where you may have held fairly rigid beliefs about the nature of God you begin to replace these notions with more expanded ones.*

Because of this dynamic of imprinting it can be difficult to determine the soul age of a person under thirty years old. They are typically involved in this process of weeding out unwanted values and behaviour patterns from their overall imprinting. The process is usually not complete until a person is around thirty-five years old, but it may be achieved ten years earlier or later.

You can often see people make a dramatic change around that age as they realize what they truly want to do with their lives. This is sometimes called the mid-life crisis.

At thirty-five the role and soul age can truly manifest. So for example an artisan who has two warrior parents will behave and appear like a warrior until this imprinting is largely shed and the true essence shines through. Similarly, as mentioned, it is common for older souls with young soul parents and imprinting not to manifest their perceptivity until about the mid-thirties. Friends and relatives notice an abrupt personality change where the person suddenly appears to be much different and often wiser.

CASTING OUT UNWANTED IMPRINTING

How do you actually dump or cast out unwanted imprinting? There are numbers of methods. First of all the method used depends upon whether the imprinting is conscious or not. Unconscious imprinting always has symptoms in terms of embedded beliefs, habits, behavior patterns, or physical ailments. These are literally embedded in the tissue of the body and as mentioned are recorded in the cells.

First these symptoms must be targeted as problems or as undesirable. They can then be focused on in a variety of ways. However let us digress here for a moment and discuss the building blocks of imprinting.

Imprinting has four main components—physical, emotional, intellectual, and spiritual. In order to cast out imprinting all four must be addressed. Many methods and therapies are only partially effective because they deal with only one and sometimes two components. If all are not addressed the imprinting is not completely removed and has a tendency to come back and affect personality again.

Traditional psychotherapy usually seeks to address the intellectual and emotional levels of imprinting. This is an effective method for making unconscious processes concious and for releasing repressed emotions related to imprinting.

Body oriented therapies have seen the need to release imprinting imbedded in the musculature and cellular structure of the body. However they sometimes neglect the intellectual and emotional levels of imprinting.

Traditional religions have sought to help people release imprinting through prayer and ritual but have neglected the other critical levels of imprinting.

Past life therapies seek to address the spiritual component that other methods have neglected and attempt to tie this into the emotional, intellectual, and physical levels with varying degrees of success. This represents a further evolution in the complete eradication of unwanted imprinting. However past life therapists often neglect to understand the tenacious nature of some forms of imprinting and rely too heavily on a quick-fix approach.

Because few therapies offer a complete approach to dumping imprinting it is up to you to design a unique method that works for you. This may involve work with several practitioners skilled in dealing with one or several levels of imprinting.

The most important ingredients in casting off imprinting are desire and timing. With these you will be able to eradicate undesirable imprinting with almost any method you choose.

One Method of Casting Off Imprinting

Begin with a physical ailment, tension, center of pain, or tender place in or on your body. Focus on this place with closed eyes and begin to visualize it as a shape, size, texture, color, temperature etc. If you are not good at visualizing then hear it or sense it tactically. Get a sense of the emotion related to it; sadness, anger, hopelessness, fear, a sense of being trapped or frustrated, or what have you. Allow the feeling to emerge and allow it to be.

At this time let yourself have a memory from the past or a symbolic picture or image. Take the first one that occurs to you without censure no matter how silly or seemingly inane. This will be the right one. Scan it over in detail and allow yourself any insights that occur to you, however do not strain at this. In particular check to see if you made any life decisions if you are scanning over a memory. Notice your emotional state of being. If the emotion has cleared and you feel lighter and freer you have released the imprinting. Check the original body sensation or pain. If it has reduced or disappeared, you have succeeded. If the pain persists or the emotional state intensifies, continue the process by allowing yourself an earlier memory or a second image. Continue until you experience a release and feel flat or neutral.

To complete the exercise, go to the area of your body where you focused on the sensation and using your imagery fill that area in with your personal golden energy that you draw from just above your head.

Variations

1. When you have retrieved a memory after following the above exercise you may wish to dialogue with whoever appears in your memory. If you remember being a little child being scolded by your father you may wish to talk with that little child that is you and give him advice and comfort. Also speak with your father as you would as an adult and see if you can understand his point of view. Perhaps you need to yell back at him or set him straight on your feelings. Maybe you need to apologize to him or forgive him for his frustration. Do whatever completes the business. Deal with all characters in the image or memory. Continue with the exercise as described.

2. Begin the exercise as before. When you allow yourself to have an earlier memory or image, specify that you wish to see any past life images, memories, or patterns that are related. Work with these as described above.

3. You may begin the exercise by focusing on a physical sensation, a preselected memory or image, or an emotional state. If you begin with an emotional state or preselected memory then try to ground it by discovering what area of your body reacts when you focus on it.

STORING PAST LIFE EXPERIENCES IN THE BODY

Just as you are imprinted in one individual lifetime by parents, culture and society, so you carry with you influences and conditions from many previous lifetimes.

And, just as with imprinting, the emotions attached to the experiences have a physical representation in the tissue of the body similar to a knot in a piece of wood. Both are infusions of energy and are there physically in the cellular structure of the body or in the wood.

These past life experiences carry a certain energy charge with them. This charge attracts a similar experience again this lifetime. So you may become injured in the kneecap and it is a reminder of a severe past life experience which hadn't been fully resolved on an emotional level. It is common that such an injury would not heal fully and the ongoing ache would be an inner prompting for you to conduct an unconscious review of the original event. The past life experience could be brought into conscious awareness through meditation, channeling or regression therapy.

Scars are often guideposts to memories stored in that area. Some injuries mend and the evidence disappears—that is because it did not relate to past life experiences. Other wounds, even trivial ones, leave a prominent scar and are a manifestation and reminder of unfinished emotional business.

In your left heel for example might be stored the experience of being dragged behind a chariot many centuries ago. Marks on the ankles can be a reminder of lifetimes spent in slavery.

The most storage occurs in the softest tissue of the body, such as the colon, the intestines and so on.

Older and deeper unresolved past life issues will be stored in increasingly hard tissue over many lifetimes. One of the most common is knee joints. The experiences that have been intensely traumatic and so emotionally charged that they have not been unconsciously resolved for hundreds or even thousands of years, are stored in the hardest tissue of all—the bone of the skull, in the teeth and in fingernails.

Sometimes people report going to the dentist with recurrent pain in their teeth and the dentist can find no specific cause. That is sometimes a manifestation of unresolved past life experiences.

It is common for past life issues to lie dormant for a long time. When you encounter the individual who caused the trauma of that past life it may be awakened. It then may manifest as pain in the relevant part of the body.

Suppose you were female in the third century and because of your intransigence your volatile lover broke your arm in a fit of jealousy. When you meet that person this lifetime you may experience inexplicable and severe pain in your arm. This is surprisingly common. It occurs because essence has decided that it is appropriate to meet this person again in this lifetime and the associated pain prompts the unconscious part of the personality to conduct a review. The meeting again may or may not also involve the creation or payback of karma.

Headaches, stomacheaches and the like are often related to this. All gout is in fact past life related and can be treated in this context.

Sometimes there is acute discomfort between two people for no apparent reason. They in fact would perhaps like to be friendly toward one another but past life fears and memories raise fears that feel real but come from an unconscious level.

For example you may be introduced to Susan who seems nice enough. But after a few minutes you experience back pain and excuse yourself. Every time you find yourself in the company of Susan you develop back pain so you learn to avoid her. Upon developing awareness of this situation you may discover that in another lifetime Susan was responsible for tripping your horse which resulted in a fall that broke your back.

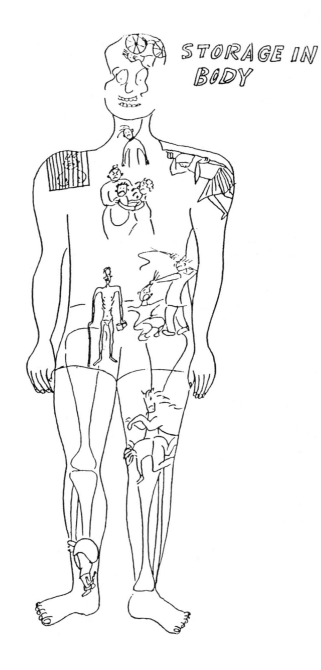

STORAGE IN BODY

RELEASING PAST LIFE STORAGE IN THE BODY

Techniques such as massage, acupuncture, Rolfing, Heller-work, and so on, often stimulate the energy such that it surfaces into conscious awareness. The energy can be released in this way.

Past life memories can be found by using the exercise described in the section on casting off imprinting. You focus on and stimulate certain areas of the body releasing the images and memories stored there.

Past Life Regression Technique

One means of handling unresolved past life issues is through past life therapy or regression analysis. The approach is to get essence agreement to look at the issue. Here are the mechanics of it.

The memory is retrieved from where it is stored in emotional part of the instinctive center and brought into the intellectual or emotional center of the conscious mind via the exercise described earlier. You see the event as it occurs in your mind's eye, including the garb of those times and the surroundings, and the background that gave rise to that past life situation.

You then relive the emotions surrounding the event. You look at why you did what you did. You realize the trauma was stored in the body because forgiveness was not complete. You examine who you were and the purpose of that life time, and if the karma was being created or paid back. Then you consider if you are able to forgive yourself and the others involved in the context of all this information. If you are able to actualize and feel a sense of forgiveness it is likely the past life issue is resolved. You may however mull it over for weeks or months before being able to feel forgiveness. Most people can arrive at forgiveness but if not, then the matter is rested until it arises again.

Meditation is another way of arriving at the understanding and forgiveness around past life issues. It is a ready approach for issues that are less traumatic or severe. Hypnosis and light trance work is also used. Frequently simple attention and awareness of one's feelings is sufficient for identifying and resolving minor occasional "upsets."

You now have a basic understanding of the imprinting process and how you get rid of unwanted imprinting. Now let us look at how you go about selecting that family that imprints you.

FAMILY SELECTION

How do you go about selecting the family you are born into? When do you make these decisions and what are the considerations that contribute to your choice? Here we will examine these questions for a fuller understanding of the spiritual nature of the family.

First of all family selection is usually done between lifetimes on the astral plane. Alternatively it is done by scanning the potential candidates already on the physical plane who are open to having a child. The choices are based on a variety of considerations: affinity, agreements made, outstanding karma, desire for specific conditions, imprinting wishes, and genetic makeup to name a few.

You select your parents for their genetic contributions and for the specific conditioning and imprinting that they can offer. This means that you will want to know what bodytypes they will have and what overleaves they have chosen for the particular lifetime in question.

For example if you wish to be born with a physical disability such as dwarfism then you must choose parents who have this potential in their gene pool.

Sometimes you choose to be born to parents knowing they will put you up for adoption. In this way you arrange your genetic background to be totally different from the people who act as parents, raise you, and imprint you according to your desires. This is never an accident.

Sometimes you choose your parents for purely karmic reasons. If your parent is hostile and beats you, it may be the repayment of a karma where you once were the abusive parent. Although you may feel victimized in that situation, essence has chosen it.

Sometimes when you are older and are manifesting more essence, this understanding can take place, leading to acceptance and forgiveness.

Your birth position in your chosen family strongly affects your experience. The oldest child and the youngest child are the most powerful positions. The youngest is the most powerful of all.

> *Think of the eight month old baby who has all four people in the room totally focused on him and attending to his every want. As the youngest you are in the position to manipulate the most people to imprint you the way you want.*

Kings commonly choose to be either the first born or last born because of the power inherent in these positions.

Infancy is a most powerful time of life. Infants control the atmosphere, and feelings and behavior of those adults around them. They frequently get what they want simply by crying or smiling.

Parents on the other hand are usually in the most powerless position. They get confused because they think they ought to be in positions of power and authority when they really are not. They are typically overwhelmed and distracted by responsibilities and are at the beck and call of their children.

Therefore the rule of thumb is that the older you get, the less powerful you are in relation to your family. This of course relates to your conception of being externally powerful.

Grandparents usually have a better relationship with children because they have slowed down and have accepted their powerlessness in relation to the children's power. They know that children are incredibly powerful at getting what they want and need despite the rules and regulations imposed by the desperate parents. Grandparents more often surrender to children. This is not to say that they are ineffective at bestowing discipline when it is needed.

FAMILY SELECTION AND OVERLEAVES

Families are also chosen for imprinting purposes. You usually select a family that will help you how to learn and express certain overleaves. More often than not you choose at least one parent with your same role to act as a model for you.

For example, a warrior child may choose at least one warrior parent to learn warrior-ness. A child with a difficult self-karmic overleaf like cynicism or martyrdom may learn how be that way from a similar parent. This is quite common.

Also a child may have cynicism as an overleaf to help him survive an abusive upbringing. That overleaf helps him anticipate the worst of a situation so he can avoid it or minimize it. Then as an adult he can look at shifting his attitude to the opposite of the pair, realism, because the purpose of the cynicism was achieved and it is no longer necessary or desirable.

Exalted roles usually choose one parent who is exalted, and ordinal roles usually pick one as ordinal for the same reasons.

FAMILY SELECTION AND SOUL AGE

Younger souls are more apt to make snap decisions to be born into a particular family. The younger the soul the less consideration goes into making these choices. For an infant soul almost any family will do. The younger souls are happy with almost any experience they might have because they have so much they want to learn.

Older souls put much more planning and negotiating into family selection because their karmic needs are much more specific. Old souls also tend to be born into families where they have long past life histories with each other member.

When an old soul decides to reincarnate with young soul parents it is nearly always for karmic reasons.

You have seen how you select your family for the purpose of imprinting you and setting you up in life. Before we can go further into your dynamic relationships with other people we need to discuss how you end each life. So, the next section deals with learning about the profitableness of death.

GETTING THE MOST OUT OF DYING

Recall that death is the seventh of the major rites of passage in each lifetime. It represents a completion and integration of all the experiences and lessons of the lifetime.

As such, your death can be the most influential event in your life. When you die you facilitate many karmic lessons for a great many people. Your death often creates an intense emotional experience for relatives, friends and those touched by you.

For example your death may cause a vast degree of conflict among relatives regarding the inheritance you have left them. Your death may cause friends, relatives, and acquaintances to intensely review the meaning of their lives and perhaps some life-changing insights are the result. Your death may create for them a fresh resolve to meet their potential or cause them to change their life goals.

You often arrange your death in a way that will facilitate the most karma. With the single act of dying you may pay off a major karmic debt and facilitate karmic completion for many others. Consider the impact of the death of John Kennedy, Socrates, or John Lennon.

Therefore death is not something that is predestined. In any lifetime you have a choice of taking a number of exit points you have prearranged for that very purpose. You have usually prearranged for yourself several biological weaknesses as possible causes of death. You may have given yourself a weak heart or immune system so that you could easily develop a disease and die quickly if you so choose. Others may have selected defective kidneys or a predilection for cancer of the pancreas in order to exit life with a failure of these organs.

Your astrological chart may show crises points in your life, that if you wished could be opportunities to die at those times.

You may have originally planned to live eighty years but circumstances were so difficult that it made the goal almost impossible to reach in that lifetime. You may not have anticipated how limiting your parental imprinting would be. Therefore you may decide to die at a much younger age and start over in a new body.

Your choice of when to die is planned for the time most conducive to pay off karma and to impact as many people as possible.

HOW TO DIE

As your chosen time of death approaches, you make numerous additional choices about how you wish to experience the event. You may wish to die fully conscious as would be the case in a sudden accident. Or you may choose to withdraw from life slowly and in stages to make the transition easier. At times essence will tend to withdraw from the body to lighten the intensity of the death experience. The exact event or experience of death is brief and may involve only a few seconds.

As essence leaves the body you begin to lose all sense of linear time. You are literally able to see or sense your whole life from outside of time. Often people speak of this as having their lives pass in review.

Your personality is most fearful of death and wants to believe that it lives forever. It spends most of its waking experience avoiding death. Essence on the other hand is unaffected by fear and welcomes the experience. To essence death is like removing a pair of shoes at the end of a long day.

The lessons you experience and learn each lifetime don't die with the personality but are retained and recorded by essence. This is of course the purpose of the reincarnation cycles.

Over a number of lifetimes you begin to prefer one form of death over another. We might say that you have favorites. Some individuals study or become experts in a certain way of dying. For example, you may prefer to die in water by drowning or in the air by falling from a great height. Some of you would rather die in the excitement of battle while others of you prefer to die doing your favorite thing such as making love or eating.

Death is indeed a most creative act and offers a great range of choices.

DEATH AND SOUL AGE

Infant souls are terrified by death and attempt to understand it through superstition and ritual. Ritual objects keep death away and placate the anger of spirits of the dead. Infant souls tend to believe that the dead live on in spirit form but must be avoided at all costs. In this sense infant souls believe that death is catching like the common cold.

For baby and young souls, death is a frightening affair. It is seen as an experience to be avoided and not discussed. Baby souls believe there is a simple law and order to the life after death. They tend to believe that if a person has obeyed the religious laws, they will be looked after benevolently by the gods or by God. If they have violated the rules in any way they will be subject to the most horrible of after-death experiences. Therefore death is something best not to think about too much.

Young souls often don't know what death might bring. In many cases they have given up superstitious beliefs and the baby soul belief in an orderly heaven and hell. Young souls begin to believe that death is the end of life and that there is no hereafter. This creates an intense anxiety in the young soul of a different type than the terror or the infant and baby soul ages. The young soul lives with the feeling that life must be extended in order to get the most out of it. After all it may be a one-shot deal. Death may be denied altogether.

The younger souls will tend to hang on to life as long as they can, even resorting to artificial means to do so.

> *The United States exemplifies the young soul pretense that death doesn't happen. Death is tucked away in euphemistic funeral parlors and cemetaries where the dead are purported to have a nice view from their gravesite. Even the words dead and death are replaced with "resting" and "eternal sleep." Nothing could be further from the truth.*

Mature and older souls are more casual about death because they have experienced it over and over. Old artisans and sages will even resort to creative ways of dying so as to make death a true expression of who they are. Older scholars have a tendency to want to study death as it happens to them. In general late level old souls may regard death with indifference.

In these sections we have explained the basics of each lifetime and how you go about living them. Now we are ready to go into your important relationships with others and see how these are evolved from one life to another. So, let's see how you set them up each lifetime.

PART THREE

INTIMATE COMPANIONS

Chapter Five

The Cast of Characters

PART THREE

In this section we shift the focus from the individual blueprint for each lifetime to the people whom you relate to, play with, and work with. Here you will begin to understand the nature of your reincarnational relationships and how you can best communicate with them. Here we will go into more depth to help you understand what an essence twin is and how to recognize them if they were to show up in your life. We will elaborate further on your families of consciousness, your cadre, your entity, and your specific place within them.

When you know the true nature of the people you are dealing with, you can begin to accelerate your spiritual growth tremendously. You can cut through the illusion quicker and set your sights on the goals that you wish to accomplish in each relationship. You can know whom to simply enjoy, whom to stop resisting, and when to move away from someone you are complete with. Let us begin with the simplest form of relationship, your agreements.

AGREEMENTS

Agreements are simple contracts made between souls or essences to accomplish certain ends during a lifetime.

For example, just as two people might agree to have lunch at a given time and place, two souls might agree to be born near each other, get married and carry out certain work during that lifetime. These two may also have made agreements to bring other souls into the world.

Agreements are not the same as karma and can therefore be broken by simply acknowledging to the other the desire to break the agreement. For example, as two people's lives unfold there might be unfavorable circumstances for fulfilling agreements to have children, such as the outbreak of war. So the agreement may be broken or postponed.

Often, whole groups of essences agree to work together or live together in communities in order to have particular experiences. Whole towns or tribes are sometimes composed of essences who have agreed to incarnate together again and again. Sometimes these agreements are based on accomplishing certain tasks.

A group which was responsible for the outbreak of war and the abuse of power at a specific time in history may agree to incarnate together in troubled times to work for peace. Another group which was involved in unjustly imprisoning people may work together in a later lifetime to obtain amnesty for political prisoners.

These are agreements to work on karma together. The karma could be worked out individually but there is support in numbers. If they all work together they are likely to complete their karma sooner.

Often these group agreements follow the lines of entities and cadres. An entire entity or cadre may agree to be followers of a particular guru or students of a philosophy or teaching. Others may work together to create a new type of technology that they believe will benefit the world. These activities will usually reflect the role makeup of the entity involved.

For example an entity made up of artisans would probably agree to create something new together such as radio, television, or computers. Another entity made up of scholars and warriors may agree to do research and teach some new body of knowledge.

So you can see that agreements cover a wide range of human experience, such as marriage, giving birth, becoming a student in a particular teaching or helping out someone in distress. Agreements then are basically very simple and can be broken as you might a lunch date. Your date may be neutral about your cancellation or may be annoyed with you as the case may be. You take your chances just as you would in breaking a lunch date.

Who are those people that you make agreements with? Let's take a look.

ESSENCE TWINS

What is an essence twin?

Essence twins are two fragments from different entities, that were cast from the Tao at the same time. About 95% of souls have essence twins or soulmates. About 5% have chosen not to have essence twins.

Essence twins have roughly parallel developments throughout many lifetimes. They may not always be at the exact same soul level or even soul age but they will be within a few lifetimes of each other. For example one may be second level mature while the other is seventh level young. The first may slow down while the other catches up and passes by. Then they might reverse this process, in a way similar to taking turns leading on a hike. They prefer to be around each other for some time each lifetime if they can. When one is alive the other that is not in a body may act as a spirit guide or helper. These roles may be reversed in the next lifetime.

In the many lives they spend together they experience most relationships with one another. They try being brothers or sisters, husband and wife, mother and daughter etc. until they have done every possible combination.

Essence twins do not always recognize each other during a lifetime. Much depends on the overleaves that have been chosen for that life and whether they are harmonious or in conflict. When the overleaves are harmonious the essence twins like to spend much time together. In the older cycles essence twins feel intensely understood by one another.

HOW ESSENCE TWINS APPEAR

Essence twins generally show up in each other's lives in any of three different ways—as relatives; lovers; and as pivotal facilitators.

Commonly essence twins show up as a brother, sister, son, daughter, or other close relative. This ensures a long-lasting, close relationship and an opportunity to give one another much mutual support.

This form of essence twin relationship is very close and can be exclusive or threatening to less secure family members. For example other brothers and sisters may be jealous of the close connection between a mother and one daughter who are essence twins, not to mention the husband feeling left out.

If your essence twin is not among your relatives there is a very good chance that they will manifest as a love interest, sexual partner, and mate. This form of essence twin relationship is often of maximum intensity on an ongoing basis. Although essence twins seek this kind of all-encompassing relationship, they are not necessarily easy ones or harmonious ones. At times they are difficult because of their sheer intensity.

When an essence twin shows up as a lover there can be trouble in the life pattern already established. This is especially the case when one twin is already married to someone else. The arrival of the essence twin on the scene can be highly threatening to the spouse. Here choices must be made. Either the attraction of the essence twin will be sufficient to break up the marriage and reform it with the essence twin, or the essence twins must define their relationship in a way acceptable to the spouse. The spouse is not usually successful in keeping the essence twin out completely.

> _A good example of such a relationship can be seen in the story of King Arthur, Sir Lancelot, and the Lady Guinevere. Sir Lancelot and Guinevere were essence twins and simply could not be kept apart. King Arthur was aware of their relationship and attempted to tolerate it until it became politically unfeasible for him to do so._
> _This is of course is a juicy essence twin tragedy._

Sometimes an essence twin may appear for a brief time in the other's life to facilitate a great life change or pivotal experience. Essence twins make great pivotal facilitators for one another.

> _Consider for example an essence twin showing up briefly as a mentor who advises you to go to medical school and helps you gain admittance through his special connections. You go on to a brilliant career as a medical researcher although you do not see this advisor again._

To reiterate, essence twins are drawn together because of their great familiarity, and their understanding of each other. Yet often the essence twins do not meet up until they are over the age of thirty, so that their period of intense karma and instability is generally over.

Usually essence twins are of complementary energy mixes. So if one was 60% male energy and 40% female energy, the other would be 40% male energy and 60% female energy. This contributes to their attraction for one another and their desire to be together for balance.

Essence twins can be so closely related that they manifest each other's roles to some degree. For example, if a sage and scholar are essence twins, the sage may appear quite scholarly for a sage, and the scholar may manifest the strongly expressive charactistics of the sage. In short, they generally influence each other heavily.

This cross-fertilization can affect you so strongly that you may actually think that you are your essence twin's role and have their overleaves.

If you are a priest with a server essence twin you might believe that you are a server. This would be especially true if you have a goal of submission.

On the other hand you might mistake a warrior with a mode of power for his king essence twin.

Learning to distinguish between your role and overleaves and those of your essence twin can be challenging and sometimes confusing. This is also true for understanding the role and overleaves of other people. You must look closely for the essential and core motivations and behavior.

ESSENCE MATE

Occasionally you will come across someone who feels close and familiar to you but who is not your essence twin nor do they correspond to any other position you can think of.

This person may be an essence mate, an essence twin from a past cycle where you both lived as different roles throughout an entire series of lifetimes. Here they are again, known to you in this cycle not as your essence twin anymore but simply as a well known friend.

TASK COMPANION

A task companion is a person who assists you in external tasks each lifetime. They help you to accomplish your life task and usually share major interests with you. This relationship is usually characterized by rapport and trust. It is easier and less conflicted than your relationship to your essence twin. Your task companion is usually a member of your same entity and they move parallel in your lives with you. They do not however share the same essence with you.

HEART LINKS

A "heart-link" describes the relationship between two persons who have known each other for many lifetimes and who have developed a deep and loving understanding of each other on an essence level.

Being a heart-link of someone is like being a lover or a best friend. It does not necessarily mean both are members of the same entity or that the two people are essence twins or soul mates.

It does mean that because of the many lifetimes with each other they have completed many forms of karma with each other. They have completed all the major monads such as husband-wife, father-daughter, attacker-victim, healer-healed (see Chapter 7 for an explanation of monads). The link does not imply a sexual relationship but it does imply feelings of oneness and love between two people at an essence level.

ENTITY FRAGMENTS

Each individual person is an entity fragment. Your entity is a company of about 800 to 1200 fragments who collectively compose a larger unit. The entity is composed of several essences, each with a number of fragments apiece.

Each of you upon creation from the Tao, chooses an entity to belong to as your family so to speak. You occupy a specific

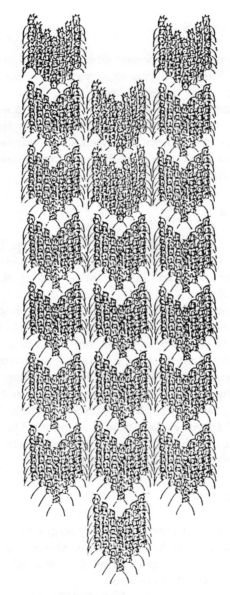

THE MICHAEL ENTITY

CADENCE

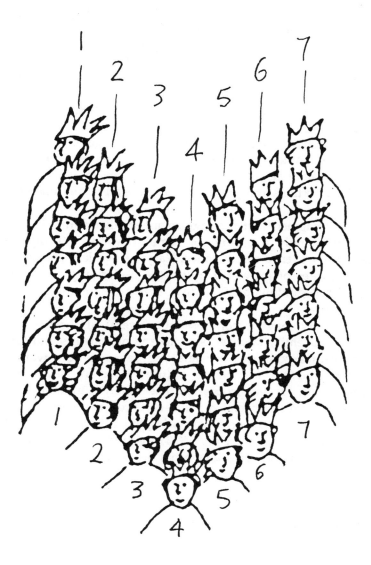

position within that entity that gives you a unique identity. This will be discussed more fully below.

The entity decides as a collective unit what experiences it wants in the universe. If for example it chooses life on earth, it divides once again into its many fragments and each begins to take a series of lifetimes for evolutionary development.

Upon completion of the various stages of development on the earth, you rejoin with all the other entity fragments to recreate the entity. This process of unification is completed on the astral plane.

Now, you do not go through the various stages on earth at the same speed. Some of your entity mates move more quickly, some will move more slowly. Those of you who cycle off first, await the others on the astral plane until you are all finally rejoined.

Entity fragments often recognize one another during lifetimes. There is usually a feeling of familiarity and affinity, and occasionally even a resemblance. Varying overleaf choices and differing rates of growth disguise the underlying similarities, making recognizing one's fellow entity fragments a test of perception.

An entity may be composed of several of the roles. For example our entity Michael is composed of warriors and kings. Some entities comprise artisans and sages, others warriors, scholars, and servers. Some entities have all seven roles represented in varying proportion. The variety is unlimited.

Each fragment specializes in a certain area of living, or in certain types of experiences. You bring this collective knowledge back to the entity after cycling off. The entity is thus enriched by all the different specializations of its members.

Suppose that you specialize over many lifetimes in music. You would manufacture, play, and master instruments of many cultures. In one lifetime you might make music your hobby while in another you make a career of it.

Another entity fragment could make a special study of certain overleaves in depth—e.g. the goal of discrimination. So this person continually attracts people with a goal of discrimination into his or her life. They might appear as relatives, friends, or as a marriage partner. This person would be exposed to them in numbers totally disproportionate to the 2% of the population that have that goal. So this fragment becomes an expert and masters all the characteristics of the goal of discrimination and brings this extensive knowledge to the entity.

When all the fragments have completed their time on earth and have reunited with all other fragments, the entity continues its evolutionary growth on the astral and then the higher planes. It joins progressively with other entities until it finally combines with the Tao itself.

Each fragment's experience of its own identity is not lost. Each fragment maintains its own integrity and memory of its experiences.

Once the entity has rejoined with the Tao, the fragments may then join together in a new entity composed of different fragments for another complete cycle.

There is another aspect regarding the reunited fragments and completed entity on the astral plane. Sometimes the whole entity chooses to manifest again on earth for the purpose of teaching or assisting others, or to complete final karma that is usually on a global scale and has to do with a great many people.

In the Buddhist tradition this is known as Bodhisattva, a high being who returns to earth to help those who are still learning their lessons. There are a number of examples of this type of being, called a Transcendental Soul. Mahatma Gandhi is an example, John the Baptist, Da Free John, and Meher Baba.

CADRE

A cadre is a group of seven entities that work together for purposes of spiritual evolution and growth. Since each entity averages about one thousand fragments, a cadre will average about seven thousand fragments.

The entities within the cadre are ordered from one through seven. The first three entities occupy exalted positions within the cadre, the fourth occupies the neutral position, and the fifth, sixth, and seventh occupy the ordinal positions of the cadre. This means that the exalted entities specialize in more big picture lessons and experiences no matter what roles are contained within it.

> *For example all the warriors, kings, and servers that make up entity number one will tend to have lifetimes that relate to exalted experiences such as politics, the change of culture, and the like. All the priests, servers, and scholars, and sages that make up entity number seven will have slightly more ordinal lifetimes focusing on smaller groups of people and more local tasks. The artisans and scholars in entity number four will act as bridge people for the members of the other entities.*

Each fragment occupies a position within its own entity and within the cadre as a whole. The relative position a fragment holds within its entity and within its cadre reflects the exaltedness or ordinalness of his experiences regardless of role.

Even so, the fragments within an entity are cast in order of role, for example all sages might be cast first, warriors second, priests third and so on. So that in a given entity the first one hundred and forty seven positions may be occupied by sages while the next two hundred and eight positions will be warriors and so on.

A fragment occupying the seven hundred and twenty fifth position within the first entity is ordinal relative to its own entity but exalted relative to the cadre at large. Most fragments then have within them both exalted and ordinal features. A warrior occupying the first position of the sixth entity would be an ordinal role with an exalted entity position with an ordinal cadre position. A priest in the nine hundredth spot of the second entity would be an exalted role with an ordinal entity position and an exalted cadre position. This specific position gives a fragment a unique flavor relative to all other members of the cadre.

Here is a chart showing the relative themes of each entity within the cadre.

Cadre

EXALTED		
Entity #1	+Purpose	- Simplicity
Entity #2	+Stability	- Balance
Entity #3	+Enterprise	-Versatility
NEUTRAL		
Entity #4	+Consolidation	-Achievement
ORDINAL		
Entity #5	+Expansion	-Adventure
Entity #6	+Harmony	-Connection
Entity #7	+Inculcation	-Eclecticism

In general fragments within the cadre will carry out the majority of their relationships and tasks with other members of the cadre lifetime after lifetime. The whole cadre may reincarnate as a village or tribe in order to experience one another and perhaps carry out certain goals that the cadre as a whole wished to accomplish.

The majority of a cadre might reincarnate on a series of islands in the South Pacific during a peaceful historical period there. On the other hand this same cadre might incarnate in a region about to be hit hard by oppression or war such as World War II. In this way the cadre gains a variety of experiences and perspectives about one historical period or event.

Sometimes several cadres will interact and cooperate together to gain experience and carry out projects. For example all followers of a particular belief or teaching may be members of seven cadres.

The positive and negative poles of the numbers apply also to soul levels and to cadence numbers as discussed below.

CADENCE

Each entity within the cadre is also divided into groups of seven fragments. This is something like counting off around a room to make teams for a game. All the "ones" have strong purpose in common, all the "twos" have stability in common and so on, as listed in the above chart.

The number of the cadence and the number within the cadence are both important. For example one server fragment may be among the first seven people to count off in the entity. That server might be number five, expansive in nature. However as a member of the first cadence to count off this server will also have a strong sense of purpose.

Another server might be among the seventh group of servers to count off. This will give that server the quality of inculcation or ability to teach. However let us say this server counts three within his group. That makes him an enterprising server or an enterprising teacher.

These positions have a powerful influence and remain with you throughout a complete cycle of lifetimes with that entity.

Essence twins occupy the exact same cadence positions within different entities of the same cadre. For example one twin might be in the fourth position of the second cadence of the third entity. His twin would occupy the fourth position of the second cadence in entity number six.

Cadence

Entity	Cadence#	Position	Entity	Cadence#	Position
One	One	1234567	Two...	One	1234567
	Two	1234567		Two	1234567
	Three	1234567		Three	1234567
	Four	1234567		Four	1234567
	Five	1234567		Five	1234567
	Six	1234567		Six	1234567
	Seven...	1234567		Seven...	1234567

You have learned so far about the principle characters that make up the cast of each of your lives. Now let's look at how you choose your important relationships and how you communicate or miscommunicate within them. Let's also take a look at your romantic and sexual relationships and understand how these are different.

Chapter Six

Learning to Communicate

COMMUNICATION AND INTIMATE RELATIONSHIPS

Why do you choose the relationships you do? Why does communication in intimate relationships break down and what can you do to re-establish it? Here we will outline the basic causes of miscommunication and describe a procedure for recognizing the problem and correcting it.

First of all, contrary to popular opinion, you usually choose your close relationships for their dissimilarity from you rather than for their similarities. You learn a great deal by being in close proximity to people whose habits and approach to life are different and sometimes opposite to your own. These people offer you the biggest challenges in the area of acceptance and they can interest you and entertain you as well. This is why you often marry someone who is so opposite to you.

Interestingly, the more alike you grow to someone, the more likely you will experience boredom in the relationship. Sometimes long-term relationships dissolve when the couple have resolved all their differences and have become similar to one another.

The older soul age you are, the more likely you will choose intimate friends for their differentness. You want to see just how much you can stretch yourself to tolerate and love those with contrary views to your own. These relationships ultimately teach you how to love yourself, because to the extent you cannot love the other, you cannot love yourself.

Therefore, although those with a similar role and similar overleaves to you are often more comfortable to be with, they do not stretch you. Occasionally you may choose to surround yourself with similar people for comfort and understanding.

For example during a life when you have a goal of flow you may choose to be with someone exactly like yourself. If you are a scholar you may choose to be entirely with other scholars in a scholarly setting.

There is a drawback to being with another who has the exact same overleaves as you or with whom you share several overleaves. You will tend to be blind about the same issues and you can get into some stuck struggles with one another and not be able to find your way out. This is often the case when two people share the same chief feature, stubbornness for example. Two obstinate people can stay stuck for a long time. If you both share dominance as a goal you can end up with some dramatic power struggles. If you both have intellectual centering you may both find it difficult to acknowledge your feelings for one another. If you are both idealists there is no one to ground the other. If you are both in passion mode there may be constant fireworks with little respite. If you are both kings you may have constant struggles over who runs the show.

Relationships between people who have overleaves on the same axis but polar to one another can work quite well. For example two action roles, a king with a warrior, can be a good balance. A person with a goal of dominance with someone in submission can make an excellent pair. Someone with power mode can be balanced by someone in caution mode. An intellectually centered person paired with an emotionally centered person makes for a more interesting relationship.

COMMUNICATION

In every relationship each person is 100% responsible for the communication. What does this mean? This means that you are 100% responsible for what and how you communicate as well as 100% responsible for your response to the other person's communication. Let us look at this more closely.

Whenever there is an upset or misunderstanding between you and your partner, there are only two possibilities to explain the miscommunication.

The first and most common reason for miscommunication is that you decide that the other person intends you harm when actually they meant none. You may have subconsciously misunderstood their communication so that you could rock the boat and have a row and some drama in the relationship. This of course can make life more interesting for you and will provide you with some learning experiences. On the other hand, it can be your attempt to protect yourself from fantasized harm based on old or faulty programs and belief systems.

An example of intentional misunderstanding is that life with your partner has become humdrum and you want to spice things up a bit.

An example of unintentional misunderstanding is that your partner can innocently say something that terrifies you, and you react in an inappropriate way. Maybe your partner says he is going out for a beer with the guys and,

based on your experience with an absent alcoholic father,
you respond with exaggerated fear of abandonment.

Here your responsibility is to work through your own issue or
to take the consequences of your decision to react.

The second reason for upset in a relationship is that your
partner is doing something to you that they know hurts you but
they do it anyway. Perhaps your partner decides to have an
affair knowing it will hurt you when you find out. This may be a
karmic payback or the initiation of new karma.

Whatever the case you are responsible for how you choose to
react. You have a choice of three responses. [A] You chose to be in
the relationship, you can also choose to be out of it if you wish.
[B] Whether your partner has willfully chosen to hurt you or
inadvertently hurt you, you choose to get over the hurt and make
further contact with them. [C] You can choose to continue to feel
hurt and remain in the relationship for ongoing pain and
suffering.

Now, all the above responses have to do only with your own
reactions and have nothing to do with blaming your partner.

Most often miscommunication happens when you are accused
of doing something that you might very well do.

For example, you do not get plugged in if you are
accused of stealing a tiger from the zoo because this is
something that you would hardly think of doing. You
may be baffled at how the other person could possibly
think that you might steal it or you may determine with
empathy that the other person is just having a hard day.
On the other hand if your partner accuses you of finding
someone else more attractive you may become defensive
because this just might be true or could be true in the
future.

So, generally speaking, the closer to reality the accusation, the more likely you are to become defensive.

THE OVERLEAVES AND MISCOMMUNICATION

Miscommunication often centers on the relationship between goals and chief negative features. Here's how this works. In a relationship one person is often being run by their chief negative feature. When one partner is being influenced by their chief feature, the other partner experiences a blockage to reaching their goal. They feel pushed into the goal polar to their principle one.

For example, let us say that you have a strong chief feature of martyrdom and your partner has a goal of acceptance. The martyrdom will tend to shove your partner with a goal of acceptance toward the goal of discrimination. Not only that but the martyrdom will push your partner toward the negative pole of discrimination, rejection. The more you act victimized and blame your partner the less accepting he will tend to be. This means that everyone ends up feeling bad. You feel bad because you feel trapped and victimized in your martyrdom. Your partner feels bad because you are blocking his goal of acceptance to the point to where he feels he must reject you.

Let us take another example to illustrate the relationship between the two overleaves in a partnership. Let us say that you have a goal of dominance and your partner has a chief feature of arrogance. The more arrogant your partner becomes, the less you will feel able to lead or win in the situation. The more you will feel pressed toward the negative pole of the opposite goal of submission, exploited. Your partner feels bad because he is experiencing the awfulness of arrogance. He feels doubly bad because within him he also knows that he is blocking you from realizing your goal of dominance. You feel bad because you are being frustrated in reaching your goal.

The Seven Goals

Ordinal	Neutral	Exalted
Expression		
+Sophistication		+Agape
DISCRIMINATION		**ACCEPTANCE**
-Rejection		-Ingratiation
Inspiration		
+Simplicity		+Evolution
RE-EVALUATION		**GROWTH**
-Withdrawal		-Confusion
Action		
+Devotion		+Leadership
SUBMISSION		**DOMINANCE**
-Exploited		-Dictatorship
	Assimilation	
	+Free-flowing	
	STAGNATION	
	-Inertia	

How do you extract yourself from this dilemma? The first step in this process is to stop engaging in fruitless miscommunication, become quiet, breathe, and observe. The second step is to review your relationship and determine whether you are the heavy chief feature user or whether you are the one who tends to slide toward your opposite goal. You may discover that you take turns with your partner doing both. At any rate, you can find the pattern in your relationship. If you are the goal slider you can begin to take steps to consciously remain in your goal no matter what the obstacles. This is your responsibility. If you are the heavy chief feature user you can embark on a campaign to be consciously aware of indulging it and extract yourself each time. The most effective way is through your attitude. This is a process that was discussed in *Essence and Personality* and we will briefly give it again here.

The Chief Features

Ordinal	Neutral	Exalted
Expression		
+sacrifice		+appetite
SELF-DESTRUCTION		**GREED**
-suicidal		-voracity
Inspiration		
+humility		+pride
SELF-DEPRECATION		**ARROGANCE**
-abasement		-vanity
Action		
+selflessness		+daring
MARTYRDOM		**IMPATIENCE**
-victimization		-intolerance
	Assimilation	
	+determination	
	STUBBORNNESS	
	-obstinacy	

To extract yourself from your chief feature you go to the positive pole of the polar attitude. For example, lets say you have a chief feature of self-deprecation and you have an idealist attitude. You tend to feel terrible about yourself because you can never achieve your high ideals for yourself. No matter how successful you become in meeting your goals, you are never quite

The Seven Attitudes

Ordinal	Neutral	Exalted
Expression		
+investigation		+coalescence
SKEPTIC		**IDEALIST**
-suspicion		-naivety
Inspiration		
+tranquility		+verification
STOIC		**SPIRITUALIST**
-resignation		-beliefs
Action		
+contradiction		+objective
CYNIC		**REALIST**
-denigration		-subjective
	Assimilation	
	+practical	
	PRAGMATIST	
	-dogmatic	

perfect enough for your self-imposed standards. A good solution for this vicious cycle is to slide over to the positive pole of skepticism, investigation. First of all become skeptical of your impossible-to-achieve ideals. Decide to investigate whether they are actually achievable or not. Investigate further and notice what you have accomplished already. This process will automatically allow your self esteem to rise, thus removing you from the clutches of self-deprecation. In addition it will allow your partner to more easily achieve his goal, making him happier and yourself happier as well.

ROMANTIC RELATIONSHIPS

Despite what your culture has to say, there is a definite difference between romantic and sexual relationships. Although both can dovetail nicely within one relationship, each has distinct qualities and a purpose of its own. First of all a romantic relationship is not limited to the relationship between two people of the opposite sex by any means. In the truest sense of the word, romantic relationships can occur between any two human beings: two children; an adult with his grandmother; a mother or father and baby; two good friends in a non-sexual relationship. How can this be?

The misunderstanding comes from your culture's confusion of the two words, romance and sex. When you think of romance you immediately tend to think of candlelight dinners or sunset walks on the beach followed by sex. However this has very little to do with true romance. Your dictionaries define romance as a fictitious and marvelous tale. And although it is true that romance is marvelous it is definitely not fictitious. So, what is romance?

Simply put, romance is a state of being fully emotionally open to another person without expectations or conditions. Romance is a state achieved through the moving part of higher emotional center. It requires absolutely telling the truth to yourself and the other person. When you are in a true state of romance you see the other person exactly as they are and you fully appreciate them for it. You know their limitations and you choose to overlook these difficulties for their sake. You choose to love them anyway without regard for how they respond or what they do. This is most obvious in the relationship between a mother and child but we reiterate, it applies to all types of relationships.

Thus feeling romantic is more of an inner state that really has little to do with the other person. Nothing is required of them. You may in fact feel generally romantic and this would include your relationship with people, animals, plants, and things. Or, you may feel romantic in a more focused way toward one individual. There is a feeling of having a crush on the person or a feeling of falling in love. Again, in your culture this is usually interpreted sexually but if you look more closely you will find that these feelings are seldom associated with erotic attraction. In fact, unfortunately many of you resist or try to crush romantic feelings toward another because you fear that you are being inappropriately sexual.

> _For example many fathers mistrust their romantic feelings toward their daughters and as a result shut them out when they grow close to puberty. Men often fear their romantic feelings for their mothers or female teachers and try to hide their love for them. Likewise men often fear they are homosexual because they feel love for another man._

Now, males and females react to romance somewhat differently because of their different biological makeups. Females learn more quickly about non-sexual romance because of their close proximity to and familiarity with babies. Men, especially since the onset of the industrial revolution, have become further and further divorced from childcare and family life, depriving them of those basic romantic feelings that begin there.

Women are stronger in nurturing and basic survival concepts because of their instincts around the birthing of children. Because the species would die if it were not for their ability to bear and care for children, women have learned to be more practical and reasonable. They have learned to compromise and get along so that life can continue. They can certainly do this without men staying around after mating. Since women as a whole tend to understand romance better than most men, they do not need to focus on it.

Men on the other hand, despite all their resistance, are much more focused on romance because this is what they need to learn more about. Whereas women are geared toward survival of the brood, men are geared toward survival of the tribe or nation. This makes men oriented toward patriotism and bravery in defense of their country, generally more romantic activities [note all the men in politics]. Since men are preoccupied with these kinds of romantic notions you tend to have a preponderance of wars. This is merely a result of a poor understanding of what true romance really is, unconditional love for another. You may have unconditional love for your country but not have it for humanity.

As you have most likely noticed, the more truly romantic a man is, the more he tends to attract women since he speaks the language that they already know. Women often love to be with homosexual men because they are more comfortable with romance and express it freely.

SEXUAL RELATIONSHIPS

So, what is the difference between feelings of romance and sexual feelings for another? Remember that romantic feelings include no expectations of the other. When you feel romantic toward another, you continue to feel whole and complete within yourself. You are emotionally open. You are essence driven.

Sexual feelings however, are full of expectations about physical liason with the other. They are also predicated on certain conditions that the other person look a certain way, dress correctly, and act in a way that appeals to you. In a word, sexual feelings are conditional. With sexual feelings you feel incomplete unless you are physically together with the other. Sexual attraction works on the personality and false personality levels.

Why then are you so preoccupied with sexual feelings when you could be feeling romantic?

Well, sexual attraction is often the royal road that leads you directly into karma. Sexual attraction often feels like a compulsion because it is the lure that draws you into karmic lessons when you might seek to avoid them. Sexual attraction also lures you into keeping agreements to bring children into the world. Finally, sexual attraction leading to sex play is often balancing to the physical body and helps to heal and ground the personality. So, sexual relationships are exciting, stimulating, and at times tortuous for many of the above reasons. It is by far one of the most exciting games on the planet right up there with the fun of making money.

Sexuality is handled differently by the different soul ages and in particular by the different roles. As the soul becomes more experienced and older over many lifetimes, the emphasis on sexuality moves from simple procreation to expression of love, and from lust to the joyful expression of oneness.

A late level infant soul might mate simply for the experience (early infant souls usually do not engage in sex). A baby soul might mate out of duty, while a young soul might approach sex as a conquest. Mature souls see sex as an intense communication of emotions. Old souls use sex as a spiritual practice or meditation or simply as sensual expression.

Sexual activity is also determined in part by role. The action roles of warrior-king tend to be the most sexually active for several reasons. First of all they love physicality and the direct action oriented contact of a sexual relationship. They are more likely to say, "Let's make love first and then talk." They want to know they can trust you physically first. They find sex grounding and nurturing and often lead amazingly sexually active lives. They tend to view sex in a matter-of-fact way and tend to be direct or even blunt about it. These solid and low frequency roles are often erotically attracted to the high frequency roles of artisan and priest.

Picture the matter-of-fact attitude of a prostitute engaging in sex for business. Many prostitutes are warriors seeking action and adventure. Think of the sexual exploits of such famous warriors as Mozart and famous kings like John F. Kennedy.

The expression roles of artisan-sage see sex as a means of creative expression. As a group they are not as naturally sexually active as the action roles because they have many means at their disposal to channel their creative energy. Artisans can nonetheless be very creative in sex play and are excellent at creating erotic environments. Sages are much more likely to say "Let's talk first, then make love." They tend to view sex as a means of having fun.

> *Sages' sex lives are often public displays plastered all over the scandal sheets. They want people to know all the details of what happened. Think of the exploits of Hollywood stars and the journalists who follow them.*

The inspiration roles of server-priest view sexuality as inspirational. Servers enjoy sexual relationships if they feel they are being of service to their partners. Priests often use sex as a vehicle to teach, be compassionate, or bring someone back to the fold. Both servers and priests tend to see sex as a vehicle for healing their partner. Priests are often content to bypass sexual relationships and dedicate themselves to their congregations. They are usually happy with the celibacy of the monastery or convent.

> *Priests, like warriors, sometimes choose a life as a prostitute or erotic dancer but for different reasons. They see the job as one bringing healing and compassion to the clients they serve.*

The assimilation role of scholar is a mixed lot. In general being solid and physical they enjoy sexual relationships and find them grounding and balancing. Sex is a good antidote for their habitual studious ways. Scholars however often lean away from the more intense, wild sexual relationships that sages prefer. It is difficult for the scholar to maintain his neutrality in the face of such intensity. Nevertheless, because scholars like to study and experiment, they have a tendency to explore more bizarre forms of sexual expression just to see what they are like. Scholars often team up with artisans for this purpose. They, however, are at ease with any role as a sexual partner except for perhaps the more outspoken sages.

Sexual expression is influenced of course by the combination of overleaves chosen. Passion mode leads to wilder abandon sexually while caution mode reduces the activity level. A goal of dominance will appear different from a goal of submission expressed sexually (together they may appear as master-slave). A chief feature of greed can accentuate sexual activity whereas self-deprecation or martyrdom can retard it.

Imagine the difference in sexual expression between: a baby soul server in submission with a spiritualist attitude, a chief feature of martyrdom, a mode of repression, and intellectually centered; and a young warrior with a goal of dominance, an attitude of realist, a chief feature of greed, a mode of passion, and moving centered. The first is likely to be a cloistered and celibate nun and the second could be a rapist.

Centering has perhaps the most influence of all overleaves on sexual expression. Most sexual activity is moving centered because it involves simple motion and processes of the body.

People who are moving centered are often talented and skilled lovers because they are able to give their bodies complete expression. On the other hand they are on the go a lot and may have multiple sexual partners, finding it difficult to stay still long enough to develop a committed relationship.

Emotionally centered individuals bring intensity to their sexual relationships and will cry and laugh while lovemaking, sometimes to the bewilderment of their partners. They want their partner to be emotionally involved with them before making love with them.

Intellectually centered people are apt to have the most trouble with sexual relationships because they are used to processing their experiences through words. They are the ones most likely to want to talk before, during, and after lovemaking.

Frequently they have difficulty getting out of their heads and letting go into the experience. They want to know what it means, much to the irritation of their emotionally centered or moving centered partners. When two intellectually centered types get together they may spend more time talking about it than lovemaking.

As you probably can guess, the subject of sexual relationships is an infinite one and we have presented here only simple basics to expand your understanding of what they are about. The best way to understand sexual relationships is of course to experience them and observe them from the vantage of being in them. Avoidance of sexual relationships is not more spiritually advanced nor is it desirable for the soul's growth. Occasionally withdrawal from sexual relationships is appropriate and helpful so that certain lessons may be learned.

Remember that sex is the physical body's interpretation of combining. Energetic combining is carried out throughout the different planes and ultimate combining occurs with the Tao itself. Now how can sexual relationships be bad?

Let us now look at the different ways that the cast of characters in your life show up. The next section deals with external monads, that variety of specialized relationships that you need to master in order to cycle off the physical plane.

Chapter Seven

Karmic Commitments

MONADS

What is a monad? How do monads affect you? How do you successfully complete a monad? Let us examine these questions for a full understanding of monads.

First of all as you know by now, there are two basic kinds of monads, those that you experience within yourself, called internal monads, and those that you experience with other people, called external monads. We already covered the seven internal monads or rites of passage. Here we will discuss the set of monads involving other people.

An external monad is a type of relationship with another person with whom you have agreed to play out both sides of an experience. This relationship is specific in the sense that it has definite themes and cultural limitations. However it is subject to wide interpretation.

Some of the most common external monads within the family structure are parent-child, brother-sister and husband-wife. Other monads might include teacher-student, leader-follower, attacker-victim and so on. These may be within the immediate family or with people outside of it.

Each side of a monad carries with it a certain lesson or reward. For example in a child-parent monad the child position has the reward of being taken care of by the parent. The reward of being the parent is in the satisfaction of nurturing the child. The completion of a monad requires that you experience the relationship with your partner from both sides. When the monad is based on age and sexual differences such as father-daughter, the monad requires more than one lifetime to complete. The father will have to be the daughter and the daughter will have to be the father. You will then know the other fragment more completely.

When the monad is not limited by age or sex differences it might be completed during one lifetime.

> *For example a leader-follower monad may be flip-flopped every few days, weeks or years. Similarly the teacher-student monad is often experienced from both sides in one lifetime. You may teach a child how to play a musical instrument. That child might grow up to be so proficient that you end up taking lessons from him.*

Now, the agreement to be in a monad is made between lifetimes and it is not something you can casually opt out of once you have made the choice. To choose to be in a monad is something like committing yourself by jumping off a diving board. It is hard to turn back. Nevertheless you can resist the monad and this is usually karma-forming.

How do you know you have made an agreement to be in a monad with someone? Usually you can know by the intensity of the experience and, with many of the monads, by their

relatively long duration. Monads take a few or many years to accomplish.

> *It is important to understand that not every relationship is a monad. Not every father-son relationship is a father-son monad. The converse is also true; there can be a father-son relationship between two unrelated men that is a father-son monad. Their relationship is like that of a father and a son. So monads are not determined by traditional social roles but by a felt sense. You know you have one with someone by the way it feels.*

Types of Monads

From most common to least common.

Teacher-Student	Slovenly-Meticulous
Parent-Child	Passive-Aggressive
Imprinter-Imprinted	Adept-Apprentice
Brother-Sister,	Artist-Patron
Sister-Sister, etc	Deserter-Abandoned
Husband-Wife	Profligate-Temperate
Leader-Follower	Innocent-Sophisticate
Attacker-Victim	Promiscuous-Impotent
Healer-Healed	Master-Slave
Rescuer-Rescued	(or Pimp-Prostitute)
Integrator-Eccentric	Player-Pawn
Hopelessly loving-	Defender-Defended
Hopelessly loved	Hidden-Disclosed
Passionate-Repressive	Slanderer-Slandered
Dependent-Independent	Jailer-Prisoner
Pivotal Facilitator-Facilitated	*Lover Monad*

To complete a monad it is necessary for both parties to acknowledge the situation and what was experienced. That is, your personality must be aware of the nature of the relationship.

> *Both you and your partner must know, for example,*
> *that you are like sisters to one another, even if you are*
> *not blood related. If your partner or you do not feel it,*
> *your monad will remain incomplete.*

You usually experience many different monads with the same fragment over many lifetimes. However you rarely have two monads going at once with the same person. It would be difficult to experience the fullness of a brother-brother monad while being teacher-student at the same time. You get more out of a monad by not complicating it with too many other requirements. Every so often you might choose to do sequential monads with someone in the same lifetime, such as leader-follower for twenty years and then teacher-student for another twenty.

Most monads will be done only once in a cycle of lifetimes. Some will be done a number of times.

> *A warrior, for instance, may do the leader-follower*
> *monad often, leading others and being led off to war in*
> *any number of lifetimes. However he may choose to do*
> *the artist-patron monad only once.*

All the types of monads must be completed before you can cycle off. This takes a great many lifetimes. The fact that all the types of monads must be completed ensures that each essence, in both male and female lifetimes, experiences parenthood, leadership, and so on—a full and vivid range of experiences.

MONADS AND SOUL AGE

Monads don't have to occur between souls of the same perceptivity level. So a young soul can have a monad with an old soul and both will learn from it. However as you shall see, the complexity of certain monads requires advanced soul age for both partners. Likewise the primitive quality of certain monads such as attacker-victim makes this choice unlikely for older souls.

Therefore, certain monads need to be accomplished at various stages of development. The monads are divided into groups of increasing complexity. Roughly speaking the more aggressive monads are accomplished at the younger soul levels. These monads are more isolating and separating by nature.

The older the soul level the more integrating the monad being accomplished. For example husband-wife is more integrating than master-slave.

Nevertheless there is some attempt to balance the various monads all along the complete cycle.

Infant soul

Those monads that are the most primitive and isolating are accomplished at the infant soul level. Such monads as dependent-independent, attacker-victim, and deserter-abandoned are appropriate to the infant soul perceptivity level. These are not complex nor do they require any kind of sophistication to accomplish. They are primarily reactive and are karma-producing.

Baby soul

The jailer-prisoner monad is a good example of the kind of monad sought for in the baby soul level. This monad teaches about rules and provides structure through confinement. In a sense both jailer and prisoner are confined and limited by the nature of their relationship. Each learns something about civilization from the other.

Young soul

In the young soul stage the principal monad to be completed is that of leader-follower. This satisfies the young soul needs for striving and achievement while calling for a measure of cooperation and long-term relationship.

Player-pawn is also typical of the young soul's need to learn about manipulation and appropriate leadership.

Mature soul

The mature soul stage is characterized by relationship monads such as parent-child, brother-sister, and husband-wife. These relationships are complex and require much sophistication to work out. They are usually deeply emotional in nature, satisfying the mature soul's need for emotional lessons.

Monads at this soul age begin to be more karma-resolving rather than karma-producing. For example a variation of the leader-follower monad, honorably serving a corrupt master, must be done at the mature level. The master side of the monad is usually done at a younger soul level.

Old soul

In the old soul stage one of the principal monads to be accomplished is that of teacher-student. It is usually necessary for old souls to teach the younger souls about their lessons and help them along.

The final monad is completed in the older soul stages—the lover monad. This is only possible between two individuals who have completed all other monads with each other. The lover monad is characterized by great compatibility, understanding and acceptance. They each have known all the extremes of the other's behavior and they hold no surprises for each other. It is a powerful basis for a relationship.

MONAD EXPLANATIONS AND EXAMPLES

Teacher-Student

Here one partner teaches the other partner everything he knows. Now, this teacher-student relationship need not appear along traditional lines. For example, a therapist may occupy the student position and his client might be in the teacher position. Similarly a president may be the pupil, while the advisor may be the instructor. The same might be true of a parent and child or coach and athlete. What is important is the flow of learning from one to the other. When the flow is counter to the social roles, the senior partner may have difficulty acknowledging the monad at first. After all the coach is supposed to be the boss. Right? Not necessarily.

This monad may be traded back and forth through the lifetime or the teacher role will be held by one partner throughout the lifetime. In this latter case the reverse will be experienced in another lifetime. Usually this is an old soul monad.

Parent-Child

This monad is not necessarily experienced between blood relatives. It is typical of the mature soul level. One partner feels responsible for the other, the child feels cared for and guided. In some cases the child position may be occupied by the biological parent and the parent position occupied by the biological son or daughter. This is often the case when the biological child is an older soul than the parent. In this case the parent will always look to the child for guidance and wisdom. The child will feel a commitment to look out for the parent.

Imprinter-Imprinted

This is an infant soul monad. It teaches about how to program the next generation with a belief system. Teaches basic principles of learning to survive by being taught.

Brother-Brother; Brother-Sister; Sister-Sister.

This monad teaches about long term commitment to another. In addition it teaches give and take, patience, support, and understanding. The partners need not be related by blood. They can appear to be friends who are "like" brothers or sisters to one another. They may feel more related to this friend than their blood sibling. This is a typical mature soul level monad.

Husband-Wife (includes long term homosexual relationships)

Similar to sibling monad but includes complexity of a sexual relationship. Teaches compatibility, commitment, joint effort, balance. Typical mature-old soul monad.

Leader-Follower

Often done in conjunction with overleaves of dominance and submission. One partner breaks new ground, changes careers, gets married, decides to travel. The other taking the cue quickly follows suit. This monad teaches responsibility, responsiveness, and cooperation. The leadership position can be traded back and forth in a lifetime or carried for the entire lifetime. In the latter case the reverse is experienced in another lifetime. This is most typically a young soul monad.

As mentioned before however, honorably serving a corrupt leader must be done at the mature soul level. This side of the monad places the fragment in a situation of extreme emotional conflict, a hallmark of the mature stage. This is one of many versions of this monad.

Attacker-Victim

This monad teaches karma formation and completion. It is often carried out slowly between mates or relatives and can often be seen in courtroom dramas. The victim continues to feel victimized even though the attacker is behind bars. The attacker continues to plot against the victim. This monad is often combined with aggression mode and caution mode overleaves. Typical infant soul monad.

Healer-Healed

Usually an intense long term relationship between a doctor, medicine person, acupuncturist, etc. and his patient. However this monad may not appear in such a formal guise. The importance here is in the feeling of being healed by someone or in the feeling of healing. This feeling may appear only in the presence of the monad partner and not in any other relationship. This monad teaches giving and receiving.

Rescuer-Rescued

Not typically a one time event but a years' long process of one monad partner continually rescuing the other from difficulty. This could be seen in the relationship between a parent, social worker, or counselor and a delinquent or disabled child. Or the monad could take the form of an alcoholic regularly rescued by the co-alcoholic spouse. When this is a monad, no amount of counseling will change the pattern. Teaches patience, discrimination, and appropriate responsiveness.

Integrator-Eccentric

Looks like the odd couple. Often a business partnership in which the one wildly creative partner gets unique ideas that are then implemented by the pragmatic and grounded integrator partner. Lucas and Spielberg of *Star Wars* fame are a classic example. This monad teaches cooperation and tolerance.

The integrator-eccentric monad is often an integral part of a sextant, a group of six working together to fulfill a mission or complete a project.

Hopelessly loving-Hopelessly loved

Here one partner is hopelessly in love with the other partner who does not reciprocate the feeling but feels troubled or trapped by the other's feelings. This is a classic Shakespearean tragedy scenario. Neither partner knows how to escape the situation. Teaches acceptance and discrimination. Often accompanied by passion and repression modes or goals of discrimination and acceptance.

Passionate-Repressive

Most often experienced between mates or close relatives. One partner is wildly expressive while the other is inhibited and shy. The challenge here is to learn to live together with such opposite responses to everything. Often accompanied by goals of growth and passion-reserve modes.

Dependent-Independent

Often seen in the relationship between a disabled person and their attendant or able-bodied spouse. However it can take many other forms. The challenge is to learn responsibility as well as the ability to trust and rely on another.

Pivotal Facilitator-Facilitated

The pivotal facilitator is a person who enters the other's life at crucial moments to help them effect a life-transforming change. This is then played in reverse in another lifetime. The pivotal facilitator may function as a therapist, advisor, lover, friend, or relative who intensely influences the other's life by their sudden presence. This is usually a short-term monad but its short duration is made up for by its intensity. The lesson here is to learn how to appropriately facilitate another person's growth process and likewise how to receive this kind of help.

Because the pivotal facilitator-facilitated relationship is so intense it often is mistaken for a sexual karma. The sexual feelings usually wear off after a few weeks or months and the real nature of the relationship becomes more obvious. If either person in the monad is married this can cause trouble between the spouses, as explained above in regard to the appearance of essence twins. The monad's intensity will create change, for better or for worse.

Slovenly-Meticulous

Usually experienced between siblings or mates in which one desires order and simplicity and the other desires casualness and freedom to express. One puts clothes, papers, and dishes away neatly, the other leaves socks, underwear, and dirty dishes strewn from one end of the house to the other. Both are convinced that theirs is the right lifestyle.

The lesson here is tolerance and patience. This usually involves differing body types, typically mercury for neatness and venusian for sloppiness.

Passive-Aggressive

In this monad one partner takes a reactive role while the other is action oriented. This represents a more sophisticated and advanced version of the attacker-victim monad of the infant soul cycle. Here one partner may take on the extreme of male energy such as captain of a football team while the other partner takes on the extreme female energy role such as wilting homecoming queen. Another example might be aggressive oil company mogul and southern belle. Either sex however may take the aggressive role. Picture a dynamic female executive and her passive house-husband.

The challenge is in learning the extremes of male-female energy so that balance can be discovered.

Adept-Apprentice

Relationship between a master craftsman or teacher of any persuasion and their chief student. This involves learning to communicate clearly as well as learning to follow the rules exactly.

Artist-Patron

This monad is self-evident. One is sponsored and allowed to pursue their work while the other sponsors them. This can appear traditionally as with a patron of the arts or less visibly as one spouse carrying the financial burden while the other goes about their interests. One spouse may put their partner through medical school for example. Typically a young, mature, and old soul monad.

Deserter-Abandoned

An infant, baby, and young soul, karma-producing monad. One partner may abandon a child to uncaring relatives or abandon a colleague in a battlefield situation to save themselves. The monad may take place over an entire lifetime as one spouse continually abandons the other only to return again and again. The lesson involves learning integrity and responsibility.

Profligate-Temperate

Another monad in which the extremes are learned in order to eventually discover balance. One partner is an uncontrolled spender and consumer, the other is restrained and tightfisted. Passion mode and reserve mode are typically found here.

Innocent-Sophisticate

One partner is worldly-wise while the other may be naive and perhaps uneducated. One version of this monad would be a relationship between a counselor and a retarded person, a rich person and a poor one, an attorney and the uneducated client he must defend. Understanding and tolerance are the lessons.

Promiscuous-Impotent

Monad often within a married or love relationship. One partner may be impotent or uninterested in sex, the other may be highly sexed and looks outside the relationship for satisfaction. One partner may be highly successful such as a movie star or government leader. The other may be eclipsed by such success and experience depression and impotency. Sometimes this is the case between a highly successful parent and a child that cannot live up to such fame and fortune.

Again, the extremes are represented here. The challenge is in learning tolerance, patience, and understanding as well as coming to terms with guilt.

Master-Slave

Also includes pimp-prostitute relationship. One partner owns and controls the other in all areas of their life. Often the master has the ultimate decision over the life and death of the slave as has usually been the case throughout history. Not all master-slave relationships have been harmful or destructive to the slave. This monad has the potential for a great many lessons including kindness, generosity, selfless giving, responsibility, obedience, and understanding.

Player-Pawn

Can take a great many guises. Typically a young soul monad wherein the player manipulates the pawn for benefit. Often seen in mafia-type activities, politics, and business maneuvers. The challenge here is to learn the appropriate use of power and control. Often accompanied by the goals of dominance and submission as well as the chief feature of martyrdom.

Defender-Defended

Teaches the partners about cooperation, care, receptivity, and power. A long-term relationship wherein one partner is protected and defended by the other. Scenarios might include an attorney and his client, an emperor and his general, a retarded person and his guardian.

Hidden-Disclosed

More typically a younger soul monad in which one partner is exposed by the other. Common scenarios include the prosecution and defense in a trial in which secrets are uncovered; political ploys uncovered such as the Watergate scandal; spy activities in which military secrets are disclosed to another country; children turning parents in to the authorities for drugs; therapeutic relationships in which a hypnotherapist or psychoanalyst helps the client uncover childhood traumas.

Slander-Slandered

Younger soul monad in which one partner defames the reputation of the other. This may be passed back and forth many times in a single lifetime. The challenge is to learn integrity, honesty, and appropriate communication. Scenarios include a scandal sheet reporter and his subjects; political contenders for public office waging a mudslinging campaign; competitors for a promotion undercutting each other at the job.

Jailer-Prisoner

Monad in which one partner imprisons the other physically, emotionally, or spiritually. The imprisonment has to strongly affect both parties such that both are heavily involved. Scenarios would include a prison guard and prisoner; a sultan and harem; an administrator and an employee; a mental patient and head nurse or psychiatrist; a parent and child, a doctoral candidate and a tough doctoral committee chairperson; and occasionally a husband and wife.

Tandem Monad

A monad in which each partner's life parallels that of the other. When one leaves home the other leaves home; when one gets married the other does so also; when one has children the other does so also, within a matter of hours sometimes. This is not a conscious copying but a syncronistic series of parallel events that are noticed by both parties with some surprise. The tandem monad teaches support and connectedness as well as issues about competition.

Lover Monad

When all monads have been experienced between two people over many lifetimes they have nothing left between them but to love one another completely. There is nothing they have not done to each other or experienced at the hands of the other. They know everything about the other. This is called a lover monad and continues as long as both live lives together. Needless to say the lover monad is experienced only in the older soul ages because of its time-consuming prerequisites.

The lover monad need not take any particular form. It may be a husband-wife relationship, parent-child, or sibling relationship. It may appear as a simple unconditional friendship between two people. The lover monad teaches unconditional love ôr agape.

The lover monad is sometimes mistaken for an essence twin relationship. Indeed essence twins often do all monads together and have a lover monad as well. But many lover monads are not essence twin pairings. You may have more than one lover monad.

SUMMARY

Now you know the main categories that your relationships tend to fall into. Of course there can be infinite variations of each. The main thing is that you want to complete all monads at least once and possibly a number of times before you feel complete enough to cycle off the planet.

These monads provide you with the best opportunity to experience karma and then to resolve it. That is their sole purpose, to assist you in your journey back to the Tao by helping you to become unconditionally accepting of yourself and others.

Now, let us move to a new section that will focus on the larger group relationships that you work and play in during your lifetimes on earth. We will start with triads and move to ever larger configurations that each influence you in a different way.

PART FOUR

SUPPORT GROUPS AND PATTERNS

Chapter Eight

Triads, Quadrates, and Pentangles

PART IV:

In this section we are going to discuss all the various configurations of groups and show you how you are affected by their unique properties. Here you will learn how to take advantage of specialized groups and how to strengthen groups that need stability by adding or subtracting people from their numbers. For example you will discover that a business project will be more likely to succeed if you work with a group of four or six rather than three. On the other hand if you want to learn a valuable lesson in human relationships you have an excellent opportunity in a small group of three.

Group configurations are a much more important part of your everyday life experience than you ever might imagine. We suggest that, as you read this section, you observe the groups you interact with and learn for yourselves their special applications.

CONFIGURATIONS

TRIADS

The triad, or group of three, follows the triadic pattern that was discussed earlier. Here we will focus specifically on how a small group of three people operate.

The triad is a basically unstable group of three persons working together to learn from one another. Triads are therefore not often highly productive in a material world sense but rather more productive from an experiential point of view. Triads usually produce great intensity for its members and as a result they are highly karmic. That is, as mentioned earlier, triads are excellent vehicles for the formation and resolution of karma.

Recall that the pattern in a triad is made up of a positive position, a negative position, and a neutral position. Each member of the group takes one of these positions automatically. The positions may rotate among the members within minutes as a conversation progresses, or the positions may stay relatively stable about a particular issue.

For example, one person may suggest going to the movies to see a highly touted film. The second person will bring up some doubt about whether it really is good or note that the theatre is across town, the parking is bad, or the viewing time is wrong. The third person takes the neutral position and often mediates a solution.

Underneath the more superficial posturing there may be a deeper level position. You may be able to observe that each of the three people tends to take an overall stance which may be generalized as positive, negative or neutral. That is, each person's general way of behaving may be obviously one of those three. This has much to do with each person's combination of overleaves. A cynic will usually take the negative position in a triad while a spiritualist will usually take the positive position. The pragmatist will often be the neutral party.

TYPICAL TRIADS

Families are often made up of triadic relationships. Where there are two parents and a child you can usually observe at any time one is positive, one negative and one neutral. This pattern may fluctuate from moment to moment.

The infant is hungry and cries, the mother soothes and nurses, the father holds the neutral position.

The child wants to go swimming with a friend, the father is worried and says no, the mother is neutral on the issue.

Mother complains about the messy house. Father says it feels lived in. Child doesn't care.

Similarly this occurs where there are two parents and three children. The children can form a triad among themselves, and you may be able to observe life positions that relate each one to one of the three positions. One is the super achiever, one is the delinquent, and one holds the neutral position.

Not all triads are composed of three people however. Often the neutral position is held by an idea or by a nonphysical entity such as "marriage."

For example you may notice that one partner is positive about the marriage, the other is negative and the marriage itself (or their relationship) is neutral. They may flip-flop on the issue over a period of months and years until they are resolved about it one way or the other.

As long as they continue to have strong feelings about both wanting it and not wanting it, the karma will continue. When one or more parties arrives at what they truly want and withstands

TRIADS

being tested by others, then they have reached neutrality and are likely to stick the course that they have decided. Or when both parties get neutral on the marriage, they separate because there is no more drama in it. Other couples stay together and begin to focus on their karma in other arenas.

TRIADS AS PROCESSES

There are two ways that you can think about triads. One way is to view triads from the more concrete perspective of three people working in a group, as introduced above. The second way of understanding triads is to look at the triadic process in events and experiences.

Triads govern the very nature of human experience. An essence enters a body for the sole purpose of experiencing and learning. Your essence sets up event after event; the way in which you learn is triadic. You spiral through each lifetime constantly experiencing triads, each one leading to the next.

Problem-solving, then, is basically triadic. Overcoming one problem simply introduces another. Let us look briefly at how this process works.

The law of three as it is called comprises three lines of force or positions—positive, negative and neutral.

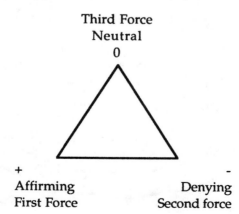

Third Force
Neutral
0

+
Affirming
First Force

-
Denying
Second force

The forces in a triad are + positive, - negative, and 0 neutral, or affirming, denying, and neutralizing. The forces change continuously from one force into another but not always in the same order. This constant shifting creates the movement of life. Without it, the physical universe would not work.

The first force is the affirmative position. It is a position of strength. It occurs when you say for example, "I want a new job." That immediately elicits the negative or second force—I don't have the skills, they are not hiring right now, maybe I will have to relocate, the commute is longer and so on. Some doubts and obstacles usually show up in some form. If not, then you immediately get your new job and there is less chance to learn from the experience—you have completed the triad instantly.

The function of the second force is to assist (through denial), the first position. It tests it, challenges it, and forces it to become stronger and more definite, or to dissipate. If you want a new career and don't believe you have the skills then you either give up or resolutely decide to find a way. The second force has compelled you to crystallize how much you desire the new job.

The third force is the most subtle. Generally humans are third force blind and easily overlook the power of becoming neutral on an issue. Being neutral is not dramatic or intense, yet, becoming neutral is necessary for change to occur. The third force, neutrality, embodies non-resistance and effortlessness.

When you let go of your fears and resistances to going for that new job, you can more easily have it. That is the neutral position. This third or neutral position is the point of resolution of the triad. Karma is resolved at that place of neutrality. Since all intensity is karma-related, all of your feelings about yourself, or another, or a situation are resolved, handled and dissipated in the neutral position.

It is important to realize that positive does not mean "good," nor negative mean "bad." The terms are only a means of conveying a sense of being opposite each other. "Good" and "bad" are subjective value judgements and as such have no place in this system of knowledge. All positions are equal and absolutely necessary for ultimate harmony.

Triadic relationships underpin the mechanism by which the universe works. The process underlies any physical phenomenon that can be experienced. Here are some examples of some basic triadic processes.

Examples of Triads

Positive	Negative	Neutral
affirming	denying	neutralizing
active	passive	mediating
yin	yang	Tao
reactant	reagent	catalyst
proton	electron	neutron
Father	Son	Holy Spirit
intellect	emotion	movement
prayer	suffering	grace
will	adversity	outcome
thesis	antithesis	synthesis
desire	obstacle	ego
you	me	us (our relationship)
Sun	Moon	Earth
buyer	seller	commodity
animal	vegetable	mineral
red	blue	yellow
father	mother	child
action	reaction	equality
solid	liquid	gas
energy	mass	speed of light squared ($E=MC^2$)

It is apparent that this list is infinite. The more you are aware of the phenomenon the more one sees it in everyday life.

OVERLEAF CHART

	EXPRESSION Ordinal	EXPRESSION Exalted	INSPIRATION Ordinal	INSPIRATION Exalted	ACTION Ordinal	ACTION Exalted	ASSIMILATION Neutral
ROLE	+Creation ARTISAN -Self-Deception	+Dissemination SAGE -Verbosity	+Service SERVER -Bondage	+Compassion PRIEST -Zeal	+Persuasion WARRIOR -Coercion	+Mastery KING -Tyranny	+Knowledge SCHOLAR -Theory
GOAL	+Sophistication DISCRIMINATION -Rejection	+Agape ACCEPTANCE -Ingratiation	+Simplicity RE-EVALUATION -Withdrawal	+Evolution GROWTH -Confusion	+Devotion SUBMISSION -Exploited	+Leadership DOMINANCE -Dictatorship	+Free-Flowing STAGNATION -Inertia
ATTITUDE	+Investigation SKEPTIC -Suspicion	+Coalescence IDEALIST -Naivety	+Tranquility STOIC -Resignation	+Verification SPIRITUALIST -Beliefs	+Contradiction CYNIC -Denigration	+Objective REALIST -Subjective	+Practical PRAGMATIST -Dogmatic
CHIEF FEATURE	+Sacrifice SELF-DESTRUCTION -Suicidal	+Appetite GREED Voracity	+Humility SELF-DEPRECATION -Abasement	+Pride ARROGANCE -Vanity	+Selflessness MARTYRDOM -Victimization	+Daring IMPATIENCE -Intolerance	+Determination STUBBORNESS -Obstinancy
MODE	+Deliberation CAUTION -Phobia	+Authority POWER -Oppression	+Restraint RESERVED -Inhibition	+Self-Actualization PASSION -Identification	+Persistance PERSEVERANCE -Unchanging	+Dynamism AGGRESSION -Belligerence	+Clarity OBSERVATION -Surveillance
CENTER	+Insight INTELLECTUAL -Reasoning	+Truth HIGHER INTELLECTUAL -Telepathy	+Perception EMOTIONAL -Sentimentality	+Love HIGHER EMOTIONAL -Intuition	+Productive MOVING -Frenetic	+Integration HIGHER MOVING -Desire	+Aware INSTINCTIVE -Mechanical
BODY TYPES	+Grandeur JUPITER -Overwhelming	+Agile MERCURY -Nervous	+Luminous LUNAR -Pallid	+Rugged SATURN -Gaunt	+Voluptuous VENUS -Sloppy	+Wiry MARS -Impulsive	+Radiant SOLAR -Ethereal

TYPICAL TRIADIC PROCESSES

Triads govern your own thought processes. You have an idea, the obstacles or negatives arise, and then you arrive at a resolution—the neutral position.

The triad governs the color spectrum where just three colors, red, blue and yellow, form all the colors of the spectrum when mixed in various proportions.

The triad governs major laws of physics. For example the atom comprises electrons, protons and neutrons—a balance of negative, positive and neutral charges.

In the triad of the solar system the Sun occupies the positive position (source of life and growth), the Moon the negative position (reflected light and rest from growth at night), and the Earth the neutral subject of this process.

Similarly triads govern sexuality—the masculine is the positive outgoing force, the feminine, the negative, receptive, passive and nurturing force, and the unification of the two gives rise to perpetuating the species.

TRIADS AND THE OVERLEAVES

The Triad is integral to the functioning of the overleaves. Each overleaf has a positive pole, a negative pole and the overleaf itself occupies the neutral position.

Take for example the goal of growth:

POSITIVE	NEGATIVE	NEUTRAL
+Evolution	-Confusion	GROWTH

Now look at the structure of the overleaf chart.

Every set of overleaves—goal, attitude, mode, chief feature, center, and body type has ordinal forms (negative), exalted forms (positive), and assimilation forms (neutral).

As a generalization, the ordinal overleaves are passive in nature and self-karmic. The exalted overleaves are active, thrusting the person out into the world and thus tend to be karmic. The assimilative overleaves are neutral and thus often correlate with non-karma, i.e. a rest position.

So for example the goals:

POSITIVE (Exalted)	NEGATIVE (Ordinal)	NEUTRAL (Assimilative)
Acceptance	Discrimination	
Growth	Re-evaluation	
Dominance	Submission	
		Stagnation

For an example, caution mode is the fear of something going wrong. So a person with that overleaf will tend to be under-confident, witheld and blocked. Its opposite is the exalted power mode. With this mode a person feels powerful, confident and an authority. He feels enabled to thrust out into the world and strive for what he wants. So the ordinal caution mode is disabling and the exalted power mode is enabling. The former is self-karma, the latter karmic in nature.

Each person chooses a balance in their overleaves for a particular lifetime, a balance of karma and self-karma.

The law of the triad can especially be seen in the functioning of the centers. The three centers that you principally operate from are intellectual, emotional and moving. These form a triad that relate to the everyday functioning of your personality. The parallel higher centers—higher intellectual, higher emotional, and higher moving—form another triad that relates to the experience of essence.

With these two clusters of three, there is also the instinctive center which is the gateway from the ordinal centers to the higher centers. So there is the larger triad of the ordinal centers, the higher centers and the neutral instinctive center.

POSITIVE (Essence)	NEGATIVE (Personality)	NEUTRAL (Gateway)
Higher Intellectual	Intellectual	
Higher Emotional	Emotional	
Higher Moving	Moving	
		Instinctive

TRIADS AS LIFE THEMES

Triads are the means by which you move through your life, spiralling from lesson to lesson. They apply to the pattern of your life.

First Position	Where you begin
	What you take for yourself
Second Position	Working with other people
	Giving what you took in (1) to others
Third Position	Understanding the whole picture

First Position

The first position is the beginning of your endeavor. For example, your childhood is a time of taking in and learning. Similarly, when you go into a training program you are starting a process that involves taking for yourself, as in the case of the psychology student who goes to graduate school and trains to become a counselor.

In the spiritual context the first line or position relates to self study and self knowledge.

Second Position

This is characterised by giving out of oneself, by teaching and serving.

The child grows up and works out in the world, using his upbringing and education to contribute to society.

The student graduates and works as a therapist for many years giving out what he has learned.

The spiritual student reaches a level of knowledge and self acceptance whereby he is self-sufficient in his state of being and is a model for those still studying. He continues to develop along his chosen path, but from a position of knowledgeable discrimination. He teaches sometimes merely by example and sometimes specifically, knowing that teaching spirituality is a part of his learning.

Third Position

The third line is characterized by understanding the "big picture." This is the perceptivity typical of the old soul, an understanding that "There is you, there is me, and there is the context in which we fit into everything."

The adult out in the world has raised a family, and reached his or her final career position or domestic stability. He has experienced all the trials and tribulations, and the joys and sorrows of family life, marriage, work, and so forth. He holds a felt perspective on all this. He is an anchor for others operating at the earlier levels. He or she has the whole picture of what life is about.

The therapist is now perhaps in middle age. He has experienced nearly all there is to experience, he has seen it all. He understands the strengths and limitations of his profession; he has developed a deep understanding about his patients and has learned to trust his intuition and not accept apparent symptoms at face value. He has perhaps lost some of the missionary zeal of his earlier years and is now more discerning. He holds the whole picture, and is relaxed, accepting, neutral and competent at a deep level rather than just at the level of technical competence.

The spiritual person has experienced his own spirituality from all facets over a long period of time. He has interacted with many people and has seen nearly all there is to see. He has a wealth of inner spiritual experiences. He is relaxed and sure of his own spirituality. He is open to teaching others and may or may not do so. He too has the whole picture of what spirituality is about and has it down on a felt or deeply instinctive level. He has a feeling of wholeness and completion.

Triads are the basic building blocks of the universe from which all phenomena originate. They are the means by which essence teaches personality. They tend to be unstable and intense and therefore are the perfect vehicle for the law of karma to ride upon.

Spiritual systems in the universe are structured around the numbers three and seven. You have seen how the law of three operates. Shortly you shall see how septants and octaves operate. First however let us take a look at quadrants, pentangles and sextants.

QUADRANTS

The quadrant is a working group of four persons who are dedicated to accomplishing a common goal. Unlike the triad, a generally unstable karmic configuration, the quadrant is stable and productive. Whereas the triad is composed of constantly rotating positions, positive, negative, and neutral, the quadrant has four fixed positions that will be discussed in this section.

Generally informal quadrants form quite readily among any people who wish to gather for a purpose and this group will find a natural ease in being together. The productive foursome need not be composed of the same four people. In the informal quadrant, members may be replaced by other people, making it a flexible unit. These are temporary quadrants that may last for a few hours, days, or weeks.

A quadrant may be formed to go on a weekend trip together or perhaps to form the work party who will set up the room for a meeting. If a member drops out, a substitute is easily found.

In a formal quadrant, members tend to remain more constant because they have made agreements to work together for many years to accomplish a specific goal. They may create music together, found and run a school, discover and implement a new scientific method or any number of human endeavors. Quadrants have wide ranging applications including business, social groups, expeditions, and interest groups, to name a few.

An example of a famous formal quadrant was the recent notorious "Gang of Four" of China.

The experience of being in a quadrant is usually fun and satisfying. As they tend to gather for a specific purpose, quadrants have the potential to be enormously satisfying to work with.

Sometimes a quadrant of four people can be identified as central figures in larger groups that gather for a common purpose. That is, one may be able to identify a core group of four within a larger context. This frequently occurs within the presidency and his cabinet.

The four positions of the quadrant relate to the four categories within the overleaves—inspiration, expression, action and assimilation. The function of each member relates uniquely to one of each of these as you will see shortly.

Similarly the functions of the positions relate to the ordinal overleaves: intellectual, emotional, moving and instinctive centers.

POSITIONS OF THE QUADRANT

The quadrant is made up of four positions, each unique and different.

The four are love, knowledge, power and support. All four positions are always represented in any quadrant and usually each member adopts one position and retains that position for the life of the quadrant. It is flexible to the extent that if one member is absent, then one of the three remaining may act both roles, or a fresh person may be invited or naturally gravitate to fill the vacancy.

Of course different roles and overleaves show a proclivity for different positions so that the positions tend to facilitate a person's natural expression.

1. LOVE   2. KNOWLEDGE
inspiration   assimilation
emotional   intellectual

3. POWER   4. SUPPORT
expression   action
moving   instinctive

1. Love

The love position is the initiator, the person who comes up with the initial ideas. He is the one who suggests a whole range of activities and goals. He acts as the source of inspiration and frequently he is the one who originally pulled the group together. He tends to be informal and likes having fun.

The person in this position frequently gets the most out the the group but is least in control of what happens. He is usually better at starting a task rather than finishing it. Sometimes this person fears not being competent. He may be seen as unstructured but forceful.

> *Marketers and advertising specialists often occupy the love position in a quadrant, where the generation of ideas is central.*

The love position correlates with the inspiration axis on the overleaf diagram and so goes well with passion mode and emotional centering.

The most common roles to gravitate to this position are priest and sage. They tend to do it well but other roles may be found filling this position as well, depending upon their overleaves.

2. Knowledge

The person in the knowledge position provides the knowledge or information that the quadrant needs to accomplish its task. The knowledge position raises questions, considers answers and facilitates discussion. Frequently he acts as a mediator or discussion group leader. The knowledge person acts as the consultant to the group.

> *In business the research specialist usually occupies the knowledge position for a management quadrant. In undercover work it is the spy or detective who provides the valuable information.*

The person in the knowledge position is good at studying the data and appraising alternatives but you may have difficulty getting decisions from him.

The person in this position fears not being interesting.

Scholars are naturally inclined to fill this position because of their propensity for study and neutrality.

3. Power

The power position is about action, production, and getting things done. This person is often the decision-maker of the group. He values results. He tends to be more quick, controlled and controlling than the other positions.

The person in the power position uses the ideas of the love position and the information of the knowledge position to get things done.

Typically, company presidents and foremen occupy power positions within their respective quadrants. They are action oriented and their job is to produce results.

The person in the power position relates best to the person in the love position, the idea generator. These two positions in the quadrant are the strongest or most apparent.

The person in the power position fears being out of control of the situation. Sometimes this person can be seen as impatient, dictatorial or intolerant, cold and uncaring, wanting results at any price.

The roles best suited to the power position are usually warriors or kings.

4. Support

The support person holds the quadrant together while each of the other positions presents its ideas, methods, and information. As the quadrant pursues its task, there are considerable stresses and strains on the relationships. A multitude of matters must be resolved in any issue—the idealists have their shoulds, the cynics are disbelieving, the spiritualists see all the possibilities and so on. Therefore, one quarter of the quadrant is devoted solely to the task of keeping it together and preventing disintegration.

The support person often finds the work space, gathers necessary materials, and provides the food and drink. He makes the others feel nurtured, cared for and wanted, and wants the group to be cohesive and sustaining.

He more than any other group member desires harmony; he fears not being liked.

Secretaries and administrative assistants commonly fill this position. Within the structure of the organization they would appear to hold menial positions but in fact their contribution is crucial. Salaries do not reflect the importance of the support position, despite the modern myth that this position is not as substantial as the others.

For example, the executive secretary of the president of a major corporation may fill the support postion for the quadrant that runs the entire company. The president may be in the power position, two other executives may fill knowledge and love (perhaps the Marketing Director and the Production Director) and the secretary sits in on meetings among the three taking notes and playing an almost invisible facilitative role.

Often people in the support position are taken advantage of because they do not stand up for themselves and can be exploited.

The roles of server and priest have a natural aptitude and flair for this, and to a lesser extent scholars because of their neutrality.

This position is the number four position and gets on best with the number two or knowledge position.

In summary the love position is the one that generates the ideas and provides the inspiration. The knowledge position brings in all the information. He considers the myriad of ideas that the love position generated and reduces them down to the few options that are likely to work.

The person in the power position helps the group to decide which will be the final path chosen to achieve their goal. Ultimately the person in the support position holds the group together through the period of resolution of conflicting ideas.

You can see the value of knowing about quadrant positions in the average workplace. Observing the quadrant positions that people fall into enables you to relate to them in the way that reflects their natural function. If you know a person is in the love position, you can go to them for ideas, not information, decisions or support. If you know who occupies the power position, you go to them to get the job done. You know to approach the support person when the cohesion of the group is threatened. And you can arm yourself for this by consulting the knowledge person for the proper data.

If one position of the underlying quadrant is absent or neglected, then the group cannot function. So any organization needs groups of people to align with each of the four positions if it is to be successful. Businesses that are successful intuitively do this. This natural breakdown of tasks into quadrant positions also applies to families and social groups. In a family it is easy for a young child to be in the love position and to generate new ideas through their creativity and spontaneity. It may be natural for the mother to be in the power position, deciding what the family should do. The father could be in the knowledge position or the roles could be reversed, and so on.

You will not always occupy the same position in the different quadrants that you participate in. You may be in the knowledge position in the workplace and in the love position in your family. This is because the characteristics of the people comprising the groups varies widely and quadrant members' roles are determined by where the need is in the group.

As we mentioned earlier, overleaves have an influence on the quadrant position chosen. A person with the goal of dominance will tend toward the power position, and someone with the goal of submission would naturally gravitate to the support position. This will be the tendency regardless of role.

PENTANGLES

A pentangle contains the same positions as a quadrant, with one additional. That fifth is called the eccentric.

A pentangle can either comprise five individuals or four persons, the fifth position occupied by their common goal or purpose. This is similar to the process in a triad exemplified by a married couple that have their relationship as the invisible third element.

> *For example the Beatles formed a quadrant but their music occupied the fifth position, turning it into a powerful pentangle.*

Pentangles are inherently unstable. They can appear eccentric, strange or unusual. The natural instability of the pentangle means the group must have a strong purpose or intention if they are to stay together. When they do stay together they can be extraordinarily powerful.

If the pentangle is not gripped by a strong sense of purpose then it is common for one member to drop out or be absent, resulting in a quadrant.

> *For example if five people have an informal evening gathering it is common for one to fall asleep.*
>
> *If the five go on an excursion one will take off on their own leaving the others to sightsee together.*

A pentangle works by taking the seed of an idea and blowing it up to a grander scale. It is frequently the most effective vehicle to get a concept out to the masses. Therefore it is unusual to find pentangles in ordinary situations.

The number five has an ancient tradition in the practice of magic. Five in the Tarot deck relates to the Hierophant, the spiritual teacher and the keeper of esoteric knowledge. The five-pointed star in witchcraft is another example of the eccentric and powerful use of the number five.

Chapter Nine

Sextants, Septants, Octaves and Nontets

SEXTANTS

The sextant is formed when one adds a further member to the pentangle—this new element is called the *integrator*.

The six positions are:

LOVE
KNOWLEDGE
POWER
SUPPORT/COMPASSION
ECCENTRIC (often an odd bodytype)
INTEGRATOR

As with quadrants and pentangles, the love position comes up with many creative ideas. The knowledge position refines these ideas down to a few possibilities based on the data. The power position decides what is to be done and moves the group toward achieving it. The support or compassion position holds the group together as conflicts are resolved.

The eccentric position has the innovative wild invention or idea: Steve Wozniak for the Apple computer, Steven Spielberg for films, to name two.

The integrator takes the eccentric's novel idea and makes it palatable or acceptable for public consumption. The eccentric comes up with wacky way-out ideas that do need modifying in order to become viable.

> *George Lucas, the integrator, worked with Steven Spielberg, the eccentric, to reformat his wild ideas in a style that was brilliantly successful as the movie* ET *and the* Star Wars *film series.*

Integrators are highly valued in our society. They have the skill to turn ideas into marketable products and money. They sometimes move from job to job, changing companies as they complete setting one company up with a direction and thrust. Some Chief Executive Officers are professional at doing that. They seek out prospective situations, take on the challenge, set up the pathway, train their successor and move on.

That is the professional integrator.

The sextant often breaks down into an exalted and an ordinal triad depending on the essence roles of its members. Not infrequently the exalted roles lose sight of the value of the ordinal roles. They can get quite caught up in their grand schemes and lose track of practicalities and the nuts and bolts of the operation. Many a project has gone down the tubes when this has happened.

> *A good example of this was the Chuck E. Cheese venture that started out with a zany high tech format for*

serving pizza. The innovative creators of this project lost track of the ordinal food aspect of the business and concentrated on the exalted wild crazy atmosphere. The consequence was high-priced, poor pizza that resulted in financial reversals.

Often whole organizations operate according to the sextant model. For example there is the common structure of a Marketing Department (ideas), Production Department (power), Personnel (support), Research Department (knowledge); the integrator may be a single person such as the Chief Executive Officer. Usually the eccentric position is not a high profile and obvious role.

For example, once the automatic can opener was invented, the eccentric's job was done. It remained for all the other elements to get one or more of these installed in every home, an on-going task of some magnitude.

A further example of a sextant is the specialized musical group, the sextet. The sextet was the original orchestra. It is built upon the quadrant, a stabilizing force with an an eccentric added to make each session interesting and different and an integrator to make the session meaningful. From the basis of the six, people were merely added to the functions for volume, variation and fun. The integrator became formalized as the conductor and the eccentric as the lead part.

In the context of the traditional jazz group, each member takes a turn at being the eccentric as he does his solo.

Identifying the roles of individuals and groups is immensely useful as it enables people and groups of people to be utilized in a way that facilitates their natural inclinations. This also makes it possible to identify specialists such as the eccentrics and innovators and give them the room they need to excel. Nothing could be more wasteful than to try to fit an eccentric into a limited and formal structure where creativity is stifled.

Priests and sages are the roles that gravitate to the part of integrator.

Now we are ready to discuss septants, the other configuration that operates as a basic building block to the universe.

THE SEPTANT AS A GROUP

Groups of seven are not an ordinary occurrence compared with quadrants and sextants that form naturally and easily. Septants are highly effective as a team if they choose to operate as such and their goal is most often a highly exalted one involving dedication to the realization of some great accomplishment.

The septant is an inherently unstable group like the triad and the pentangle. Nevertheless a highly dedicated crew can keep a septant together for a major task.

Not all the members of a septant are highly visible so that you may not easily identify them publicly as you might with a triad (the Three Stooges) or a quadrant (the Beatles).

The septant is a sextant with the additional position of "observer," a spot often taken by a scholar.

The septant has of course seven positions.

POSITION	RELATED ROLE
LOVE	ARTISAN
KNOWLEDGE	SAGE
POWER	WARRIOR
COMPASSION	SERVER
ECCENTRIC	PRIEST
INTEGRATOR	KING
OBSERVER	SCHOLAR

Any group of seven tends to fall into the seven positions, and there is a tendency for people to select the position that relates

to the natural function of their role. However there may be other factors that override this, such as the combination of their overleaves or specialized knowledge or experience that determines the position that they are best suited for.

THE SEPTANT AS A PROCESS

As stated in the section on triads, spiritual systems are based on the numbers three and seven. They work together to form the building blocks of the universe.

The law of seven combines two triads and a seventh step representing the integration of the whole. This is called a septant and governs the unfolding of spiritual growth. The signs of this integrative number are to be found everywhere including the seven days to the week; seven orifices in the human skull, seven major colors in the spectrum, seven chakras, seven sets of overleaves, seven stages of development, seven levels to each stage, seven internal monads, and so forth.

As white light divides into seven as it passes through a prism (a three sided crystal or triad), so the analogy holds that when fragments leave the Tao they pass through a prism effect and the fragments split up into seven types of roles. It is correct to say that any one role is merely a particular frequency of energy.

THE SEPTANT GROWTH PATTERN

The septant is a specific cosmic law governing all developmental sequences. Everything on the physical planes corresponds with a septant pattern.

The septant growth pattern governs the way in which all things evolve or change. The law applies to the development of human activities or relationships. It includes the development of projects, the growth of corporations, the course of marriages, the unfolding of your life, and so forth.

The septant can be divided into two triads and the neutral position. As mentioned, the basic patterns for the physical plane are based upon the triad and the septant. Two triads equal six steps, and the seventh step is completion.

The first triad is the ordinal experience and upon resolution the person moves to the second triad, which is a higher (exalted) lesson built on the first. The seventh step is the integration of the ordinal and exalted triads.

The Elements of a Septant

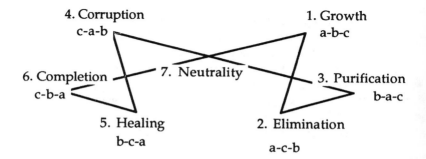

4. Corruption
c-a-b

1. Growth
a-b-c

6. Completion
c-b-a

7. Neutrality

3. Purification
b-a-c

5. Healing
b-c-a

2. Elimination
a-c-b

The Triad

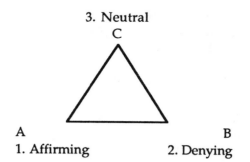

3. Neutral
C

A
1. Affirming

B
2. Denying

The triad sets up conditions that facilitate karma. The septant sets up long range patterns of growth—i.e. evolution into new forms. In other words the septant integrates the lessons learned in karma and develops the experience into higher more refined ways of being. It is a long path and the steps are small. The path is the septant and the steps are triads.

The steps of the Septant Growth Pattern form an enneagram. The seventh step, shown at the crossing point of the figure, may also be represented as the circle around a symmetrical design.

The Seven Steps

1. GROWTH, INCARNATION

An essence incarnating as an infant soul
A person starting a lifetime
A couple starting their relationship
The beginning steps toward a lifelong career
The beginning of a business
The start of an administration or government

2. ELIMINATION, DISINTEGRATION, DECAY

Getting rid of unwanted stuff
Dumping imprinting
Clarifying one's purpose by discriminating
Clearing out distractions
Unloading unwanted merchandise
Firing unproductive staff

3. STABILIZING, PURIFYING, REFINING

Improving on what already exists
Self education
Beautifying the environment
Refining goals
Gaining experience

4. CORRUPTION, DISEASE, REBELLION

Illness, disease
Unfaithfulness

Dishonesty
Threatened bankruptcy
Scandal
Theft
Catastrophe, natural disaster, war

5. HEALING, RENEWAL, ADAPTATION

Healing
Rest
Recovery process
Adaptation
Coping with change
Reform

6. COMPLETION

Finished product
Recovery
Health
Lesson learned
Culmination
Transformation

7. NEUTRALITY

Everything recorded
Integration
Stasis
Examination of all events
Remembering
Readiness for something new

You can move into this seventh position at any time without affecting the position where you are on the septant.

Example of a Septant Functioning in a Relationship

1. Let us take a simple example of boy meets girl. They start off with meeting each other and the relationship starts to grow. This is stage one, the initiating and growth point.

2. After the first few dates they discover that they have differences. They are faced with either parting ways or negotiating a workable partnership. This is step two and is characterized by eliminating unwanted stuff. The instability of this creates a feeling of disintegration.

3. If their differences are resolved the couple reaches the third stage. They build on what they have and make the most of it. It is a stage of harmony and stability. They have decided to stay together and they proceed with raising children or whatever. This phase can last a long time.

4. In stage four the universe throws in a wild card. The relationship has been stable and everyone thinks it will stay in that way for ever. But one of the partners falls madly in love with someone else, or gets cancer. There is often an issue around morality and truth. The survival of the relationship is at stake.

5. Stage five is the healing process. If the relationship survives then it adapts to the new situation. The issues are resolved, cleaned up and healed.

6. Stage six is completion. Following this the relationship may end, or it may start a fresh cycle at a higher level.

7. Stage seven, as described earlier, is a neutral resting place where a person can move to for a short time at any point in the process whereupon he or she returns to that point.

These steps apply to relationships, marriages, careers, groups that gather for a specific purpose, spiritual growth and so forth. In fact the septant describes the human growth process in all its shapes and guises.

Although there are hosts of influences on the development of relationships, the pattern of the septant is usually discernible.

THE LIFETIME SEPTANT

Here is the septant at work in its ideal state throughout a lifetime. Of course not everyone follows the entire course of the septant each lifetime. In fact it is more usual for younger souls to keep repeating the first three steps over and over until they die. Eventually souls reach the fourth step as a prerequisite to moving into the exalted steps.

1. Intellectual center: You decide upon your overleaves; where you will be born; who your parents will be; what you want to learn about this lifetime, and so on.

2. Emotional center: You are born and form emotional relationships with family and peers. You begin to create and resolve karma.

3. Moving center: You go to school; learn; participate at many levels socially, academically, athletically; find a career; cope with a job.

4. Instinctive center: You reach middle age. You ask yourself what life is all about. You make great changes in your life, career, relationships, goals, all characteristic of instinctive center. This sets the course for the rest of your life.

5. Higher intellectual center: From here on you can have a more higher centered approach to life. You have the opportunity to look back on your life, and tell the truth to yourself about how it all works.

6. Higher emotional center: In this stage there may be new types of relationships, including grandparenting. You can accept the whole family setup and encourage the strivings of individual members. Retirement with satisfaction. For younger souls there can be great dissatisfaction at that point and sometimes they die as they feel no further purpose in living.

7. The final and seventh stage is your opportunity to integrate the experiences of your entire lifetime. You can accomplish this by reflection and reminiscing about your life. You feel philosophical and complete and you share your wisdom with others.

To summarize, the septant is a group formed for an exalted purpose. It is also a growth pattern that builds upon the triad, the foundation stone of the universe. The septant is a fundamental developmental process underlying all life changes.

THE OCTAVE

Groups of eight break down into two quadrants so that they can function more effectively and more easily. Therefore the octet is not so much a group configuration as it is part of the process of evolution, for the number eight forms the octave.

Now an octave is the bridge between one septant and the next septant. You could even say that the first step of the next septant is the same as the eighth step of the octave preceeding it.

An excellent example of an octave is the notes of the musical scale:

1. *Do* 2. *Re* 3. *Me* 4. *Fa* 5. *So* 6.*La* 7.*Ti* 8.*Do.*

The note Middle C is repeated as the same tone but one octave higher. The eighth and first tones are the same, but separated by a unit of pitch that divides into eight. In other words there are seven different notes.

The notes of an octave are different because they occupy different frequencies. As you evolve through the soul levels from infant to old, you gradually occupy different frequencies or levels of beingness. When you evolve from infant to baby soul perceptivity, you have completed an octave by going from first level infant to first level baby over a series of lifetimes. You are simply changing tone and frequency.

When you have completed a septant process in your life experience, you change frequency because you have also completed an octave. You end at the beginning of the next lesson. So it is the octave that accounts for evolution. Triads are the steps, the septant is the path, and the octave is the foothills you are climbing on your way to the mountain top or the Tao.

The octave makes evolution possible.

NONTETS OR LADDERS

The function of a ladder or group of nine is to move a group toward a specific goal. Once that goal is attained, the nontet has no further purpose.

This configuration of nine is most common in the business world but can occur for private or social purposes as well.

The appropriate synergy among the nine people is a prerequisite for the status of a nontet. In other words the nontet does not exist simply because nine people are together. They must be nine people who work well together and every single one is motivated to achieving the goal. They must trust and accept each other to the level of mild tolerance.

> *Let us take the example of an investment group. Let us say a group of nine people gather together to invest and make $10,000 apiece. Given that they have a common goal and basically share a similar investment philosophy (high risk or long term gain) they compose a nontet. Once they achieve their investment goal of $10,000, they can disband or form a new goal. If one person's heart wasn't in it, the group would be less likely to succeed.*

Often a group of nine comes together to discuss ideas without reaching a conclusion and it dissolves. It fails to become a nontet.

There are no positions in a nontet as there are in the quadrants, sextants, and some of the other configurations described. Instead the members tend to act out of their role. They provide what they are best at providing with their special talents and needs. So a group of artisans would probably set about accomplishing a creative project; a group of scholars might do research together; and in a mixed role group each role would offer what he does the best.

Likewise members do not always perform the same duties in the group. They flow and change, contributing appropriately from their roles and talents. Because of its size the nontet does not operate as tightly and formally as a group of six or less.

> *Corporations are often formed around the configura-tion of a ladder. The president, the various vice-presidents and the board of directors may comprise a nontet that sets out to achieve the corporate plan. The plan will succeed as long as there is a single purpose or goal such as the creation and distribution of a product such as a computer.*

Ladders can get stale when motivation falls off. Likewise ladders fall apart if some members begin to pursue a different goal without the agreement of the whole.

In summary, a ladder comprises nine people who trust and tolerate each other with a keen enthusiasm to achieve a single specific goal.

Chapter Ten

Support Circle and Group Process

GROUPS OF TWELVE—SUPPORT CIRCLES

Often we suffer from the illusion that our journey through life is painfully marked by loneliness and isolation. This is of course part of the maya of the physical plane and helps to keep the Tao hidden in the great game of hide and seek. As essence gains experience it gradually perceives that not only is life less joyful when we try to go it alone, but that in fact true separateness is impossible. In fact we are not only connected with others but every one of us is surrounded by people that offer support in very specific ways.

These support people fulfill a similar function as does one's family of origin. The difference is that they are drawn from a much wider source—families over many lifetimes, comrades at arms, teachers and so on. A blood relationship with these support people is not necessary and often is not desirable. Support people are free of the cultural duties and expectations that society places on familial ties. This allows support people a greater range of interaction with each of us.

Let's see how these support people help us and discover what categories of assistance they fall into. Let us also learn how we can find out who is in our personal support group and how we can use them.

THE TWELVE SUPPORT POSITIONS

Each person has twelve support positions to draw from for assistance. These positions cover all of a person's basic needs in daily living, making them a practical tool for coping with and enjoying everyday life.

Once a person has identified the positions of his family and friends on the support circle, then he or she can call on them specifically to help out. Nevertheless, even if we do not consciously know who they are, they are available and help out whenever they can.

> *Jesus knew his twelve supporters and in his final years surrounded himself with them. Because everything he taught, he taught by example, his twelve apostles were a hint that these supporters are available to each of us.*

Needless to say, just as each of us has twelve helpers, each one of us are members of other people's support groups. Knowing who we support and in what position can be enormously helpful in our interrelationships.

The twelve positions group themselves into triads that work together. On the next page you may see a summary of the positions, followed by a brief discussion of each.

The Twelve Support Positions

Power	Your position
Love Knowledge Compassion	Get things done: intimates
Mentor Beauty Child	Inspirational
Humor Discipline Anchor	Assist in physical plane lessons
Healer Enlightenment Muse	Assist in spirit-plane lessons

Love

The love position is filled by one who truly loves you. He is willing to promote you and allows you to completely love him in return. This love does not mean romantic love but agape, unconditional love. This person teaches you what love truly is and is not deterred by your resistances, prickliness, or warts. From the love person you learn forgiveness and compassion.

Imagine someone that you always feel more loving around. You feel safe with them and because of this your best traits shine when you are with them. You are always inspired by their patience with you and you learn about love by watching their gentleness with other creatures.

The person filling your love position is a source of inspiration and ideas, an exciting and invigorating person to be around. Not surprisingly the love position is commonly filled by essence twins or people whom you have spent many many lifetimes with—

especially if you have attained the relationship of the lover monad (see Chapter 7).

Any role can fill this position but priests, servers and artisans have a proclivity for it.

Knowledge

The person in the knowledge position provides information, helpful advice or a fresh perspective when you are confused. This person provides the necessary perspective and often helps to facilitate your decisions by providing the facts of a situation.

Knowing who is in your knowledge position is exceptionally helpful because it helps you get things done in your life. When you have a problem, you simply call them up and you have tapped into that person who is uniquely placed to help you the most.

> *For example, to solve a practical problem, you can call a person in your knowledge position and discuss it. Maybe you like to call your Aunt Maybelle, your minister, or your therapist when you are struggling with a decision like whether to change jobs.*

The person in the knowledge position may or may not provide that piece of information that cracks the problem, but his or her perspective alone may be sufficient to see the matter in a different light and solve it. The knowledge position facilitates the problem solving, albeit indirectly.

Scholars commonly fill this position because they are the ones that assimilate vast amounts of information and are truly knowledgeable.

Compassion

The person in this position provides truth and understanding. The compassion person keeps the individual awake, pushing them to look at their limits.

It may be filled, for example, by a zen master. His compassionate support may not always appear gentle and kind but perhaps firm, direct, and even confronting.

Imagine a friend who loves you enough to tell you the truth about the destructiveness of a bad habit like drinking to excess. This might make you angry at first but in the longer run you learn that you are loved and cared for by this friend.

The customary interpretation of a compassionate person is one who tolerates another's foibles. This is not necessarily the characteristic of this postion. The person filling the compassion position is more concerned with pointing out the foibles, gently and with what has been called ruthless compassion.

This position can be filled by person's psychotherapist, counsellor, or teacher. In terms of roles, compassion is often filled by priests and servers.

These three support positions, love, knowledge, and compassion, form a cluster which help you to resolve karmic situations. The three people plus the person who is being supported form a quadrant, with the subject of the support in the power position. This power position is the thirteenth position in the support circle.

This quadrant is the facilitating center of the support circle, and these four are the key people of your support group.

Mentor

This person acts as a parent or a model to the subject of the circle. The mentor acts as a role model as well as guide and council. The mentor can be a major imprinter during childhood and as such is often the same role. If for example you are a server and both of your parents are artisans, you may gravitate to your server uncle, who as mentor helps you to manifest your server nature.

Mentors can be parents, coaches, teachers, relatives, professional or academic advisors, or friends. As mentor however, they will usually have great impact on you and the relationship is usually lasting whenever possible. It is a person who is experienced and has walked the path you are on now.

On occasion your mentor may be a long way away, but, because the relationship is recognized on an essence level, a meeting is usually arranged. Sometimes there is a "chance" encounter or an unexpected trip which is a manifestation of essence arranging for a meeting with the mentor, an opportunity for recharging inspiration and renewing ideals.

Any role can fill this position but kings excel.

Beauty

This person epitomizes what is beautiful to you. They teach you how to see beauty all around you in your daily life even in the midst of a seemingly ugly city. Often they themselves have great physical attractiveness or a beautiful personality that inspires and supports you. They teach you how to see the beauty in yourself.

This person might be an art teacher, a musician, a craftsperson, a fashion designer, a beautician, an architect, an actress, a model, or almost anyone.

Artisans, priests and sages are commonly in beauty positions.

Child

This position helps you build responsibility by getting you to take care of them. You feel parental and nurturing and are driven to care for and support this person.

The child position can be filled by an actual child but anyone can fit the bill, even an adult or elderly person.

For example your father or mother could be in your child position and you would end up taking care of them more than they take care of you. A father could feel like a child in the presence of his son despite the age differences.

The child position might be filled by a mentally retarded brother or sister that you care for for many years or similarly by a disabled person. Where a marriage has a great disparity in ages one of the couple may fill the child position for the other who acts as parent.

Your child position is obvious and easy to spot. That person feels like a child in your presence. This is exactly the way you feel in relation to the person whose child position you fill. Most of us fill both positions during every lifetime. In fact, often the positions of mentor and child are reciprocal.

Transactional analysis focuses on the potential for each of us to be in the child position.

This concludes another triad, or quadrant if the subject is included.

Humor

The humor position supports you in your physical plane lessons by getting you to lighten up in the midst of difficult karma.

This is one of the people in your life that naturally makes you laugh and of course he or she is a pleasure to be around. They bring a lightness and a gaiety into your life, and indeed comic relief when circumstances might be trying.

It is easy to recognize who it is that makes you laugh.

The fun loving qualities of sages make them the most common roles in this position although any role can meet it. Most often this will be someone you know personally but it can be a professional comedian like Woody Allen whom you have never met but whose films you enjoy.

The humor position may not be humorous to other people but they succeed in making you laugh.

Discipline

Where the humor position brings lightness, the discipline position brings organization and reminds you of responsibility.

The first attribute of this position is that this person compels you to decide whether or not you are going to act.

> *For example discipline is a fairly common position in marriage, where one partner tends to press the other to meet his or her obligations. Another example would be that the discipline position holds the subject to the repayment of a debt.*

A second way the discipline position manifests is that they force you to focus your thinking in order to work out exactly what you want.

Your children often cause you to think out the basis of your values. The child asks "Why?" and you have to come up with reasons. This thinking through of where you stand on any issue is characteristic of the position. The response calls for intellectual discipline.

The position is often filled by parents, your spouse, children, business relationships where you are called upon to produce the goods, and so on. Probation officers, therapists, ministers, teachers, coaches and consultants often fill the position well.

Because discipline relates to being grounded and working out where you stand with the reality of a situation, the solid action roles, kings and warriors, flourish in this position. The most fluid roles have the greatest lessons—artisans, priests and sages.

Anchor

The person in this position provides groundedness, safety and rock-solid support in the subject's life. One has the sense that they are always there and one can always turn to them, especially in times of crisis. They will always provide food and shelter, and the basics as a brief respite for the subject in their time of need.

The person in the anchor position can always be counted on and will never reject the subject.

Another role that the anchor plays is as a "listening post." They ground the subject of the support circle, making them aware of what is impractical and helping them reduce their options to a realistic set of choices. The anchor is a wonderful person to talk to and "nut out" a problem with.

Scholars absolutely excel at this function. This is their major contribution to civilization over aeons of time. If you wish to evaluate an idea, develop a project or crystallize some embryonic notion, talk to a scholar. They will tell you what works and what doesn't in a neutral and disinterested way, leaving you with the best of one's notion and how to implement it.

Healer

The person in this position may heal you directly by providing physical assistance such as your personal physician, body worker, or acupuncturist. However you can be healed merely by the presence of your healer, who might be a counselor, friend, or relative, who heals you through a brief talk for example.

You feel physically better and emotionally balanced and healed as a result of being with them. They may also teach you about self healing or instruct you in methods of healing others.

The more fluid roles—priests, artisans and sages—excel in this position.

Enlightenment

The enlightenment position is filled by a teacher. In their presence you frequently experience the higher centers—higher emotional, higher intellectual and higher moving center.

In the presence of your teacher you seek only to drink at the fountain, to take in all you can. This can mean learning from an obvious and public spiritual teacher or simply an old lady next door that teaches you about gardening.

Spiritual guides such as Meher Baba, Werner Erhard, Yogananda and so on, fill the enlightenment position for many individuals.

Enlightenment means to make light. That is, enlightenment is a matter of gaining a philosophical perspective on your experience. The enlightenment position in its simplest (and lightest) guise can be about helping you to let go, loosen up, relax, and take time out.

> *So going to Aunt Edna's beach cottage for a weekend might be where you simply step out of your life, forget it all completely, lie in the sun and fish and relax totally for two days. She would be enabling you to lighten up.*

Muse

This position need not be filled by a person who is currently alive on the physical plane (in a physical body) nor does it need to be filled by a person at all.

The muse represents your highest values in life. These can be embodied in a person for example and you might say "I would like to have my life just like that person's—I would like to be like them." Their model gives you a goal and a target in the development of your life.

On the other hand the muse can be an abstract concept—"I want to be a concert pianist"—without a specific role model.

The infinite souls such as Buddha or Jesus Christ fill the muse position for literally millions of people.

The Muse then is your goal or highest aspiration. Common muses include the ambition to become the Chief Executive Officer of a company, or to make lots of money, or to raise a happy, warm, and loving family.

Younger souls will tend to select a muse that reflects ambition, whereas older souls will seek a muse that is more spiritually oriented.

Power

You, the subject of the support circle, occupy the thirteenth position, the power position.

When you are truly supported you become powerful. As the power position you live your life and integrate your ideals with reality.

> *As mentioned earlier a great example of the archetypal support circle in operation is Jesus and the twelve Apostles. They supported Jesus in his life's work. He occupied the thirteeth position, the power position.*

Remember that each person has their twelve apostles to assist them. The task then is to identify them so that they the way is cleared for them to serve more directly.

Young souls often allow the positions on their support circle to lie dormant and go it alone. That is partly due to a sense of competition and the feeling that the other person is a threat.

Older souls tend to seek support more than young souls. They recognize how the game of life works, that we are all in the game and it is more fun and works better if the challenges are shared. Doing it all alone is a hard path and often stems from feelings of competition.

Older souls let go of the fear (despite being surrounded by the young imprinting) and acknowledge and use support. They know that sharing their life and supporting others is the easier path to tread and raises the amount of love in their lives.

Old souls have had so many lifetimes that there is a tendency for the same people to fill the same position lifetime after lifetime.

These familiar folks tend to form an inner circle or primary circle that we could call the first string.

When a person in the first string is not present in one's life the position is filled by someone from the second string of supporters. There is a third string as well as a fourth, fifth, sixth, and so on.

First string supporters can be recognized by the intensity and enduring nature of the relationship with the supported person.

The first string child position will be a close, intimate and ongoing relationship over many years. The second and third string positions lack the intensity of the first string and may show up for a shorter period of time.

Up to a quarter of all the support positions are filled by the subject themselves because the other individuals are not available on a day to day basis.

> *A woman may have a retarded son at home who is in her first string child position. She may work at a hospital and a long term patient may fill her second string child position, and so on.*

By the mature soul stage the first string positions are permanently filled by specific individuals based on many lifetimes of accumulated support. That is to say, one has had sufficient lifetimes to have built up some deep and long term relationships over many intense experiences.

Occasionally one person can fill more than one position on another's circle. For example in a marriage, one partner might fill the love position as well as humor for the other and so on. This makes for a well rounded and interesting relationship. The love position teaches how to love and gives emotional richness and the humor position makes it all fun.

It is unusual for one person to fill more than two first string positions on another's support circle, and he or she normally fills one position only.

On the other hand a therapist may fill the compassion position in the fifth string for a large number of people; being in the first string for that number of people would be much too intense and taxing.

In summary the importance of support circles lies in using the people in your daily life to share experiences and lighten the load. You live in a society that values independence and competition. The path to warm and loving relationships lies in supporting others and being supported. That means contacting people and actually telling them you want their help.

The people that fill the positions on your support circle have made this agreement with you and they derive great satisfaction in fulfilling the agreement. They experience frustration when you block them or disallow their help. Likewise you experience frustration when you are resisted in your attempts to assist another. This is analagous to the feeling you get when someone refuses to accept the gift you have bought for them. Remember that surrendering to assistance equals becoming powerful.

The support group is the last configuration of great significance in your life. There are larger groups but they have less impact on you than the ones described thus far. In addition, all larger groups are made up of combinations of these smaller groups.

Let's, however, look at the processes that groups of any size go through in their evolutionary path.

GROUP PROCESS AND STAGES OF DEVELOPMENT

Small groups follow a definite and specific plan of evolution. This evolutionary pattern is common to groups of any number and with any agenda or focus. This growth curve is in addition to the characteristics of quadrants, septants, and so on discussed in these chapters.

In their development, small groups age and go through the same process as souls go through in their many lifetimes.

1. Infant group

The infant stage of any group is characterized by superstition, fear and distrust of one another. The group is unsure of itself and its direction. The motto is, "You're a stranger and I don't trust you."

2. Baby group

The group evolves over time to the baby stage. They decide in favor of some distinct structure and so rules are made. The group becomes less random and more civilized. There is an attempt to get the group to all focus on the same goal and there is a heavy emphasis placed on agreement. The motto is, "I might trust you if we can agree to the same rules."

At the baby level the group is quite dependent on the group leader for guidance and structure and there is little individual initiative. The tendency is to look to authority.

3. Young group

When the structure has been set the group develops into the young stage. It is characterized by ambition and attempts to move out into the world and make others aware of the group and its goals. They will tend to create events and experiences that impact other people.

At this young level they form a conviction of their own rightness and they slip into the belief that other people are wrong and need to be shown the error of their ways. The group begins to become successful and people feel they are achieving the goals that they set out to achieve.

There can be intense struggles for power and leadership within the group at this stage, even to the extent of creating factions. The group may split off and form other groups with different goals. The initial leader may be challenged for strength or deposed. This is the third developmental level.

The group motto is, "We're right (or I'm right) and you need to be shown the error of your ways." Individuals may adopt the same motto in their struggle for power and control in the group.

4. Mature group

When power struggles have been processed the group evolves gradually to the mature stage, characterized by more democracy, shared leadership, and an acceptance of more responsibility by each member. This is a new arena of difficulty as the group questions and re-evaluates its purpose. There is a measure of introspection and much emotional processing. In the mature group major conflicts arise and are resolved—the group learns it can still go forward despite differences of opinion.

The lessons of the mature group involve tolerance and acceptance. There is an interest in sharing within the group and with other groups. The motto is, "We have a point of view and you have yours—let's share." There is a renewed sense of community and commitment on a deeper level than before.

The experience of the group is mixed and vivid. Members decide that they would like to be closer to one another but then encounter the differences that exist. There is a struggle with intimacy. Some members leave and others join. There is a reshuffle; those that decide to stay with it generally feel rewarded with close emotional bonds as the group unifies.

5. Old group

Finally the group moves into the old stage. This is characterized by a redoubling of efforts to leave the chaff and keep the essentials. The group is casual with one another as there is usually a cosy intimacy and close friendships. The friendships start to extend outside the group as well as within it; members meet other members' spouses or lovers, and circles of friendships develop that transcend group boundaries.

Old level groups are highly accepting and live their philosophies. The earlier levels strive for but do not actually achieve this level of effectiveness. Old groups living their philosophy have a powerful effect on the outside world. These old groups are models for proper living.

GROUP PROCESS

Old groups have a wide vision and a broad perspective on their place and of the world at large. They are aware that they can facilitate the world in its lessons as they have already been there.

Groups generally do not attain the old stage—the challenges and obstacles on the way are formidable. Most groups dissolve before then.

GROUP PROCESS AND CENTERS

Another way to trace the development of groups is to look at the seven steps that groups go through according to centering. These roughly correlate with the soul perceptivity stages— infant, baby, young, mature, and old, but they add another dimension to our understanding of group dynamics.

Developmental Stages of a Group According to Centering

1. Intellectual	Conception, creation
2. Emotional	Forming relationships
3. Moving	Getting things accomplished
INTERVAL	Process (octave) may or may not continue
4. Instinctive	Reorganization - bring in new material,bring in basic issues.
5. Higher intellectual	Examining the truth, obtaining objectivity
	Getting rid of what doesn't work
6. Higher emotional	Perfecting relationships
	Higher connections
	Emotional productivity
7. Higher moving	Examining beauty, sexuality, prosperity
INTERVAL	Move into next lesson or higher octave

1. The intellectually centered group

The group starts at the intellectual center, and members begin to look at why they got together. They examine the ideas that brought them together and study how to accomplish their goals. This applies to all groups, including academic and school classes. The members are not connected to each other emotionally and the group is not at all personal. The group is dealing with abstract concepts that are outside the group—this creates a safe atmosphere for the group.

As the group focuses on a topic there may be a certain amount of conflict from one or more members. This member can be identified as the "group goad." The role of the goad is to be obnoxiously negative—other members feel that this person is totally unreasonable. The goad often attacks the ideas of one or more persons. The rest of the group is mortified at the unreasonableness and unpleasantness and springs to the defense.

2. The emotionally centered group

Thus the group enters emotional center. Instead of the goad, one member may become a scapegoat who is prickly or disagreeable, a chafing member of the group. The attention that the scapegoat generates draws out people's emotions.

The process in the group in emotional center usually becomes quite intense. There is a wide variety of emotions experienced—humor, anger, uncertainty, etc. There is a chance that the group will break up as people would rather part ways than resolve the issues.

The intensity causes the group members to interact much more closely, thus forming a cohesive group.

3. The moving centered group.

This propels the group to the third stage of group growth which is that of moving center. The group has been through emotional intensity and now wants to do something active as a group. They may set up social events (parties, potlucks) or decide to get more involved in the outside world.

When people form a group to start up a business, this is the stage where the first actual business is done. Before this, the activity was conceptual. It dealt with such questions as "How is it going to work? Who will do what (with perhaps some disagreement)? Where will we do it? What shall we call ourselves?" These are all intellectual considerations that give rise to some emotional interaction and eventually result in moving center activities of doing business.

The group may continue at the third level of being active for a long time. In fact businesses may continue at that level in perpetuity.

4. The instinctive center group

The third level often leads to a period of rest, the instinctive center phase. Underlying this quietness the decision is being made whether or not to forge ahead to new and higher levels. It is a time of review and re-evaluation. The members withdraw somewhat and are a little more separate from one another. There can even be some depression, a let-down feeling or apathy, perhaps lethargy.

Sometimes this instinctive center phase is brought about by a crisis, a major obstacle, a wrench in the smooth functioning of the group. The group's product may suddenly become obsolete in the marketplace, surpassed by unforeseen developments from the competition. The group leader may fall ill and be forced to leave the group. The results can be devastating to the group.

Needless to say, groups often break up in the instinctive center phase.

5. The higher intellectually centered group

If the group proceeds to the next level, if they have the intention of breaking limits in terms of any kind of non-material growth, there is a period of intense new realization; the group may discuss new ideas and feel inspired. The group members examine the truth—specifically, what is true for them. At first glance this seems obvious. But it is really a lesson in perception, about perceiving what is truly happening. There are no limits to this level of processing. The group members reach to achieve insights. There are plenty of traps (maya) along the way.

> *Let us use the example of a business striving to achieve this stage. It may be constantly struggling to improve profits, and it frequently re-examines its role in an ever-changing marketplace. One trap is to engage consultants and pay them a lot of money to tell the firm what it already knows but doesn't want to believe. Having completed that circle the firm then accepts that information as the truth.*

Sometimes during this higher intellectual phase, group members are totally honest with one another and are able to share things they felt unable to share in previous stages. There is much more trust and group members tolerate helpful criticism from one another. The group attempts to become more objective, clarifies their goals and focuses on what they truly want.

6. *The higher emotionally centered group*

After a period in higher intellectual center the group moves to higher emotional center. A higher emotional experience in the group is characterized by deeper connections between members of the group, stronger emotional lessons about one another, and the deepening and perfecting of relationships.

In the higher intellectual center group members had made decisions about which relationships they wanted to nurture and pursue, and those they would let drop. Higher emotional center concerns furthering those relationships where the truth has been examined. There is a richness and potential that distinguishes these relationships from the ones that were dropped. There is more energy focused on these friendships and they can be immensely rewarding as they have been chosen in the context of furthering the individual's deeper purposes and enlightened self interest.

The quality of these relationships extends to outside the group as well.

7. *The higher moving centered group*

On completion of the general development of emotional connectedness (although the theme never stops) the group moves to higher moving center or sexual center.

The group at this level examines high levels of energy. It arranges group activities—parties, travel, workshops—and it does this in the context of experiencing and enjoying the beauty of each member of the group and the beauty of their accumulated and hard-won intimacy and knowledge. This is quite an advanced level for a group to be operating within. It is rare for groups to hold together through their own resistances and attain this level.

8. *Rest*

After this developmental sequence has been experienced the group slides into a rest period. It has completed an octave. The members have learned from their very mixed experiences and will always remember some of that knowledge.

This is a natural ending point for the group and groups often part ways here. Members remain lifelong friends. It is a quality of friendship that some know well from college or high school, or from being comrades at arms in war: the common enemy facilitates and speeds up the process and resistances to intimacy melt beside the perception of a larger threat.

If the group should continue, it will start again at a higher level of the same process, starting at the intellectual center. However the speed of the process doubles and the group will move through the stages twice as fast. The group's members have learned how to learn.

As a generalization, the first octave takes two years. The second can take place in a year and the third, if at all, in six months. After that the processes and stages merge. The speeding up process is exponential.

GROUP DYNAMICS

One important dynamic of groups has been called the hundredth monkey phenomenon. When a certain number of individuals collectively experience a lesson or master an aspect of their consciousness then it seems the larger group of friends and relatives of the people in that group also receive the lesson. So if for example a group is learning a lesson regarding self-esteem, the members might find that their family and friends are also tending to have experiences that raise issues of self-esteem—even though they are not members of that group.

An analogy to this might be the splash that a rock makes when it lands in a pond. That splash makes ever-widening circles throughout the pond.

In each group there is usually a core of four people (quadrant) who generate the energy, direction and stability of the group. If the core quadrant members do not show up, the group may have the experience of being fragmented, divided and even uncomfortable. If a group loses one or more members of the core quadrant, other group members will adapt and change their behaviour within the group and fill the gap. In other words the group finds replacements. If it doesn't, it may disintegrate.

The people who show up for a particular meeting are definitely meant to be there—their presence reflects agreements made on an essence level. There are no accidents or mistakes. Those that are missing usually get the lesson anyway but have the disadvantage of not having consciously studied how to handle the experience. Those people who are present are there in the right mix so as to facilitate the purpose of the meeting.

Groups tend to create a lot of maya about their size, who to include and who to exclude, etc. It seems however in practice that the group will balance itself and find its own size and composition appropriate to its purpose. Experience suggests that this in fact happens regardless of any efforts to control it.

Small groups of eight to twelve people tend to be the most cohesive. Groups of up to about thirty-five people can still be quite effective even though this assertion is contrary to studies conducted in Western psychology.

MICHAEL STUDY GROUPS

When people become Michael students and meet regularly to discuss and learn about this system of thought, they make an agreement on an essence level to accept lessons in their daily lives that makes use of the information.

This implicit agreement holds whether the lesson given at the group meeting is channeled, or taught. In this way spiritual growth is accelerated for those who wish it.

The agreement with Michael, if made, means that you experience the lessons and specific situations within them, but consistent with the energies that are out there on the planet at the time. You can pick up the threads and use them in your life.

If for example a group discusses unconditional love or tolerance for others, then, in the following days, members will tend to find themselves confronted with people who for them are most difficult to tolerate.

Through this practical and experiential approach you learn how to handle life better. The overall object of the philosophy is to promote love and acceptance through finding out your true essence and purpose.

If you choose not to become a Michael student then you will tend not to have those lessons in a group context unless you are a member of another spiritual group. These same dynamics tend to apply to all spiritual development groups regardless of the teacher.

You have seen how group configurations influence your life and how you can use them for spiritual growth. You have also seen the process that groups go through in their own evolutionary patterns.

Now we are going to shift gears and focus more directly on methods to accelerate your personal growth and development. This will include knowledge about the care of your physical and energetic body, because you evolve in the context of your body on the physical plane. We will also discuss methods that can increase your effectiveness in the world and expand the scope of your personal power as well.

PART FIVE

GROWTH

Chapter Eleven

Body and Energy

PART V.

In this section we will focus on the avenues open to you for personal growth. Here you will learn about the properties of the human body and its energetic counterpart. We will discuss ways that you can maximize its potential and we will present you with methods of keeping it healthy and balanced.

Ultimately, personal growth is based on your ability to have more love, satisfaction, and joy in your life. So, here we will also describe the principles that allow you to manifest more of what you wish for in your life. You will discover as well that personal power goes hand in glove with increased prosperity. Mastering these is a prerequisite to handling the most challenging and satisfying lessons of all, unconditional love for self and others.

AWARENESS OF THE PHYSICAL BODY

Your body type, one of the seven sets of overleaves, chosen prior to birth, helps to give you an earthly personality. Remember that these body types reflect a combination of three planetary influences, Mars, Jupiter, Venus and so on (pure types are rare). Here we will discuss the role of the body in spiritual development and the various influences that keep it healthy or blocked. In addition we will present a variety of methods to support it and keep it in balance.

The human body is not just an accident of nature no matter what the scientific community may say. Nor was it popped into existence completely formed as the creationists would have you believe. The truth about the development of the physical body is actually much more interesting. It was evolved over millenia with the help of Devas to sustain sentience. This process occurs throughout the universe with many species, some successful, some aborted. The experimentation is rampant. Some life forms, developed for sentience on a particular planet, are moved to other planets with similar conditions, if the original planet has become too crowded to sustain yet another sentient species. Such was the case with the human body.

The human body was developed for life on a planet of the Dog Star system, Sirius. It evolved with the help of Devas from life primarily in the sea to habitation on land. Because several species had already attained sentience there, conditions were not good for yet another apelike creature to begin infant soul cycles there. Earth, by space standards, was not far away and already contained some apelike creatures not yet ready for sentience. The only sentient race was aquatic, leaving plenty of room for development on land. So, infant soul, primitive men were introduced to earth by technologically advanced, older soul, Sirius sector beings.

Gorillas are currently in much the same situation today on earth, but with little possibility of transport in the near future. Will they be promoted by humans or enslaved by them during their early infant soul cycles?

The human body has a planned design and structure. It is a function of the interaction of a number of complex energy systems which are an integral part of the universe. Let us here examine these in light of the whole teaching and then discuss ways that you can care for your body.

The human body is a highly complex, bordering on magical, receiving and generating station. Your body absorbs natural forms of energy such as light, sound waves, moisture, chemical compositions, oxygen, etc. Your body then processes these ingredients and from them generates emotions, expression, productive work, as well as physical by-products.

Now, your body acts as a support vehicle on the physical plane for the higher purposes of your essence. The physical body is the means through which the lessons and the karma are experienced on the physical plane. Your body is an integral part of false personality which is the vehicle for the lessons and opportunities on the physical plane.

In Essence and Personality *we gave you the analogy of a horse and rider for personality and essence. This same analogy applies to your body and essence. The horse, your body, comes into intimate contact with the terrain—rocky ground, mud, grass, etc. Essence, the rider, experiences these encounters through the horse. When both function in harmony the body can operate magically. If the communication between them is poor the body is much more vulnerable to disease.*

Your body type facilitates the use of the overleaves you have chosen for this lifetime. It has an important role to play in working out karma and self-karma.

For example a large imposing body will facilitate your goal if you have chosen dominance. However it may frighten other people thus serving your self-karma issues about intimacy.

Your body has such an intimate relationship with essence that it is able to reflect your soul development. Essence can be more readily seen in older souls than in the younger cycles. As mentioned when your body is acting in harmony with essence it begins to manifest magical properties. The physical body becomes capable of instantaneous healing, superhuman feats of strength, and extraordinary athletic capabilities.

BREATH AND THE BODY

At the core of the life of the body is the breath which is the origin of the word "spirit" (Greek *spiritos*, breath). The quality of the breath in the body relates to the quality of essence expression through it. The quality of breathing depends on the capacities developed through the disciplines of conscious exercise and conscious relaxation.

Aerobics are necessary to strengthen the circulatory system and the cardiovascular system. Aerobics increase the flow of energy through these systems, flushing the body of toxins, and releasing the stresses that have accumulated.

Aerobics are a function of the moving center which finds its expression through physical activity. For most bodies, twenty minutes of strenuous exercise a day satisfies the needs of the moving center. Consciously stressing the body in this way without stopping or resting keeps the body healthy and functioning smoothly.

Aerobics increases both the rate of breathing and the volume of breath. Because fear tends to inhibit breathing over time most people chronically breathe shallowly. The increase in breathing that aerobics brings initially can cause feelings of fear before feelings of well-being can be experienced. This causes many people to fear physical exercise and resist it on an unconscious level. The only solution to this dilemma is to move through the fearful feelings. This process is also experienced in different sorts of meditations which involve breath work.

Initially when a person begins an exercise routine, the body may experience stiffness and pain due to the number of toxins it has stored. Physical exercise works to release these toxins, and discomfort may be felt for several days. This physical discomfort needs to be experienced in order to achieve the feelings of well-being and clarity which comes with regular exercise.

Your body can be harmed by too much exercise and physical duress. Different body types have many different levels of endurance and knowledge of your own type will help you determine what you are capable of (see "Body types" in _Essence and Personality_). You need to find your own appropriate, healthy level of exercise. Just as aerobic exercise is important for the body, conscious relaxation is necessary for a healthy body.

DIET AND THE BODY

Your chosen diet is heavily influenced by your role in essence, your body type, your frequency, and by your relative balance of male and female energy. These four factors interrelate with climate, weather patterns, and seasonal changes to determine the balance or imbalance of your diet. In addition certain foods directly effect specific organs of the body no matter what the other influences are.

For example certain foods are useful for the cleansing of specific organs of the body. Lemon juice cleanses the intestines; cranberry juice cleanses the kidneys; vegetable oil detoxifies the liver.

Food can be divided into male and female types as well as a balancing neutral type (Refer to Chapter 12, on balancing male and female energy).

Certain body types are best suited to certain types of food.

Each of the roles also prefer certain foods. For example the more solid roles prefer more solid foods and more fluid roles prefer lighter foods such as vegetables and fruits. Solid roles prefer meat and potatoes.

Hot climates require more yin food while cool climates require more yang food. Seasons also determine the appropriateness of yin foods and yang foods. The reader is referred to the vast body of literature on this subject.

One of the ways essence makes use of the characteristics of food is that it will use different foods to trigger past life experiences.

> *If, for instance, you eat a lot of rabbit, it will tend to bring up past life associations of a country and time in which you had a similar diet. You may experience types of feelings similar to ones you had at that time. This would be useful if you were working on a lesson related to that lifetime or completing a karma begun at that time.*

There is a second way in which essence uses forms of food and that is as a means of bringing up issues which need to be dealt with.

> *For example, you may drink milk without event until you are thirty years old at which time you may start to experience an allergic reaction to it. Essence wishes to introduce a new reaction to encourage you to look at why you are suddenly getting headaches when you drink milk. Now, as a result you may get in touch with a past life when you had negative mothering and nurturing experiences; or perhaps you yourself did some poor parenting of babies. This then causes you to review and consider on a personality level the whole issue of babies in preparation for having your own children.*

SEX AND THE BODY

Sexual tension and release for the human body is tremendously important for its well being and satisfaction.

While it is true that certain individuals benefit from the experience of focusing their energy away from sexual expression this is not true for the vast majority of people. Sexual expression is the body's way of expressing its desire for unity consciousness. Sexual play is both receiving love and nurturance as well as generating it. Sexual play is a highly creative act which is appropriate in its many forms.

Sex forms a function of balancing the male and female energy. Sex is very important for the solid roles (scholars, warriors and kings), since they approach life more physically.

It can be a more abstract experience and less focused for the more fluid roles. The solid roles tend to function best if they enjoy sex with the opposite sex as often as every day or every two days. The solid roles often tend to find that if they do not have that amount of sexual experience their daily functioning starts to decline. This is not to say that homosexuality is inferior, it is merely that there is a measure of balancing between sexes that is healing.

Since sex play is so balancing to the physical body it can be used as a spiritual practice or tool. Some spiritual traditions such as tantra yoga focus specifically on the energy surounding sexual activity as a means for spiritual development.

STRESS

Relaxation and psychological stress are polar states that together form balance in the human body. This type of stress is a physical manifestation of anxiety or fear. Anxiety comes about when you experience something new in your life, something unknown. Thus stress comes about when you are trying to expand your awareness of yourself, to be even more conscious than you were before. Stress is caused by such things as starting new relationships, taking a new job, or handling the ups and downs of everyday life. Stress can be caused by the anxiety of meeting deadlines, meeting other people's expectations, or handling a huge workload.

Stress is always manifested by a physiological reaction in your body. This reaction keeps your body balanced and in limited amounts is actually healthy for you. However, when stress is intense and chronic it can make you ill and can shorten your life. This chronic stress level makes you less aware of what is going on around you. Your energy is being used to cope with anxiety, so the stress can become a form of inner preoccupation.

The rubber band is a useful analogy to illustrate the influence of stress. When it is unstretched it has only potential but it is not useful. When stretched within its limits, for example around a newspaper, the rubber band holds energy and is fulfilling its potential. If stretched or stressed too far it breaks, resulting in a loss of potential.

Stress accumulates in different parts of your body; muscles, joints, organs, glands, tendons, etc. This is a result of residual energy from the continual processing of information through the centers. Thoughts and emotions generate energy which is often not completely expressed and released from the body. This accumulated energy acts as a blockage to the natural flow and harmony of the body. Often the accumulation of energy in body parts results in disease, inflammation, and illness.

Muscles that have been constantly stressed due to habitual thought and emotion can become chronically contracted or tense resulting in bent over posture, scoliosis, and disharmony of muscular patterns. These patterns or muscular tensions in the body can be read as character structure, and character patterns in the personality. You can determine that a person is chronically fearful by simply looking at their physical posture and the set to their expressions. You can see the chronic anger or sadness withheld in the person's unique muscular patterns.

Under heavy stress the chakras come out of alignment. When you undergo an extremely stressful situation such as awaiting news of an endangered loved one perhaps, your first chakra or instinctive center is activated to send powerful messages to the other chakras.

> *Suppose you are awaiting news of a friend or relative who is aboard a hijacked jetliner overseas. Or you may be awaiting the outcome of your father's heart transplant operation.*

The third chakra which relates to the moving center or power chakra is especially misaligned by this kind of stress because it is motivated to act without having anything to do but wait. As the chakras come more and more out of alignment awareness suffers and consciousness is reduced. This is why normally aware people often make foolish decisions when under stressful conditions.

You will tend to manifest stress according to your centering. If you are intellectually centered you will tend to discuss your stress at length. If you are emotionally centered you will tend to feel stress and it manifests as depression or anger. If you are moving centered you will tend to put stress into your body through ailments such as stomachaches, headaches, ulcers, and colitis.

Let us now look at how to reduce stress.

STRESS REDUCTION

You can begin stress reduction by identifying the stress points in your daily life. The starting point for this is a brief daily meditation, no matter how busy you feel you are. In meditation or concentration you can focus your body and find out where the stress is located and how it is manifest. The meditation is a means of being aware of the form of stress and a focus on releasing it. The meditation also allows your body to experience soothing, centering and calming, and gets you back into balance.

In concentration you do a brief mental check-up. You examine your emotions, thoughts, and what you are doing in your life. Check to see if any of these areas are feeling out of balance. Questions you might ask yourself are: "What are the things that are worrying me today? Is there anything that I can do today to release stress? Are the things I am worrying about necessary? Can I get less identified or less plugged in? What are my priorities? What do I want?"

As part of your concentration you can get in touch with your instinctive center. As a product of young soul culture you probably have deep programming that a high degree of stress is necessary to your survival. This deeply held conviction may go back to primitive society when you needed to be able to move quickly into fight or flight. You can talk to your instinctive center to reassure it and bring it up to date.

When you emerge from meditation in a calm and neutral state you are likely to perceive more clearly and objectively what you want from your life and how you are going to go about getting it.

After you have identified the stress points in your life you can begin to reschedule your life to remove stress producers and include more relaxation.

One means of lowering stress is to assure that you get a reasonable proportion of rest. In general older souls need a ratio of one to two of rest to work:

> *For example you need to rest one day for every two days of hard work, or rest one hour for every two hours of work. In terms of a monthly basis, the ratio means about twenty days of work and ten days of rest. You can determine your own schedule as long as you maintain the same ratio. However we would not recommend a breakneck schedule of two years with no breaks and one year of doing nothing.*

It is important to note that rest here is not defined as spending a weekend painting your house or making substitutions of one type of work for another. Old souls are natural experts on the subject of rest and many have pioneered the subject to new pinnacles of excellence. Rest means either doing nothing or pottering around doing some mild activity.

If you should try to work more than this ratio, you will tend to become unproductive. So, unlike most Western concepts of efficiency, productivity is maximized by taking proper rest periods: two days of work for each one day of rest.

You can be overworked and continue to function but this will make you unbalanced. In fact overwork will eventually result in high blood pressure, heart attacks, ulcers, depression, and lowered productivity.

In summary stress is counter-productive and quite unnecessary in day-to-day life. Stress is the creation of a young soul society belief system that it is necessary for productivity. Older souls especially do not have to accept this belief system and can learn with some practice to minimize the amount of stress in their lives and live in gentleness and joy.

When you have identified the stress points in your life and you have restructured your schedule to include more rest, you can turn your attention to reducing the stress in your body.

Remember that chronic psychological stress produces structural tensions in your musculature. These energetic blockages in the body can be released through specific stretching exercises or yoga postures. This is an ancient science called hatha yoga. Specific stretching exercises can be geared toward areas of chronic stress in the body. For some people the shoulders and upper arms are the areas of stress whereas for others the legs or pelvis may contain the most blockage. If the blockage is chronic, deep stretching must be done gently at first and then deepened over a long period of time. Unless you are already knowledgeable this should be done under the guidance of a teacher.

In the last few years we have seen the development of deep tissue manipulation systems—Rolfing, Hellerwork, Reichian therapy, and Feldenkrais, to name a few—geared to release deep muscular tension and liberate the body from stress. Not every system is good for every body and of course the sensitivity of the practitioner is most important no matter what the method.

STRESS AND SOUL AGE

How you perceive stress and how you respond to it depends a great deal on your soul age. Here is a rundown on how each soul age approaches stress. Since the older soul levels are the most complex, we will spend more time discussing their stress issues than the younger soul levels.

Infant soul stress

Infant souls try to keep the stress level low in their lives so that they can get used to their bodies and learn how to survive. They are easily stressed and fare poorly in highly complex and stressful societies. They prefer out of the way, equatorial climates where change is minimal and survival is assured.

Infant souls cope with excess stress by withdrawal or by striking out desperately. The response is not unlike a frightened or cornered animal responding with paralysis or panic.

Stress is eliminated by complete removal of the feared object, environment, or by total restraint.

> *Think of a terrified little child who curls up in a fetal position or screams uncontrollably. That child needs total support or loving but firm restraint.*

Baby soul stress

Baby souls likewise prefer less stressful environments and gravitate to small communities where traditional life prevails. Near the end of the cycle baby souls begin to experiment with higher stress levels to prepare themselves for the high-stress young soul cycle. They may get themselves jobs in government positions, especially the court systems, to raise their level of stimulation. However, if stressed too much, they may respond like infant souls, either exhibiting great confusion or attacking the perceived threat fiercely.

Baby souls do not look internally for the source of stress in their lives. They react to stress with physical symptoms and require surgery and medication to treat it. They seek to reduce stress by calling for more safety in the environment such as implementing more law and order. Structure reduces their anxiety.

> _Baby souls feeling anxious about the presence of homosexuals or unfamiliar racial types in their midst, will attempt to create laws banning them from participation in their community._

Young soul stress

Young souls use stress as part of their ambition to make them achieve. Young souls are famous for exceptionally active lives that often include a tremendous measure of external stress. They play the big time games of national and international politics, high level academia, professional athletics, corporate warfare, and the flash and sparkle of entertainment stardom.

Because of the intense competition and cutthroat pressures of these arenas, young souls often resort to external means to reduce their stress levels. Alchohol and drug abuse are common results of these lifestyles. Until the final levels, young souls do not see the source of stress coming from themselves and their own choices. They prefer quick solutions to their stressful conditions and often these solutions lead to more stress in a vicious circle.

> _Consider a corporate executive under heavy stress as predatory companies are attempting a corporate buyout, a move that if successful would result in the loss of his job. He works endless hours and his wife and children never see him. As the stress mounts, he has an affair_

*with his secretary to take his mind off the problems.
However this raises more stress around his home life and
so he begins to drink more and more to reduce the tension.
You can see where this scenario will probably end up.*

Because the United States is a young soul country we all have
a measure of young imprinting which says stress is useful in
getting things done. Therefore many older souls fall into similar
traps as the executive just described. This will be discussed in
depth shortly.

Mature soul stress

Mature souls tend to accept stress as being necessary because it
allows them to have a full, varied, and exhaustive array of
emotional experiences. Stress facilitates both the highs and the
lows of experiences so they often choose to have stress in order to
create drama in their lives. In fact, early level mature souls,
having just arrived from the young soul stage, are good at
generating stressful situations. Daytime TV soap operas are
excellent at depicting young and mature soul drama.

Because of the difficulty of the cycle, mature souls tend to
retreat from time to time to less stressful environments. However
these retreats are generally short-lived and they return once
again to the bustle of action-packed drama in the big city.

To reduce stress, mature souls are more apt to seek out
psychotherapy and philosophy as coping mechanisms. They begin to look inside themselves for the source of their difficulties
and may even resort to blaming themselves excessively.
Occasionally internal stress mounts to such a degree that personality breaks up under the strain and hospitalization is required
for a time.

Old soul stress

As the internal pressures to complete karma and pursue
spiritual development mounts, old souls actively begin to eliminate external forms of stress in their lives. They are often torn

between the need to create a peaceful and harmonious environment and their need to complete outstanding karma before they can cycle off. Completing karma often requires an active life in the external affairs of the planet. Therefore, it is not uncommon to see old souls flip-flopping from quiet to busy from one lifetime to the next. Often this pattern is visible within one lifetime.

Because of their many active lifetimes in the earlier stages, old souls are confronted with several dilemmas. First, they carry with them the memories of age-old, high stress patterns of their former lives. Secondly, these patterns are reinforced by many of the younger soul societies where they live. Thirdly, old souls begin to tire of the rat race and tend to feel lazy when it comes to external achievement. All this produces a perfect scenario for intense self-karma about low self-esteem.

Old souls tend to accept stress as necessary because they feel that because they are lazy they are inadequate. That is, they equate self-esteem with productivity. The fact of the matter is that old souls do not have to accept this illusion as a necessary part of their life. The quintessential old soul seeks nothing more than to act like somebody who is retired and he may even feel this way at an early age.

> _You can ask a 14 year-old, old soul what he wants to do and the answer is that he wants to retire. He may not know at that tender age exactly how he is going to do that but his intention is firm. This is because the tendency for the old soul is to wake up at the beginning of each lifetime and feel that he is already in his fifties or sixties. Old souls constantly hold to the prospect of giving up their job as soon as possible to go and bask in the sun in Tahiti. However they rarely allow themselves to do this._

So, old souls tend to produce stress to compensate for being old souls in this society. They believe that stress will light a fire under them and make them ambitious and productive like everybody else. Because there is a strong social push to be successful with three cars and four houses, anything less than that can produce feelings of failure.

The bottom line desire to turn inward and feel peace prevails despite the self-induced stresses.

COPING WITH STRESS

In general, for younger souls, stress facilitates the kind of experiences that essence wants to accumulate over its many lifetimes. We have already discussed how younger souls tend to handle stress in their lives. However, for older souls, stress is not a particularly good motivator and must be reduced for spiritual development to take place.

If you are an older soul, then there are several things to consider. First, doing what you don't enjoy doing is stress-producing and therefore unproductive. If you don't like where you are living or if you hate your job you will tend to dislike yourself as well, thus paving the way for increased self-deprecation and less spiritual insight. Secondly, being spiritual is not putting up with negative situations because "you feel you ought to." Thirdly, you have the internal power to transform your life situation any time you wish because you are an experienced planetary pioneer. Personal power is tapped by pursuing what brings you harmony, beauty, and satisfaction.

The starting point for looking at stress in your life is to look at your survival fears. What are your fears attached to? Is it your job? Are you intensely afraid of being without work; without money? Or are your fears related to being abandoned in relationships? The greater your fear the more stress you will tend to create in these areas. Operating out of stress in a relationship impedes completing the karma because you will be uncentered, less aware, and less able to reach the neutral position necessary for completion.

So stress does not make you more productive and it does not help relationships. It does not help you survive. Working harder is not necessarily the solution. Often stepping back and giving yourself a rest or a break is vastly more productive in the long run. Examining your survival fears and challenging them is the most productive path you can take.

STRESS OR TERROR

Facing your fears and reducing stress at the same time appears to be a curious paradox. Putting up with a bad situation is stressful and does not produce spiritual growth. On the other hand facing your fears about leaving the situation is equally stressful but with an important difference. When you put up with a bad situation you not only feel stress but hopeless or even bored.

> _For example if you feel stuck in a destructive marriage where your spouse drinks, gambles away all the money, and beats you, you may feel terrible stress. However you will also feel bored, apathetic, or powerless to leave._

On the other hand, should you face your fears about leaving you will feel an underlying level of excitement. You will begin to feel empowered no matter how frightened you are. This is where great spiritual growth lies and this is why we suggest you live on the edge of terror rather than put up with the dullness of stress without transformation.

What most old souls truly want is a situation where they can follow their own preferred work schedule doing something that feels spiritually enhancing for them. This is usually oriented toward increasing the beauty of the environment, or serving others in a myriad of ways.

For further information about how to manifest what is wanted, the reader is referred to the section on prosperity in Chapter 13.

Now let us proceed to discuss your other body.

YOUR ENERGETIC OR SUBTLE BODY

The subtle body is a magnetic and energetic field that inter-penetrates and surrounds the physical body. This energetic body or aura acts as a vehicle for the essence to communicate with the physical body. It is however impermanent and dissipates with the death of the body along with the false personality.

The aura has properties which are both physical and astral. The aura is occasionally sensed or felt by others and even seen at times but usually not in ordinary situations. The aura expands and contracts: when you are awake the aura may flare out from eighteen inches to three feet around the body. When you are asleep it contracts to a thin, often blue, glow at the surface of the skin. This also may occur in times of illness.

The aura changes colors and shifts in pattern according to your thoughts and feelings at the time. Healers and different psychics who perceive auras will be able to see in your aura whether you are under stress or whether you are experiencing a joyful state or an angry feeling.

The aura is made up of concentric bands, each of which is connected with one of the seven chakras located along the spinal column. The chakras act as a communication link between the essence and the physical body. These seven chakras correspond with the seven centers which were discussed earlier. The band in the aura related to the root chakra is located closest to the body, whereas the band related to the seventh chakra or the crown of the head is farthest out from the body.

THE AURA BY ROLE

Each role exhibits a different pattern in the aura and therefore the aura is a good clue to determine the role.

Imagine the different frequencies of the notes of an octave and you can get the idea. Each note makes a different pattern when vibrated on a plate of sand.

AURA

The overleaves and false personality can then be seen as an embellishment of this particular frequency. This gives the aura a distinct and unique appearance for each person.

In general the solid roles—server and warrior—have more compact auras that appear to be moving inward. The exalted roles—sage, priest, and king—have expansive auras that appear to be moving outward. The ordinal artisan aura is also expansive and the scholar aura just appears to be neutral.

The action roles, warrior and king, have solid-looking auras that appear grounded and stable. Generally they completely surround the body, including the feet. The aura of the king is expansive, solid, and impressive. The aura of the warrior is compact, solid, and grounded.

The inspiration roles of server and priest have energy fields that are more fluid than those of the action roles. The priest has an expansive, high frequency aura that radiates high above the body, but often does not reach below the chest area or even below the neck. This gives many priests a floating appearance and at times makes them ungrounded. More than any other role except artisans, priests need to actively work with their auras to include their whole body.

The server's aura is more compact and tends to be fluffy or full of coil-like shapes of inspiring energy. Because their work is more service oriented in the physical sense, their auras are much more grounded than priests and usually extend down to their feet.

The aura of the expression roles is of course highly expressive and is characterized by much personal creativity. Sages have dramatic, expansive, and colorful auras. Artisans have huge auras that constantly change pattern and hue like chameleons. The artisan aura can be a problem because it is so large that it is constantly invaded by the people nearby. In order to maintain their sense of identity artisans change their auras constantly to suit their own changing mood and creative urges.

Scholar auras manifest a great range of size and shape depending on the relative exaltedness or ordinalness of their overleaves. Nevertheless, scholar auras are typically neutral in appearance, tending to blend in with the environment.

THE FUNCTION OF THE AURA

The aura acts as a receiver of impressions, both from the external world and from the inner world of essence. It is a vehicle for expression as well, communicating instantly what you are feeling and thinking. The aura tells all so that you cannot lie through your aura. The best you can do is to attempt to obscure what is there by shielding yourself. Older souls are usually adept at reading auras (albeit subconsciously) and determine whether to trust someone on the basis of their aura communication and not on what they say in words. On the other hand they may choose to ignore what they see in another's aura in order to fulfill a karmic debt.

The aura is capable of rapidly assimilating information during intense experiences overwhelming to the body. Gradually this information is filtered into the physical body so that insight and understanding occur after a period of several days.

Imagine you attend a weekend intensive consciousness-raising group and at the end of it feel overwhelmed and uncertain about what you learned from the experience. In the days and weeks following the event you may begin to realize everything you gained from the rapid learning that took place over a few hours.

The aura can be affected by external events and thrown out of balance. For example, a verbal insult may create a hole in the aura or cause the aura to contract. So the aura has expanding and contracting qualities. A series of such events may show up as a chronic dark spot or vacant spot in the aura. This gradually filters into the physical body and manifests as a malady or disease. You will usually find the disease in the part of the physical body closest to the affected aura position.

AURA CLEANSING

Aura hygiene acts as a prevention to a physical illness and certain practices are helpful in its cleansing. Since the aura reacts to thought and feeling, meditation and visualization are excellent ways to cleanse this energy.

> *Imagine a flow of comfortable healing color filtering down through the energy body starting from above the head. Allow it to pass all the way down the body and around it down to the feet, releasing all the disharmony down into the ground where it is neutralized. This is an example of one of the visualizations which can have a healing effect. Refer also to the chapters on the healing masters and spirit guides which can be used to facilitate this process.*

The burning of certain herbs and plants such as sage can be used to cleanse the aura as well as showering or bathing in water. Certain crystallized minerals and gems are helpful in healing the aura. Fluorite, for example, can be held to the top of the head for fifteen seconds. The energy within the crystal becomes discharged in that time and will take ten to fifteen minutes to recharge itself.

Much has been written about the nature of the aura and its healing and we refer you to the many books offered on this subject.

CHAKRAS

Chakra is a Sanskrit word which means vortex or circle of energy. These are like the aura of the subtle body and are not seen by the average naked eye. The major chakras are located along the spinal column from the base to the top of the head.

The chakras and the aura cannot usually be seen by the naked eye because they vibrate at a frequency beyond the band frequency which is normal for visual perception. Occasionally certain optimal conditions make it possible to see them and highly sensitive individuals can discern them through their greater range of perception. This is very similar to the ability of a dog to hear high frequency sounds which humans cannot.

The first chakra is located at the base of the spine and is related to the instinctive center. It governs basic survival and is related to the infant soul age.

The second chakra is the spleen chakra is related to higher moving or sexual center. It is located in the abdominal area just below the navel.

The third chakra is located at the solar plexus of the body and relates to the moving center. It governs power and distribution of energy throughout the body. It relates to the young soul age.

The fourth chakra is located at the sternum and is known as the heart chakra. This chakra corresponds to the emotional center which is at the mature soul age. It governs affinity and self-esteem.

The fifth chakra, located at the throat, corresponds to the intellectual center and governs speech and communication. This chakra is related to the old soul age.

The sixth chakra is located at the brow and corresponds with the higher intellectual center. In this system of knowlege the perception of truth is a core tenet and this sixth chakra is the chakra which governs it.

The seventh chakra is located at the crown of the head and corresponds with higher emotional center. This is the chakra often depicted in religious paintings of many cultures such as pictures of Jesus of Nazareth, the Buddha and various saints. They are usually shown with halos or fire above their head. This indicates the development of the seventh chakra or higher emotional center.

Like the aura, the chakras can be out of balance with one another because of overuse or under-use. When this occurs, one chakra may become disproportionate in size relative to the others either by becoming overly activated or closed down tightly. Since the chakras, like the organs in the physical body, are made to work together, such imbalance causes the other chakras to shut down or compensate in ways not healthy for them.

> *If your self-esteem is low, your heart chakra will tend to close down. You may attempt to compensate for this imabalance by increasing your use of the power chakra in your solar plexus, resulting in competition and power struggles with others. Or you may overcompensate by increasing your use of the throat chakra, resulting in intellectualizing about your experiences without feeling them.*

Meditation and visualization can heal and balance the chakras. As with the aura, there is a great wealth of information about working with the chakras which is not presented here and can easily be found in other spiritual texts.

There is a great deal of communication between your auras and chakras. Sometimes this takes the form of intrusion or cording which is the next topic.

CORDING

"Cording" is a type of communication taking place on an energy level (not strictly physical), between two or more people. The most basic form of cording is between a newborn child and his mother. There is an energy cord between the child's first chakra at the base of his spine, and the mother's first chakra at the base of her spine.

This energetic cord is analogous to the umbilical cord; however the energy cord remains in place for several years, whereas the umbilical cord is cut at birth. With this energy cord the child feels secure and connected with the mother. The mother experiences and is able to respond to any threat or danger to the child. Both are intimately connected through this channel of communication.

The communication channel is not limited by distance or physical objects.

> *For example, the mother may be in one room and the child in another and the energy cord still exists. This is how the mother knows instantly when baby is in distress even if they are physically separated. Without such a communication link survival would be much more tenuous.*
>
> *Infants are experts at establishing communication cords with whomever they are with. Fathers, aunts, babysitters, older siblings, and friends are all seen as potential cordees.*

Usually this umbilical type energy cord is dissolved at two to three years of age. Sometimes because the mother has a difficult time letting go, or the child has that difficulty, the cord remains in place for many years. Then we see grownup individuals tied very closely with their mothers in usually unhealthy ways. Symbiotic relationships are examples of prolonged and development-arresting cording.

Sometimes such a first chakra energy cord remains in place between twins, who may remain in intimate communication with

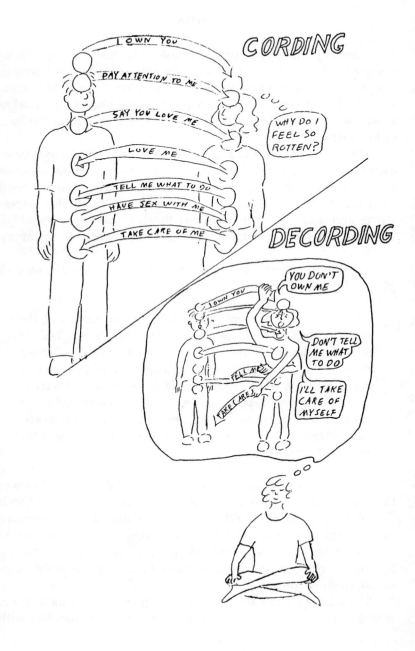

one another even though they have been separated by thousands of miles.

Now, temporary cording takes place between people all throughout life. The cording takes place between any of the principle seven chakras and may be initiated by either party or mutually by both.

The reasons for cording are many. Affinity, control, knowledge, and curiosity are the main motivations for cording between people.

Lovers are often corded between the fourth chakras and are immersed in their warm feelings of affection for each other. Competitors may try to dominate one another or control submissive types via the third chakra, center of power. Teachers and students may be corded via the fifth, sixth, or seventh chakras, all centers of higher learning.

Cording need not be accepted but because it is so subtle it often occurs without the recipient noticing. You may end up with cords from many people jamming your chakra system like an overloaded switchboard. You may feel excessively tired or overwhelmed not being able to think clearly or feel present.

Emotionally needy individuals do send out cords to those they feel dependent on and this can result in a feeling of tiredness or drain in the recipient. Teachers, counselors, parents, and healthcare workers of all types are often prone to this kind of stress.

At times the cord can be so intrusive that it can cause an intense headache, stomachache, or other physical distress, especially if it has been in place for a long period of time. It is important to remember, though, that you are never a victim of cording. You allow it either through agreement or lack of awareness. Cords are usually placed into the front of the chakras but they can enter from the back as well. Usually those entering from the front are there by agreement whereas those entering from the back are sent covertly. Typically these cords are sent by those who are good at covert control or others who feel fearful of communicating more directly.

Cording is most frequent in the following situations:

1. Between friends and lovers or mates: these cords usually say "I love you," or "What do you feel for me right now?"

2. Between teachers and students: these cords say "What do you know?" or "Know this."

3. Between those with sexual interest in one another: these say "Are you interested?" or "Yes I am."

4. Between enemies: these cords say "You will do as I want," or "What is your strategy?" or "Take that!"

5. And finally in crowds: crowds are favorite places for people to check each other out clandestinely or even openly. There is a feeling of safety in numbers. This kind of cording is usually undertaken to satisfy curiosity. The cord may say "What are you like?" or "What do you believe?" or "Who are you?"

DE-CORDING

Cording is a necessity between infant and mother and in circumstances where someone's survival truly depends on a cord to another. These cords tend to dissolve naturally when the need has ended.

Beyond this cording is not necessary even though it is a common practice. Cording has the advantage of obtaining information rapidly without time-consuming verbal and social communication. Cording is equally effective in communicating to another over great distance or when social barriers prevent verbal contact.

However cording is intrusive and can produce physical irritation. In addition it can create confusion and can definitely be karma-forming if it is registered as an emotional intensity by the other. Respectful psychic communication can take place without the penetration of a cord and can be heard or ignored by the recipient as he chooses.

> _Cording is a bit like grabbing someone by the arm so that you can speak with them. Sometimes it can be appropriate if done with permission or by agreement._

De-cording is a hygenic exercise that leads to a feeling of harmony and balance. Basically when you rid yourself of all unwanted cords you recreate yourself as you wish to be. You once again establish yourself as the leader in your own body and the one who decides where your energy will go. The main exception to this are mothers who have agreed that their infants decide where their energy goes.

De-cording is a simple mental exercise that is best done at the end of the day or after much interaction with other people. Or it can be a specific exercise to cope with an intrusive individual.

Sometimes you will find that you can't get someone out of your mind. You may even find your sleep disturbed by the constant image of someone you know or even someone you have just met the day before. This is usually a sign that the person is attempting to communicate with you via a cord. Simply close your eyes, visualize your seven chakras, and notice where that person has entered a cord. Gently remove it, making sure you have refilled the opening with your own essence. Mentally tell the person whatever you wish to communicate.

> _You might, for example, wish to tell them that you would prefer not to communicate with them at this time. Or you may want to ask them what they want and reply to them, remembering to tell them that they need not cord you to get your attention. Sometimes a simple_

"Hello, I know you're there," or "I love you" is sufficient to send them on their way and let you sleep, or read, or carry on your business.

On the other hand you may feel the presence of a painful or intense cord without knowing who it is from. Simply put your attention on the physical area where you feel the sensation and ask for a picture of who it is. You may be surprised. It is always the first person that occurs to you without fail. Do not censure. Ask what they want and what they are doing there. If you do not want them there tell them to leave. If you wish to speak with them tell them to give you more space first.

For general de-cording follow the same procedure: however you may not wish to speak with each individual corder because there may be hundreds. Simply methodically remove all cords from all chakras, front and back, and send them back with a gentle goodbye. Fill in all openings with your essence. Leave any cords you have agreed to retain.

Occasionally de-cording will produce immediate reactions. If you have removed a persistent cord from your mother you may get a quick phone call from her asking if everything is all right. The same might be true for a mate or lover. De-cording will produce feelings of lightness, clarity, and relaxation. However you may have to deal in person with those whose cords you removed. A panicky client may have to be calmed, a mate reassured, an enemy or associate dealt with as you see fit.

Chapter   Twelve

Balancing Yin and Yang

MALE-FEMALE ENERGY

You cannot truly understand yourself and others unless you know something about the balance of male and female energy that encompasses all aspects of the physical and astral planes. When you know about this relative balance that exists within you, you are in a better position to move through your life more effectively. Here we will focus on male and female energy so that you can get a sense of their effect on your life.

Each essence is unique in its particular combination and balance of male and female energy. This balance was chosen at the beginning of the current cycle of lives that essence is involved in. What is this male and female energy and how does it affect you?

Male energy corresponds with the Chinese word *yang* for dynamic, focused, assertive, and action oriented energy.

Female energy corresponds with the Chinese word *yin* for magnetic, unfocused, receptive, and passive energy.

Male Energy	Female Energy
man-made, refined	pure and natural
thin (focused)	large (unfocused)
fashioned, as carvings, sculptures	raw natural materials, as wood & rocks, or asymmetry as in gems
bright shiny clear colors	soft, diffuse colors
man-made environment, city	nature; trees, flowers
birds and fish	cats and dogs
baby, young, and early mature souls	infant and old souls
root vegetables, e.g carrots	above ground, quick-growing plants
meat, nuts, chocolate, coffee	alcohol
grains	water

These two forms of energy are in a constant state of tension and balance within the Tao. On the physical plane you concentrate on experiencing them in a state of imbalance. The imbalance that you perceive makes experience on the physical plane interesting. You are always attempting to right the balance and the result is forward motion or progression.

When you choose percentages of male and female energy for a cycle of lives you set up a condition so that you can learn and have physical plane experiences.

Each of you consciously or unconsciously attempts to balance your male and female energy with the foods you eat, the clothes you choose, the colors you wear, and the jewelry you select.

For example, you can dress to match your own male-female energy balance. You may wish to choose a balance

of synthetic (male) and natural (female) materials. Or
you might choose a symmetrical or asymmetrical gem for
a ring, or a balancing color and so forth.

Now your balance of male-female energy is not altered by the
sex of your personality for a given lifetime. It basically has
nothing to do with whether you are in a male body or female
body.

For example you might be a warrior with 95% female
energy and 5% male energy. Whether you are male or
female will not change this basic balance of energy.
You may be a 60% male and 40% female energy sage
in a female body or a in a male body. The ratio will
remain the same for the cycle of lifetimes.

So an individual with more male energy is more directed,
focused and specific in their experiences no matter what their
sex. The higher female energy person has a broader, more
creative vision, and is less focused no matter what their sex.
Some essences have chosen to be specifically male energy or
female energy whereas others choose a more equal balance, or
fifty percent of each.

You will tend to be attracted to another with the complementary balance of male-female energy. For example an artisan
with 80% female energy and 20% male energy will find most
compatibility with someone having 80% male energy and 20%
female energy. This is the most comfortable pairing in terms of
the male-female energy balance.

This optimum between couples does not always eventuate
because of other factors such as karma or agreements. Two high
female or male energy types may choose to be together for
purposes of learning.

Often you can sense a person's balance of male-female energy
simply by looking at them. Males who appear highly feminine
often have a high proportion of female energy. Similarly

females with a masculine appearance may have much male energy.

This may influence sexual preferences. A life in a male body with a high proportion of female energy would be more karmic than a life in a female body that might prove more comfortable and familiar.

> *A high male energy king might prefer male bodies for its first series of incarnations, leaving female lifetimes for later. Likewise a high female energy king might adopt more female incarnations early on.*

There is no correct ratio of female sexed lives and male sexed lives that you elect to experience. This is totally a matter of free choice. One fragment may feel balanced with 80% male lives, 20% female lives whereas another might feel better with an exact fifty-fifty balance.

SOUL AGE AND MALE-FEMALE LIFETIMES

Infant soul

The infant soul age is a survival oriented sequence in whch action karma predominates. Therefore, regardless of your male and female energy ratio you will tend to have more male bodies during this time than female ones. Male bodies facilitate the learning of survival lessons. If more female lifetimes are taken at this age, then more survival lessons will have to be experienced in later soul levels. There may be more self-destructive tendencies later as certain survival lessons have not yet been learned.

Baby soul

This marks the beginning of diversification. Those with a preponderance of male lives will begin to have female lives.

Young soul

Fragments who have had a preponderance of male lifetimes thus far (the majority of fragments), will tend to be poor at communicating with females. They will see females as different and alien and perhaps not as good. When they are in female bodies they will feel less comfortable and will buy into the program that being female is not as good as being male.

Those with a majority of male lifetimes under their belt will be much more ruthless as young souls.

By the same token, those with more female lives thus far will see males as strange and alien. They will have difficulty relating to them.

During the young soul cycle sexual chauvinism is played out to the extreme.

Mature soul

At the mature soul stage imbalances begin to be rapidly made up. Those with more female lives now choose more male lives and vice-versa. This adds to the discomfort of this soul age. In addition much karma must be repaid here that relates to the need to be in an opposite sexed body.

> *For example if you have been male in most of your lives you have accumulated a great deal of imbalanced experiences and have fulfilled only one side of many monads. To complete these experiences you must be female and experience situations from that perspective.*
>
> *Often females in this circumstance have a constant string of love affairs with males to make up for all the times their sexes were reversed.*
>
> *They must be mothers, sisters, aunts, and female lovers to get the full range of lessons available.*

Because the mature soul age is the most emotional, those who have been women more often have an easier time of this sequence.

Those who have been men more will have additional challenges in learning to handle intense emotion.

Old soul

During the old soul sequence all imbalances must be righted and completed. Those with a preponderance of male lives will tend to suffer more from self-deprecation than those with more female lives.

MALE-FEMALE ENERGY OF THE PLANET

Historically the planet itself goes in cycles of male-female energy. During a high female energy period, matriarchy, creativity, intuition, and the arts predominate. During a high male energy period patriarchy, aggression, logic, and science predominate. There is a shift occurring at present from male to female energy predominance. It is characterized by, for example, the growth in feminism and the rise of more women to positions of power, the environmental movement, and a shift in health and nutritional patterns. This is a long-term cycle that takes thousands of years to complete. For a time male and female energy will appear to be balanced as they hold equal sway. However gradually female energy will predominate as the next cycle goes into full manifestation.

Within these greater cycles cultures express greater female or greater male energies.

For instance, even though the planet has been in a male energy cycle for many hundreds of years, the culture of India has been characterized by female energy. They have carried the female energy expression within the greater expression of male energy demonstrated by Western and other cultures. This allows for the experience of both male and female environments at all times during earth's history.

In summary each of you carries a percentage of male or focused energy and female or unfocused energy. The ratio that you carry gives you a unique outlook and form that you carry from one lifetime to the next regardless of your sex. You seek to balance your percentages of each through your relationships with other people.

MALE AND FEMALE CYCLES IN ONE LIFETIME

Males and females, regardless of their percentages of male and female energy, experience regular cycles throughout life.

Male cycles

Males pass through three approximately eighteen day cycles that repeat in a regular order over and over. The three cycles are 1. an *aggressive* (moving) cycle; 2. an *intellectual* cycle; and 3. an *introspective* (emotional) cycle.

During the aggressive cycle males are more energized and awake; sleep less; have a stronger scent; assert themselves more; initiate relationships, projects and the like; can be more belligerent and warlike, are more sexually active, create more testosterone, take more risks, indulge in romanticism, and act heroic.

This aggressive cycle has given males a reputation of being bad boys as well as great accomplishers. Because of the negative connotations of baby soul aggression, modern Western man often attempts to repress this cycle, a reaction that only breeds intense stress. Repression of this cycle also prevents males from getting the necessary formative experiences with male and female relationships that create balance. As a result males are often confused about their appropriate sexual response.

During the intellectual cycle males consolidate their experiences from the aggression cycle; strive for balance; plan their next courses of action; organize their lives; and communicate rather than act.

Men are conditioned to favor the intellectual cycle and thus many men will attempt to prolong this cycle or mask the other cycles with it.

During the introspective cycle males reflect more on their internal states; focus on emotions; become moody or cranky; prepare for the upcoming aggression cycle; accomplish less in the world; sleep more.

Men have been conditioned to enjoy this cycle the least and they often try to ignore it to their own detriment.

Female cycles

Females, in contrast to men, pass through two major cycles of two weeks' duration in a repeating pattern. These cycles like the male ones correspond to processes within the physical body. The two female cycles are 1. *inspirational,* and 2. *emotional.*

During the inspirational cycle females prepare for, experience, complete, and move away from ovulation; have more vision; experience expansiveness, sleep less, are more sexually active; and accomplish more in the world.

During the emotional cycle females: prepare for, experience, and move away from menstruation; sleep more, are more moody and cranky, accomplish less in the world; and focus more on internal states.

Because male and female cycles are on different schedules they do not operate in a parallel fashion. Thus males will eventually experience both female cycles in all three of their own cycles and vice versa. This makes for a varied and fascinating array of emotional states and facilitates the formation and completion of karma. Remember that the physical universe by definition is in a constant state of imbalance seeking balance. Male and female cycles reflect this constant universal tension.

FREQUENCY

Frequency is another important characteristic of essence. Frequency is not determined by the balance of male or female energy that you carry and has no relation to whether you are in a male or female body. Frequency is autonomous, separate and distinct. Then what is it?

In simple terms, frequency is the specific rate of vibration that characterizes your essence. This frequency manifests through your physical body and through your personality lifetime after lifetime.

The easiest way to speak of essence frequency is through percentages, one percent being the lowest frequency type and 100% the highest. So, essences are distributed in frequency according to a bell curve. Few essences are found at the lowest frequencies and few at the highest frequencies. The most common frequency level is 50% and the numbers reduce away from that.

Frequency is best descibed as how you present your energy. Remember that it is the speed of vibration of your essence and is carried from lifetime to lifetime.

Frequency tends to correlate to some degree with role. The more fluid, high frequency roles are artisans and priests. This gives these essences more vision, a quickness, however it also makes staying in the body more difficult and less comfortable.

Low freqency, solid, roles are warriors, kings and scholars. They tend to be the most grounded and comfortable in the physical body but not as quick and fluid.

Servers and sages tend to fall in the middle ground.

In the old soul cycle many of these distinctions break down and frequency is less important as a difference.

Now each plane of existence vibrates at an ever increasing rate of vibration or frequency. The physical plane of course vibrates at the lowest frequency. Since the astral plane is a higher frequency than the physical plane, those roles with higher frequency tend to be more comfortable doing astral work and less comfortable doing physical, in-the-body work. Those roles of a lower frequency have a more difficult time doing astral work and are not as comfortable out of the body.

However this is not to say that higher frequency essences are in any way more evolved or better than lower frequency essences. You might say that frequency is more like color preference. Blue is not better than yellow, only different. Each wears better or worse under varying conditions.

Each role tends to occupy a given range. Low frequency for a priest might be at the same frequency level of a high frequency scholar. A high frequency warrior may overlap with a low frequency server. This similarity in frequency tends to give them a better understanding of each other.

The greater the difference in the frequency of two essences, the more difficulty they will have understanding each other. On the other hand the more interesting they will be to one another. This can be seen most blatantly in the relationships between warriors and priests.

Often people with opposite frequencies are attracted to one another and are fascinated with each other's differences. Marital discord is often related to this differential in frequency because each sees and acts in the world so differently.

A high frequency king and a low frequency artisan might get together quite successfully. They would both operate at a similar pace and agree on the wide vision they both see. On the other hand a low frequency king and a high frequency artisan might have trouble. The low frequency king might see the high frequency artisan as flaky and flighty, having no substance. The high frequency artisan might see the low frequency king as a slow-moving stick-in-the-mud.

Your frequency is quite flexible and can be altered at will to fit in with the company at hand, or by the choice to do a certain kind of work. If you are a scholar with a 50th percentile frequency range and you are in the company of several artisans with a frequency level of 80%, you can temporarily rise up to perhaps 75% in order to match them. Eventually you will slide back down to your usual range that is more comfortable for you.

It is important to remember there is nothing better or worse about high or low frequency—it is a matter of preferences.

To summarize, your essence frequency is a vibration or speed that characterizes you lifetime after lifetime. It determines how comfortable you will be in a physical body and enables you to take on tasks suitable for your frequency range.

FREQUENCY AND MALE-FEMALE ENERGY RATIO

Now let us put together these two qualities and see how they interact with one another. Let us examine examples of the most extreme types to see how they operate.

1. A high frequency, 90%, makes this artisan fast moving and highly fluid. In addition this artisan has 75% female energy and 25% male energy. This combination of high frequency and high female energy makes this artisan much more comfortable during her female lifetimes. Her male lifetimes will tend to be more challenging in terms of self karma. She will tend to leave her male lifetimes for later in the cycle. She will have more difficulty relating to low frequency roles but will be more attracted to them. She will have more ease relating to high frequency ones.

2. A low frequency, 15%, makes this warrior solid, stable, and slower moving. This warrior also has 90% male energy and 10% female energy making him more comfortable during male lifetimes. His female lifetimes are usually left for the later soul ages and these will be more challenging in terms of self-karma. He will have more difficulty relating to high frequency, high female energy types but will be attracted to them. Relating to low frequency or high male energy types will be easier for him.

3. A mid frequency of 50% makes this sage flexible, with the ability to appear both solid and fluid as the case may be. In addition having a balanced male-female energy ratio of 50%-50% makes him equally comfortable with male and female bodies. He will be able to relate to all frequency ranges and male-female energy ratios. He will not have the particular skills that go with the extremes. This is a popular position for many roles, especially scholars who like neutrality anyway. This is the center of the bell curve.

In addition there are all possible combinations of these variables. There are high frequency roles with high male energy and low frequency roles with high female energy. Each will have characteristics that benefit them and some that hinder them.

Now that you know something about male and female energy properties you are ready to learn something about the principles of prosperity and manifestation.

Chapter   Thirteen

Manifesting

THE NATURE OF PROSPERITY

What is prosperity? How can you be more prosperous? Why do people have trouble with prosperity? In this section we will discuss with you all the properties of prosperity and give you a new perspective on how to have it.

Many of you automatically think of prosperity as something primarily financial. However, this is simply not so. Prosperity encompasses much more than money. In fact prosperity is synonymous with self-esteem. Prosperity is manifesting what you feel you are worth. It is success by your standards: it could mean lying in the sun for an hour a day without having to feel you should be somewhere else; knowing that you can lie there and congratulate yourself on having your life so well handled that lying in the sun is a celebration.

PROSPERITY

Prosperity or havingness (the ability to have) is a pervasive thing. You limit your success according what you think you are worth. This occurs unconsciously and it so happens that you have that level of success or richness of relationships that matches your self-esteem.

> *Imagine a family with low self-esteem winning a million dollars in a lottery. Within twelve months it is all gone and they are back to the old lifestyle. They couldn't have that level of success because their self-esteem was not high enough. Their energy level could not contain the huge increase.*

Limits to prosperity are imposed by the false personality and come from fear. There are real and specific fears of what may happen to you if you have high, high havingness. For instance, people kill other people for their possessions. If you don't have much you won't get killed. One can look at the specific fears in your conscious mind and dispose of them.

The converse of this is that if you love yourself then all things are possible.

So, prosperity is about feeling worthy enough to have life be the way you want it. On this account prosperity fills lack; lack of time, lack of things, lack of relationships, lack of love, lack of creativity and so on. Prosperity is then about having an abundance of anything you wish you had more of, including more spiritual insight.

PROSPERITY AND HIGHER CENTERS

Spiritual prosperity, as with spiritual power, has to do with being in higher centers, gaining that distanced perspective on yourself and your life to see how it all fits together. It is about feeling a sense of oneness with other people.

Not surprisingly, prosperity is a matter of how you handle the three components of the higher centers and of the universe—truth, love and energy.

Truth

The focus of higher intellectual center is truth. Prosperity is a matter of having truth in your life. You can tell the truth to your friends and family and they can tell the truth to you. This is the prosperity that truth bestows.

When you have told the truth and have heard the truth you can then act on it. You can then decide what relationships you want in your life. When you tell yourself the truth about your job you can decide to change it or to keep it. Having done this weeding out you are automatically a more powerful person. You are not spending time with people you don't want to, so you have more time and more energy. In short you have higher havingness.

Having seen where you fit in, you can then see the whole, and open yourself up as a spirit without boundaries to your guides, channeling, and connectedness, and away from pain, fear and suffering. From this space you can make powerful choices.

Love

Remember that higher emotional center manifests unconditional love. Prosperity is dependent on having more love in your life. It is about feeling that you deserve it and loving yourself enough to let yourself have it. As will be discussed later, fear blocks higher havingness levels and the remedy is learning how to love yourself.

Love yourself and all things are possible.

Energy

Prosperity is about having the energy to manifest what you want. The energetic quality of the higher moving center makes the integration of truth and love possible. When truth and love work together in your life you can become as prosperous as you wish. Remember the example of the family with low self esteem who could not take advantage of their good fortune. The energy of higher moving center raises your capacity to have, do, and be more.

INTEGRATING HIGHER CENTERS FOR PROSPERITY

How do you learn to love yourself? Self-acceptance is the first step. Self-agape requires that you accept yourself as you are, warts and all. This means dropping every particle of self-deprecation you can find. Now, many of you, especially you older souls, think that putting yourselves down has value. You may think that feeling bad about yourself will motivate you to do better or be a better person. When have you ever seen this work? Or you may feel that trashing yourself will prevent you from being an even worse person. The truth is, punishing yourself will probably make you into a less happy, less spiritual person. In fact self-deprecation is never, never of value.

> *Here it is useful to think of dog training. Beat a dog into obedience and it will cower and hate you. It may obey out of fear but one day, given a chance, it will turn against you. Train a dog with kindness and rewards and it will love you and do almost anything for you. You may argue, "But I'm not a dog!" Your body is like a dog and deserves to be treated at least as well as one. It likes to be petted.*

Step two in learning self-love is to learn to suspend judgment of what is good or bad about you. It is arrogant to assume that you can stand as judge of yourself and put yourself on trial. It is also arrogant to stand in judgment of others or of your experiences. Therefore dump every shred of arrogance you can find and you will also eliminate your judgments and criticisms. You can then have more love, more experiences, and more awareness.

Step three in learning to love yourself more requires that you begin to experience yourself as being cause and not effect. This means being out there having your life run the way you want it to, rather than being at the effect of what others want. Stop yourself in any situation and ask yourself whether you feel you are causing what you are experiencing or whether you feel you are victimized by it. You may be uncomfortably amazed at how often you find you are in effect.

Step four in learning self-love is that you allow yourself to see all the good you have created. Everything in your life has served you in some way, even the most horrific negatives. Find out what you have learned from those negatives and see that they have served you. Your essence set it up that way because essence wanted you to learn certain things. When you can see that, then you know you are on the right track and you can validate yourself for a job well done.

Step five is accepting experiences and not blocking or fighting them. Flow with the experiences your essence has set up and experience them fully so that you won't be repeatedly confronted with them until you finally pay attention to them.

Step six is composed of several substeps. It involves not falling prey to one of the four victimizations:

a.   Not enough time
b.   Not enough money.
c.   Not enough sex.
d.   Not enough love.

Now, almost everyone has one or several of the above. Almost no one has enough of all four. You either have plenty of time and no money, or plenty of money and time and no love, or plenty of sex but no money and so on. The truth is that you can have enough in every category. To get there however you must change your beliefs to the contrary. Let us now examine each of these in more detail.

a. Not enough time

When you do not give yourself enough time to relax, get your work done, or be with good friends you literally rob yourself of the opportunity to have more in your life. This is the activity of impatience, the rush to pack so much into your schedule that you do not enjoy any of it. Drop impatience and take time. Paradoxically when you relax more and take the time you need to enjoy your work or relationships you become much more productive.

Do you take the time to dress well? Do you take time to take care of your body? Do you take time to reflect and enjoy being?

b. Not enough money.

Having enough money is a product of feeling you deserve it and allowing yourself to have it. If you are programmed to think that people who have money are evil or have sold their soul to the devil then you will never allow yourself to have it. If you feel that if you had money you would abuse it you will likewise see to it that you have very little.

In Western culture and throughout history, having money has been seen as having power. If you believe that you are powerless then you will probably also be without money as a result.

The truth about money is that it is pure energy and as such it is neutral. How you use it is what makes the difference. Allow yourself to have as much of it as you can handle. Having money requires you to have a great deal of responsibility if you are to use it appropriately. There is even a lesson in wasting it so you can't lose by having more.

Contrary to what some of you think, having more money does not necessarily deprive others of having it too. True prosperity includes sharing and has a way of growing rather than diminishing.

Now, some of you choose not to have it, not because of low havingness but because it is not where you choose to have your lessons this lifetime. This is a legitimate choice.

c. Not enough sex.

When you deprive yourself of a satisfying sex life out of guilt, self-righteousness, or fear, you contract your ability to have, do, or be more. Your capacity to enjoy your body and express energetically through it is in direct relation to how much you can have. Through satisfactory sexual expression you communicate and share yourself with others.

Now a satisfactory sex life is up to you to define. For some people (especially the solid roles of warrior, scholar, and king) daily sexual activity feels right for full satisfaction. For other people (especially the fluid roles of priest and artisan) less frequent sexual activity feels prosperous. For a few souls total abstinence is appropriate for the lessons they have chosen to focus on.

If you feel frustrated that your sex life is paltry then you are creating a condition of scarcity out of low havingness. You are probably operating out of fear or guilt. A thorough examination of these feelings and their source will pave the way for greater abundance. Intending to feel satisfied and actively seeking it will ensure it. The truth is that there are partners for everyone.

d. Not enough love

Love is everywhere. So, if you are experiencing a scarcity of love, you are blinding yourself to it for your own reasons. Often these reasons include the belief that you are just not lovable. Simultaneously you may fear the intimacy that love brings. Or you may fear abandonment and the pain of losing love so much that you avoid it like the plague. Whatever the reasons, scarcity in love reflects a temporary limitation in your ability to be more of who you are.

As with sex, money, and time, raising your ability to love requires that you give yourself more of it. The cure for fear of water is learning how to swim. The cure for scarcity of love is learning to love yourself more. When you love yourself you charge yourself like a magnet. Others are drawn to love you as they would be to a magnet.

To summarize, prosperity is about truth, love and energy. Prosperity is a result of telling yourself the truth, caring enough about others and trusting them to tell them you love them, and having the energy available to act. The aim is to have an abundance of all three.

Phrasing all this in other words, you are here to learn about handling the physical plane. Prosperity is the measure of how well you do that.

> *Let us look briefly at love in a relationship. One way of looking at love is to see it as the ability to resonate with the other person, not only a spouse or lover, but say someone in your family or a friend. Love is about looking after them, being aware of their needs and knowing where they are . So when they come home tired, you are aware of that and respond so that they feel nurtured.*

> *It is a useful tool to be able to ask this person, "What can I do for you today so that you will feel nurtured?" You can also observe any resistance you may have to asking that question, or to actually doing the nurturing.*

PROSPERITY AND SOUL AGES

Infant Souls

Infant souls can be prosperous in the sense that they often choose benevolent tropical environments in which their survival needs are met. However because infant souls are fearful and inexperienced they are rarely prosperous in the intentional sense of amassing wealth or power. Near the end of the infant soul cycle they may become able to exercise some limited power in their tribe or locale.

Baby Souls

Baby souls can and do become prosperous in a material sense although this is not the norm. Near the latter part of the cycle they sometimes gain prominence politically and can have a hand in international politics. Again their lack of experience and fearfulness make them no match for the expert young souls with whom they must compete.

> Khomeini of Iran, Botha of South Africa, Kadafy of Libya, and Idi Amin of Uganda, are examples of politically prosperous baby souls in power. Some of the most outspoken fundamentalist church leaders in the United States are prosperous baby souls. However they often have a hard time hanging on to their power and wealth as can be witnessed by the South African example. They seldom use enough good judgment to sustain their positions.

Young Souls

Young souls are usually oriented toward amassing wealth, power and fame as an end in its own right. They are the experts in this arena because they have experience and are incredibly motivated to succeed in a material sense. They are often spurred by the belief that life is a one-shot chance at the big time. On the other hand, since their motivation is often fear of losing, the prosperity they gain has a way of running them, creating a measure of misery along with the pleasure.

Young souls are sophisticated in their techniques and know how to have a good time manipulating the physical environment to maneuver themselves into positions of power, wealth, or fame.

In general they are not deterred by low self-esteem or goals of internal growth. This is an extroverted cycle.

Yours is a young soul society and even older souls have a measure of that young soul imprinting. Young souls are characteristically at the effect of their overleaves or personality traits. This means they are out to win. Often they are not concerned about other people's feelings as much as being successful.

Mature souls

Mature souls tend to shun materialism and its association with winning at any cost. They have moved from extroversion to introversion, seeking self-knowledge and spiritual awakening that often leads them away from the pursuit of material prosperity. The mature soul looks suspiciously at fame and fortune as diversionary and potentially karma-creating. However, because they are neophytes on the spiritual path, they seldom allow themselves the luxury of spiritual prosperity either. Therefore the mature soul cycle can be the most impoverished cycle of all.

Mature souls often make the mistake of thinking that retreating to a cave and living in austerity (poverty consciousness) is somehow more spiritual. It may be indeed appropriate at times to experience solitude and simplicity. However, as the mature soul gradually learns, living on the physical plane is about mastering it externally and internally. And of course the external mastery, for older souls, reflects internal mastery. The mature soul learns that it is OK to be prosperous; that prosperity is not the enemy of spirituality. On the contrary, affluence and well-being provide a basis for extensive lessons, whereas poverty and frugality are more limiting in their challenges.

Old Souls

Old souls have perhaps the greatest challenges of all in mastering prosperity. They have a wealth of experience to draw from and this is both a help and a hindrance. They tend to remember their abuses of power, wealth, and fame from earlier incarnations and take great pains to avoid repeating these errors. Often they unnecessarily withold material prosperity from themselves for this reason. Eventually they learn that avoidance does not produce mastery.

Old souls also can be lazy in that they do not want the responsibility and distraction that can go with material prosperity. In the earlier stages of the cycle they prefer to pursue spiritual development to the exclusion of worldly possessions. Eventually they realize that prosperity in a spiritual sense and prosperity in a material sense can not necessarily be isolated from one another.

Old souls are busy developing mastery of their overleaves and personality. They hold an awareness of the greater picture. In this context they can achieve prosperity through enjoyment and developing the ability to share their fortunes on an "I win and you can win too" basis.

Older souls have a knowledge and mastery of the basic laws of prosperity. They know that like attracts like, and that the secret of prosperity is giving away what they want the most.

To receive love, give love. This applies to oneself as well.

To be powerful, share and delegate power. This is not the same as giving up power.

To have more of anything, such as money, share what you have first.

They have learned the hard way that "What you sow is what you reap." So, regarding money, power, or love, old souls gradually learn that the goal is to have these flowing through them. That means you must have them coming in steadily and leaving readily. Holding on to money, power, or love blocks the flow and makes it more difficult for more to come in.

Old souls know that thoughts are things. So through intense visualizations about their goals they can manifest what they want if they can first dump their imprinting about limitation.

Old souls gain an intuitive perception of the more subtle ways in which the universe works. So older souls can use the natural laws of the universe to their advantage. There are various forms of energy manipulation (such as certain meditations) and aphorisms that neatly sum up particular laws such as the ones above.

These kinds of techniques recognize that the old soul is indeed a part of the universe and consequently can control a part. There is abundant energy in the universe and the aim is simply to have more of that energy flowing through.

Old souls are capable of detachment. The neutrality that comes with detachment is an important law of prosperity. It is described as that place which is between total relaxation and total effort. The notion of surrendering and letting go, of letting the universe provide, is critical to having absolute prosperity on every level.

BECOMING MORE PROSPEROUS

In order to become more prosperous in an integrated way, balance is required. Each axis must come into play. There must be inspiration, expression, action, and assimilation. Inspiration needs action. Action needs expression. Expression requires assimilation first and so on. All are interrelated. When satisfying prosperity is blocked, usually one of these four axes have not come into play.

> _Imagine that you are inspired by a vision of what you want your life to be like. You assimilate the vision and express it to other people. However without a plan of action it is unlikely that your vision will manifest to any degree. Likewise if you go into action without an inspirational vision you will probably only manifest chaos._

The following is a pragmatic step-by-step approach to having, doing, and being more in your life.

What to do:

1. Work out exactly what you want and write it down as a series of goals.

2. Create positive affirmations about these, stating them in present terms, as "I am now enjoying wonderful health and good relationships."

    This will instantly bring up the negative beliefs that have held you back in this area. Those beliefs can then be listed, acknowledged, and let go of. New positive affirmations can take the place of each one.

3. Regularly visualize mentally being the way you want to, having what you want, doing what you want.

4. Persist in doing this despite current circumstances and absence of immediate results. It takes time for thoughts to manifest on the physical plane.

5. Make a plan of how to meet the goals. Check off each step as accomplished.

LIMITATIONS TO PROSPERITY

Know what your comfort zone is. Pushing beyond your comfort zone and having more can be quite uncomfortable, believe it or not. Do you truly want another forty thousand a year? Do you truly want a committed love relationship? Are you prepared to handle whatever discomfort comes with it?

Ask yourself first, "Can I have it?"

- too much
- comfort zone
- too little

Look at what you have to give up to get above the comfort zone limits of your ego. List the items. Look at how other people rely on you to not increase your havingness. If you do it, they will have to look at theirs because they are often competitive. This may make them angry with you.

You need to give up the belief that you can't have it.

Note that your ego simply wants to be right.

There are two attitudes to money:

1. Spend now and trust—make the space for it. (positive)

2. Expense control—governed by the fear of running out (negative)

Note that these work in a kind of dynamic tension with one another. One does not work without the other.

Look at the structure of the universe. Does anything run out? No, it doesn't. The law of the universe is that it will replace whatever you spend. What you sow you shall reap. Look at your experience. You can run low on things and stay there, but you never actually run out. You never actually starve to death unless you have specifically chosen an environment to promote this experience. You can trust in this process.

One of the governing principles of this teaching is neutrality, that is, not hanging on to things. There may be pleasures, sadness, money or whatever. The aim is to experience them as they occur. Let them in and let them out.

Often people dealing in huge sums of money work no harder than those in menial jobs. The energy input is the same. The difference is in the mental tapes they play. Their beliefs about money are different. One believes you have to work hard for a little of it. The other believes you can have lots of it for relatively little effort. They

*make it fun. They don't seek to hold on to money. They
are philosophical about it. They work hard at working
out what they want and persist until they get there.*

MEDITATION FOR PROSPERITY

The purpose of the universe is to enable you to learn.
Prosperity is the attitude that you can have what you want in
this universe. Therefore prosperity is one of the things you are
here to learn. Here is a meditation that facilitates that
learning.

Sit quietly, close your eyes and be aware of your body, your
thoughts and your feelings. Put all those things to one side.

Think of a quantity of energy. This may be easiest in
monetary terms such as an annual salary. Or you can think of it as
a quantity of love, or a measure of getting the most out of life.
Draw that amount of energy out of the earth and up into your
feet. Be aware of reprogramming the very cells of your body to a
higher level of havingness.

Move the energy up your legs to your torso. Pay special
attention to the joints, such as ankles and knees. Energy tends to
stick in the joints.

Eventually move the energy up through your head and
imagine it as a fountain pouring out of the top of your head. Let
the energy cascade down the outside all around you at about a one
to two foot radius. Pay special attention to your back.

As this energy flow hits the ground draw it around and in
again to your feet. Now increase the amount to a higher level—
for example think of raising your worth as a salary. Check to see
if you feel comfortable with this higher level. If it is uncomfortable, lower it to where it is comfortable. The aim however is to
gradually get it higher and higher.

So draw in that increased amount of energy into your feet and
up through your body. Be aware now of the overall circulation of
energy and let it circulate for a few minutes.

Finally seal off your feet and your head and when you feel complete, draw the meditation to a close.

This meditation can in fact be done several times during the day fairly quickly. You can do it while jogging, or sitting in a car in traffic, or sitting at a desk, or while walking.

It is a powerful meditation and strongly recommended. Within weeks or at most months you will notice results.

Let's look now at another method of bringing in prosperity. This involves an understanding of how you shift between parallel universes. How is that done?

PARALLEL UNIVERSES

Although your focus is in the single physical reality that you know, your essence is busy with an infinite number of others. Because essence is so incredibly energetic, and so little of essence is needed to keep tabs on the life you are living, essence occupies itself with countless other parallel existences.

These parallel existences are physical realities where you exist in ways that are somewhat similar and at the same time different from how you are now. Why is this?

Each time you make a major life decision during a lifetime you choose one alternative from two or more possibilities. You choose to live out one of these possibilities and leave the others behind. Yet the truth is that you never leave the other choices behind because you as a being want to experience and know exactly what would happen if you chose the other alternatives. In this fashion you can maximize the learning and experience that you eventually bring to your entity.

Each lifetime you have x number of major decision points that leads to splitting off a new universe. You do not split off a new one every time you decide whether to chew a stick of gum or not.

At the moment of choice you split off an entirely new universe—with the Tao's assistance—complete with duplicate versions of all the people and things that you know in your current reality. Within this new universe you play out the alternative choice with all the details and nuances that are involved with that life.

> *Let us say you are contemplating getting married and you can choose between two possible partners, John and Richard. John is a wealthy and stable businessman who will provide security and predictability. Richard is a wild artist who is exciting but totally unpredictable. You choose John and settle down to a comfortable but slightly dull existence. However even years later you dream about being married to wild Richard and imagine what it would be like. In a parallel universe you did marry Richard and your dreams are a bleed-through to that existence.*

Now the Tao functions most efficiently and therefore each choice does not necessarily split off an entirely new universe. Your decisions dovetail with other people's decisions and together many people spin off a parallel universe that meets their collective needs. For example there is an earth that managed to avoid World War II altogether. In this way, all those people who chose to be killed in the war in one reality got to live in another.

When a new universe is spun off an existing one it is very much the same as the first with minor differences. But as time passes the alternate universe begins to look more and more different and eventually there may be little that is recognizable between the two.

> *Imagine the differences between a bat and a mouse. Both are related as they are both rodents. Yet each has adapted over the millenia so that their appearances are grossly different.*

Just as each universe is distinct with its own integrity, each universe has its own karmic ribbons. You are not accountable here for what your parallel self decides to do in another universe. If that parallel version of you chooses to kill an enemy, the karma accrued exists only in that universe. You may choose to work out your disagreements in a more amicable fashion. In the end your entity will benefit immeasurably from all karma completed.

New universes beget other new universes each time there are new alternatives to be played out. You can see how incredibly infinite the universe is to accomodate all the expanding possibilities. You can also get a sense of how effortlessly the Tao creates something so vast and complex in a twinkling of an eye.

Science fiction writers are often people who are good at picking up on the interesting scenarios in parallel universes.

HOW TO USE PARALLEL UNIVERSES

A parallel universe can be of use to you in your current reality. It may be that you do not particularly like the choice you made to be a particular way. Perhaps you are timid and shy and wished that you had more courage or public speaking ability. You can be sure that there is a parallel universe where you have much more presence and where you are dynamic and forceful. You may occasionally dream about that alternate reality and see yourself being that way. However through meditation you can consciously communicate with that dynamic self and using your desire and intent you can bring over some of these abilities. Here is one simple technique:

1. Contemplate the ability you wished that you had or the trait that you would like to change.

2. Deeply relax and use your favorite method to get into a light trance state where you are highly receptive.

3. Postulate that you wish to journey to and view yourself in a parallel universe where you have the desired ability.

4. Observe the pictures that you get closely. Notice the simi-
    larities and differences carefully. You may be taller or
    heavier there or you may carry yourself differently. Notice
    how you dress, the jewelry that you wear, the style of your
    hair. Notice the environment and the decor of your home
    there.

5. Select one small item that you can replicate here in your own
    universe. It may be a simple ring, a leather jacket, a hat, or
    different hairstyle.

6. Find and carry with you a similar object or style that will act
    as a constant reminder of that parallel universe. The results
    can be most powerful.

Realize that you can draw from a parallel universe to
improve your present life. You may have chosen between law
school and being a musician. Perhaps you were a very talented
musician but completely gave up music for law. After twenty
years as a lawyer you find that you are unfulfilled and you miss
music a great deal. After a little practice you are amazed to find
that your musical abilities have progressed as if you had been
playing all along. In a parallel universe you remained a musician
and did develop this talent. So you have been able to tap this
talent when you returned to music. Recognize that you can do this
anytime you wish about a great many latent talents and skills.

When you tap into your latent talents and skills you are
exercising personal power. In this next section, then, increasing
personal power is our focus.

PERSONAL POWER

What is personal power? Who is a powerful person? What
makes you a powerful person? Here, in the following we will
delve into these questions.

In this section we will focus especially on increasing power in relation to yourself, and developing the ways you can raise your consciousness through your own means. Although this section concentrates on developing power within yourself, rather than power out in the world, the two are interwoven.

THE NATURE OF POWER

Power is often associated with such other notions as dominance, control, perhaps aggression, charisma, inspiration, presence, etc. Therefore power has many different perspectives.

In young soul society, developing power is usually thought of as gaining the ability to get what you want. This usually means striving for deliberate control over other people's lives or amassing great material wealth.

This is legitimate as a lesson and experience for essence to work with over a series of lifetimes. Manifesting what you want on the physical plane and getting to see what it means to have these things is after all one of the main experiences that the physical plane has to offer.

However, because these kinds of power bring the notions of winning over losing, amassing, and control over other people, they are usually associated with fear. For, what can be amassed to win or control can also be lost or fall prey to others. So, the pursuit of external forms of power naturally brings up a fear of that same power. Interestingly this fear paradoxically brings both the fear of being victim to it and the fear of using power.

Certain early mystic and spiritual traditions, for example shamanism, regarded power somewhat differently. For them power was seen as something that was inherent and nurtured by an intimate relationship with all of nature.

Nature was seen as containing all power, and man, being part of nature, could participate in it.

At times power was manifested from meeting nature in adversarial conditions and surviving it. Thus someone who became a shaman might have a bout or fight for survival with an

animal or a disease or a natural disaster such as an earthquake.
A person who had survived this natural difficulty would be seen
as a powerful person.

> *In other terms, power in the mystic tradition could be*
> *seen as that ability to stay present in the moment. The*
> *origin of the word mystic is from the Greek "mystos," to*
> *keep silence. The inference here is that the spiritual*
> *power or strength comes from silence and that which is*
> *hidden.*

This is often the type of power that is associated with great
figures as Ghandi, Buddha, and Jesus of Nazareth.

For these individuals power is not necessarily related to
physical strength, attractiveness of appearance, or any traditional stereotypical notion of power, but truly with a presence.
This type of power has to do with manifesting a certain vibra-
tional level.

POWER AND MODES

Now, power is generally thought of as action oriented,
something you can use to change people, events, or relationships,
or get things done. This is the power associated with moving
center and with your mode.

> *For example you might think of power as residing in*
> *political office, something that, if you had, you could use*
> *to change society. You might think of a corporate mogul*
> *as powerful, someone like Daddy Warbucks from* Little
> Orphan Annie. *With his power and money he could make*
> *almost anything right.*

However, although this may be one form of power, it
certainly misleads you into thinking that power has to look a
particular way. The fact is that your personal power is closely
related to your mode. Remember that the mode is your modus

operandi, the way you do your other overleaves. For your recall the seven modes are caution, power, reserve, passion, perseverance, aggression, and observation.

Now, you may wonder how modes such as caution, reserve, or observation could possibly lead you to the experience of personal power. The secret lies in acting from the positive pole of your mode. When you act from your positive poles, no matter what your mode, you automatically begin to tap into your personal power.

Let us look at an example. The negative pole of caution mode is fear or fearfulness, an obviously powerless position. However the positive pole is deliberation, a focused activity that seeks to avoid mistakes and maximize productivity or safe passage. He who acts deliberately, or after deliberation, is more likely to succeed than one who blunders ahead without knowing the hazards.

> _Consider a chemist working with volatile materials or an explosives expert setting charges for diminishing avalanche danger. Such people, being cautious and deliberate, act powerfully in the world._

This same approach works for all modes. Let us look at another apparently restrictive mode, reserve, and see how it can empower you. The negative pole of reserve is inhibited, again a powerless position. The positive pole however, is restrained. When you act with restraint, you can begin to refine your actions or hone them into balanced movements with a minimum of wasted effort.

> _Think of the powerful ballet dancer or figure skater who has refined his or her movements through restraint and discipline. Can you accuse them of powerlessness?_

When a person with observation mode clarifies, he acts powerfully. When he surveys he does not. The same is true for the person with perseverance mode who persists. When he is unchanging, he is disempowered. If you are in passion mode then you will be powerful when you are self-actualizing, not identifying. If you are in aggression mode, you find power through being dynamic, not belligerent.

The power mode person is not automatically powerful when acting from the negative pole, oppressive. He is powerful when he acts with authority.

POWER AND THE HIGHER CENTERS

In esoteric teachings power resides in using the higher centers appropriately with other people and being able to transmit energy through the use of these centers.

For example, the higher intellectual center is about speaking the truth with other people. Many powerful teachers, such as Lao Tsu, have transmitted their messages of truth through this center. Let us for a moment consider the power of higher intellectual center. The single most powerful concept that you have is the belief in the power to create your own life. At some point you, as part of the Tao, created what is now our universe. The universe is malleable to the extent that you can choose the way you want to move within it. It is not a static thing.

At any moment you have the power to know you can create your own universe by looking within to see what exists—examining what kind of concepts and ideas have made our universe what it is.

The higher emotional center is about sharing love, particularly unconditional love and acceptance of other people. Jesus taught powerful messages of love and worked miracles of healing through this higher center. You can experience the power of higher emotional center when you feel at home on the planet and connected with other human beings as your brothers and sisters.

The higher moving center (i.e. sexual center) is about manipulating energy. In some teachings, sharing bliss as a state of being is carried out through this higher center. Bliss is a powerful form of energy that the Buddha shared with his disciples.

You can feel the power of the higher moving center when you experience yourself as healthy and vibrant. You can tap into its power and learn to use it to manifest what you want.

The fact that you have higher centers is much more important than you might realize. They are what separate you from non-sentient life.

> _Think for a moment; what is it that makes a sentient being sentient? What is the difference between a human and a plant? The difference is a question of degree of power. The difference comes from the ability to go into the realm of possibility rather than the realm of being something defined by the blueprint of genetic makeup._

Being sentient means you have the ability to look within and create yourself according to your consciousness. You are fluid and subject to change at any moment. You are not static, preformed or set according to any kinds of rules.

You have the ability to manipulate and change your definition quickly. When there is enough energy present in your consciousness you can prepare yourself for new ways of being.

Most spiritual traditions teach discipline in terms of being able to use this form of consciousness intentionally. Meditation is a powerful tool for undefining yourself and creating room for more power to surge through you. As you become more powerful you develop more sentience and become able to redefine yourself at will.

So, it is possible to interact with other people from a more sentient awareness rather than from a mechanical one—that is, in terms of patterns or habitual behavior.

> _Let's look at an analogy for a moment. Let's say your car broke down and you had to walk everywhere. And not only that but you recently sprained your ankle and you_

had to walk slowly everywhere. From the vantage point of walking slowly you would see things you never would have seen from your car. When meeting other pedestrians your perspective would be different from the perspective a driver has of other drivers. And when crossing the street you would have to watch out for cars in a way that is entirely different from avoiding pedestrians in your car.

And that is not even taking in the cyclist's point of view who is somewhere between the slow pedestrian and the powerful motor car. As the cyclist you have a viewpoint that you are faster than the pedestrians but slower than the cars. You see and feel the environment from an entirely different perspective. In addition, you may feel an affinity for other cyclists but regard other cars and pedestrians as objects to avoid.

So there are all those different points of view. And most of you have at one time shared all those different points of view. As soon as you switch to another mode of transportation it is easy to take on that point of view and totally forget the other view existed.

Sentience allows you to remember that all three of those points of view exist. You can be in agape about pedestrians when you are the driver as you would have it be when you are the pedestrian.

APHORISMS ABOUT POWER

The central theme of these aphorisms addresses your basic choice about life, that you create it according to yourself and not according to what already exists. You create your own reality.

In order to understand how fully you have done that, you can look back into the past and see how you created what you now have and what you believe to be real in your life.

You may experience resistance to the idea that you create your own reality. Your false personality may say, "I didn't create this broken finger, this rainy day, this head cold, and so on. It is X,Y, and Z's fault that it happened." And when you experience positive events like good times with friends or a job bonus, false personality is just as likely to give responsibility to chance or someone else. False personality is afraid of real power.

In day-to-day existence the idea that you are in control of your life is unique. It is a novel concept that is brought up repeatedly in this system because it is at the core of what empowers you.

The following are some aphorisms that powerfully express the true condition in which you live.

> I CREATE AND AM IN CONTROL OF MY OWN LIFE AND UNIVERSE.

> I HAVE CREATED THE GAME OF MY LIFE AND HAVE CHOSEN TO PLAY IT AS A PLAYER IN THE GAME OF MY CHOOSING.

> I AM THE LIVING EXPERIMENT OF MY OWN CREATION.

> I CREATED MY LIFE IN MY OWN CONSCIOUSNESS AND THEN MADE IT REAL.

Now this notion that you create your reality, is readily underestimated. The way this particular universe works is that consciousness comes first. How is this so?

The universe, among many created by the Tao, grows to the extent that it becomes aware of itself. It is then able to play with what it is. This is the seeking out of "What am I?" and "Who am I?," or "What is this thing that seems to be myself?" There is a quest toward identity.

Once the universe forms a certain degree of identity, it then splits itself up into players that play games with each other. Now there is more ability to play with what it (you) are.

The causal law states that consciousness comes first. Consciousness is your perception of reality on the physical plane.

For example you might play with having a water world or a desert one. You might choose a ten-foot tall body or a three-foot one. All these things are played with on an energetic level and gradually these things become more real and solid. They become your actual experience of yourself in the world you share with your co-creators. You end up being here and it all becomes apparently real.

You then believe that you are born here and die here and so on. What do you do with it now that you're here? You can get stuck in the very believability of it.

The point is that it all came into existence first from the perceptual point of view. You create it first. Then you experience it.

I CREATE THE CIRCUMSTANCES AND CONDITIONS
THAT DETERMINE MY ABILITY TO BE SATISFIED
WITH MY LIFE.

All that is around you is a product of intention. Intention is power.

You have the ability to be more creative by being more intentional about what it is that you want to create.

If you wake up and say, "I would like to have this kind of day" there is more possibility of having this kind of day simply because you had that thought.

If you wake up and all these dreadful things happen to you—you are out of Wheaties, out of milk and other traumas—and you say, "My God, I'm having a rotten day," you are more at effect and you are more likely to have that kind of day because you already believe it.

> I CAN HAVE WHATEVER I WANT IN MY UNIVERSE
> EITHER BY PLAYING THE GAME AS I HAVE
> ALREADY ESTABLISHED IT OR BY RECREATING THE
> GAME ACCORDING TO MY WISHES.

Since the world around you is the product of thought and intention, you can manipulate it in the same way that you created it in the first place.

This means you can have or do or be anything you choose. It is the difference between paying attention to the game you are playing and letting it play itself—as in pinball; you can shoot the ball and not touch the flippers or you can play with the flippers.

When you play with this more fluid state of consciousness you can set about manifesting what you want. Because you are in the time-oriented physical plane, however, it may take you minutes, months or years to manifest what you create. It could also take you three lifetimes to manifest what you want. Now, you can choose to feel a victim of time and say, "If I can't become a millionaire by tomorrow then it's beyond my control." The fact is that if you were not on the physical plane time would not matter. You may not remember but you agreed to live in the illusion of time. Remembering that you did gives you power.

> I AM LIMITED ONLY BY THE CONDITIONS BY
> WHICH I HAVE LIMITED MYSELF.

This aphorism deals with the fact that you perceive things largely from habit. What you think is reality is just habitualized imprinting. You do not actually see what is there because you have learned to see it only a certain way. Reminding yourself that this is so, empowers you to break through the limiting beliefs and truly manifest what you want.

> **MY UNIVERSE PROVIDES ME WITH EVERYTHING THAT I NEED TO GROW ALONG THE PATH CHOSEN BY ME.**

Power comes from knowing you are supported no matter what the circumstances, no matter how dismal events seem to appear. Traditionally this has been called faith.

> **MY FRIENDS FACILITATE ME IN LEARNING THE LESSONS I WISH TO LEARN IN THIS LIFETIME.**

Your best friends empower you. They are the people who present you with your most difficult lessons because they care about you the most on an essence level and wish to see you grow the most.

> **THE POINT OF VIEW FROM WHICH I HOLD MY LIFE IS SUBJECT TO CHANGE ACCORDING TO MY STATE OF CONSCIOUSNESS.**

Going into higher centers does change your point of view.

> **EVERYTHING IN THE UNIVERSE CAN BE LOOKED AT FROM A DIFFERENT POINT OF VIEW.**

To be able to look at yourself from different points of view is a form of power. Personal power allows you to break through the concepts of what brought you to where you are now, and to take a new direction to where you would like to be. When something comes forth in your path and brings a new point of view, you get the opportunity to say, "I could see myself in a new situation just by allowing this different point of view to exist, rather than the old traditional patterns."

Finding more examples gives you the opportunity to play with altering your perspective on a daily basis. As a result you can change your life and take up opportunities that you perceive.

Clearly all teaching is pitched at this. You walk out seeing things differently from when you came in.

Sometimes instinctive center finds this frightening or life-threatening. Then it needs to be spoken to kindly, soothed and balanced.

> THE ONLY THING THAT CAN TRAP ME IS MY POINT OF VIEW.

> I CAN ACCEPT, REJECT OR FEEL NEUTRAL ABOUT ANY OF THE LESSONS I CHOOSE TO CREATE FOR MYSELF.

> ALL THINGS ARE CHANGEABLE.

All these aphorisms relating to point of view address the power of your attitude. Remember that your attitude is your primary perspective and the key to eliminating your chief negative feature: self-destruction, greed, self-deprecation, arrogance, impatience, martyrdom, or stubbornness. Erasing your chief feature is not only an act of incredible power but releases the unlimited power within you.

> I AM HERE BECAUSE I WISH TO BE.

You would not be here if you did not still have something to do. Do not worry about not being in the right place. If this were the wrong place you would be some place else!

In this section you have been familiarized with forces in life that provide much personal growth. Your physical body and your energetic body are excellent tools for such growth. You have seen how knowing the principles of prosperity can accelerate your growth lessons and you have discovered how personal power is the result.

In the next section we will shift our focus very slightly from personal growth to methods that emphasize more spiritual growth. This is at best an arbitrary distinction because all growth is ultimately spiritual.

PART SIX

INTEGRATION

Chapter Fourteen

Putting It All Together

Part VI: INTEGRATION

The previous chapters have described the social structure of the physical plane and the basic rules that keep the earth school a productive and evolving one. You now have the opportunity to understand the deeper nature of your relationships and to become aware of how they help you to grow. Now you can consciously gravitate toward productive relationships and support people who will give you what you need to reach your goals. With the knowledge in these pages you can accelerate your evolution toward unconditional self-acceptance and the joy that springs from accepting your fellow travelers.

> *Imagine that you have been stumbling along with many large bundles and parcels in your hands, on your back, and hanging from your neck. You have been able to negotiate generally in the direction you wanted to go,*

yet you have had to stop frequently for rest and to rebalance your load.

Now imagine that a number of helpful friends appear from the forest around you and distribute the load among them allowing you to proceed more quickly and enjoyably with their company. They were there all along but somehow you never noticed them.

In the following pages we will review the basics about karma, imprinting, relationships, groups, and communication. We will show how they provide the environment and structure that allows you to use your overleaves to gain experience from life to life. Furthermore you will see how you get closer to essence through your relationships with others.

KARMA

You have seen how karma acts as the glue that holds the game of life together. It insures that cause will be followed by effect and that there will be consequences for your actions. Remember that karmic activity follows the laws of the triad and the septant. Every action has a reaction and then there is resolution. Resolution always sets up another action, and another reaction, so that the play is eternal. The lessons follow the septant growth pattern leading to the next higher octave of lessons. The result is that you evolve.

Remember also that karma takes time, a central feature to physical plane experience. Within this context, all the lessons of life are played out. When you are totally in the present, you step outside of time and are free from the suffering that you perceive karma to be.

The overleaves are the tools used by essence to facilitate karma. The overleaves mean nothing unless they have context to operate within. The overleaves have to act against the environment and must be bounced off of other people in order for there to be experience and learning.

For example a goal of dominance would be difficult to experience if you spent your life in isolation on a desert island. Furthermore you could not incur nor repay karma in such an environment. The best you could do is experiment with self-karma.

The overleaves, relationships, and karma form a triad that is a building block for your physical plane experience as humans.

MAYA

Maya is the great forgetfulness that allows you to play with karma. Maya is illusion and without it there would be no game. Remember that maya becomes more subtle as your essence evolves throughout its many lifetimes. Maya is an exact measure of your ever-expanding awareness. It becomes more subtle in exact proportion to your developing consciousness.

Overleaves, relationships, and karma are all ultimately governed by maya and how they manifest is another exact measure of the level of maya that you are playing with.

VARIETIES OF REINCARNATIONAL RELATIONSHIPS

The lessons moving you toward evolution are not experienced in isolation but rather in relationship with others. Relationships are not randomly experienced yet they are freely chosen. You make agreements of many kinds with other essences to assist one another and facilitate certain experiences for each other.

For example, without an agreement with a potential mother you would not have much opportunity to be born.

The relationships that you learn the most from are often with individuals that you have chosen to be with in a specific type of relationship. Monads are a principal, structured kind of relationship that provide a vehicle for developing and completing karma.

The monads have a building quality that takes you from more primitive types of relating in your younger soul lives to more complex and sophisticated relationships in your older soul lives. Since you do many of the monads with the same people over many lifetimes you get to know them and yourself very well. You discover your uniqueness and your essential oneness with the other at one and the same time.

Your essence twin provides you with a best friend and a pivotal facilitator, that is, he pivots you into growth oriented experiences. He knows you well enough to make sure you live all of life like you said you wanted to when you agreed to be a human being.

If you have chosen to have an essence twin or soul mate, then you will suffer his influence, feel his support, and experience his magical attractiveness over and over.

Your task companions will join you in creative and pioneering projects that you agree to carry out each lifetime. They are there to work with and support you in your projects and schemes. You facilitate each other's fortunes and failures and either way you are furthered by your relationship.

Your cadre is your cosmic family with whom you were once united and with whom you will ultimately reunite to become greater than you ever were. These are the fragments that you play out many of your monads with and the ones that you support and assist between lives. Remember that your cadre has a personality of its own that you participate within. Your unique personality reflects the larger personality of your cadre. You never exist in isolation.

Your cadence is your special subgrouping within your cadre and this gives you another special orientation. There is no limit then to your uniqueness and your ability to specialize. After all, the Tao is not interested in exact copies, only unique forms and new creations.

FREQUENCY AND MALE -FEMALE ENERGY

Your frequency and percentage of male and female energy gives you a unique essence fingerprint or scent that figures significantly in your relationships. Your level of frequency determines the comfort zone and challenges that come from relating to others. Recall that high frequency folks understand each other but high frequency people feel balanced by low frequency people. Likewise for low frequency types. Difference in frequency makes for interesting differences in temperament and style. A high frequency priest and a low frequency warrior are about as different as you can get. This is great for karma formation.

The same can be said for male and female energy percentage. Your percentages of each determine what kind of relationships you will seek for balance, what kind you will feel comfortable with, and what type you will find excitement with.

Remember that frequency level and male-female energy proportion are a function of your role and remain the same throughout your entire cycle of lives on earth.

HANDLING IMPRINTING

Each lifetime you want to insure that you will have the personality that will give you the best opportunity to handle karma and to have the kind of experiences that you desire for essence growth. In addition you want to make sure that you are going to be in the right environment to carry out your monads and agreements with others. You choose your earth family to provide you with this ideal environment and to imprint you in desired ways.

Your childhood years are spent becoming imprinted with overleaves, beliefs, habits, and behaviors that contribute to your decision-making process on a day-to-day level. Your decisions then contribute to the karma and self-karma that you wish to learn from. The imprinting gives you an exact level of maya to live within and to cut through.

> *Here you have your triad of relationships, over-leaves, and karma in the context of maya.*

You have seen how you begin to sort out this conditioning in your twenties and how you can cast much of it off by your mid-thirties. This leaves much of your adult life free for direct essence work.

You will see that occasionally you bypass the birth and childhood process by walking into a body that another essence chooses to abandon. Thus you have several options for coming to the planet.

GROUPS AND CONFIGURATIONS

One of the main ways that you forge ahead with your evolutionary process is through your participation in groups of various sizes and functions. Over lifetimes you occupy each of the different positions in the groups you work with and of course you develop favorites. In addition you get to work and play with others who occupy different positions in those groups and you discover how they work together to produce results.

    Monad   Already mentioned above. These are paired relationships of a specific nature experienced from both sides, e.g. mother-daughter or leader-follower.

    Triad   Recall the purpose and operation of the triad, a group of three. This is an imbalanced group with affirming, denying and neutral positions. Triads are building groups, karmic in nature. Remember also that the triad is an evolutionary process that affects relationships and most physical plane experiences.

Quadrant   Remember that the quadrant is a balanced and productive work group. Recall its four main positions: love; knowledge; power; and support. Which do you do best?

Pentangle   Recall the eccentricity of the pentangle, rarely lasting but spiritual in nature.

Sextant   Remember that the sextant is a stable quadrant with two added positions: Eccentric and Integrator. Use it to accomplish major tasks.

Septant   Like the triad, the septant is both a spiritual group format and an evolutionary process. Recall the steps of the septant:

1. Growth
2. Elimination
3. Purification
4. Corruption
5. Healing
6. Completion
7. Regeneration.

Remember that these seven positions are the steps in the evolution of any group process whether familial or business oriented.

Support group   Recall the twelve positions of your support group. Remember that they are there to remind you that you are not alone on your path of evolution. Which have you not yet identified in your life? Can you bring them in?

Power	Your position
Love Knowledge Compassion	Get things done
Mentor Beauty Child	Inspirational .
Humor Discipline Anchor	Assist in physical plane lessons
Healer Enlightenment Muse	Assist in spirit-plane lessons

ASTROLOGY

Your astrological chart is a representational map of the influence of the stars and planets on your personality at the moment of your birth. Again you are reminded that you are related to all of nature. The relationship of planets determine influences in your life that contribute to your forming and resolving karma. You can find your overleaves in your astrological chart as well. Remember that astrology does not dictate your choices, only influences them. You are always free to choose. Astrology ultimately is governed by maya.

COMMUNICATION AND INTIMACY

Relationships depend upon communication as does intimacy. You have seen that communication requires 100% responsibility on the part of each party. Miscommunication is usually intended by the false personality to keep the karmic game going. Miscommunication is of course a product of maya.

You have seen that cording is a definite kind of energetic communication that is necessary for infants and their mothers for survival purposes. A cord is an energetic type of communication between two people's chakras that is intrusive in nature. You have learned to be aware of cording and you have learned ways to disengage from other people's cords if you wish to.

Recall that relationships on the physical plane take place through the personality overleaves. The way you and your partner use these overleaves determines the nature of your relationship and the resulting karmic lessons.

Intimate relationships are usually chosen for their challenges and differentness. These are the contexts that produce the most effective lessons and evolution. These relationships are also the most fun in terms of karmic process. When the intensity of a relationship is released through the completion of all karma, all that is left to experience is love.

Love ultimately ends maya, karma, and the entire physical plane game. When you experience unconditional acceptance of yourself and others you have achieved total communication, total relationship, and the game is over. You have reunited with the Tao. That is the ultimate goal of the physical plane game. Getting there is a thrilling experience. If it were not, no one would bother to play. All you have to do is look around you at the number of your fellow beings to see how popular the game is.

RELATIONSHIPS AT WORK

The following vignette is an example of how relationships actually work in relation to karma, agreements, and overleaves. Remember that the possibilities are limitless here and that these are only some of many possible scenarios. As you read, see if can begin to grasp the larger context of relationships and how they further you in your path of evolution.

The player

Sixth level mature warrior.

Female this lifetime. Usually male.

Frequency of 10; male energy 60%; female energy 40%. This is the maya level being worked with.

Overleaves: Goal of growth, passion mode, idealist attitude, chief feature of impatience, emotional centering.

Relationships: Sage essence twin; two task companions, one warrior and one artisan; one major quadrant with a goal of education; three major monads: mother-daughter; teacher-student; healer-healed; agreements for two children.

Karma: Desire for 200 karmic debts to be repaid this lifetime. 35 major karma, 165 less intense karma, sundry minor karma. Several major karma including: marriage to unfaithful spouse [reversed from prior lifetime]; intense caretaking relationship with disabled brother; helping relationship with daughter [all reversed from prior lifetimes].

The big picture

Notice that this warrior is at the highly karmic sixth level. Not only that but she is in her mature soul cycle, the difficult adolescence of soul ages when relationships are intense and everything is emotionally charged. She has selected a goal of growth, passion mode, and emotional centering for the occasion. This will ensure that she grows spiritually through emotional lessons and an attitude of idealist will get her to forge ahead and keep her constantly dissatisfied with her lot thus facilitating her goal of growth. The chief feature of impatience is a natural with the other overleaves. This will give her a sufficiently hard time to feel challenged during this life.

These overleaves are good for the level and amount of karma she has chosen to handle this lifetime. Being a solid warrior with slightly more male energy will help to keep her focused on her goal and to handle the wildness and fluidity of passion mode, idealism, and emotional centering.

She has decided upon some juicy challenging relationships that are sure to produce growth through emotional lessons and she gets to repay karma at the same time. She has armed herself for the journey with a couple of good task companions and an essence twin to help out. In addition she has a quadrant to work with that will assist her and ensure more growth.

The lifetime

You have selected a family situation that immediately casts you with a major monad and the kind of imprinting you need to develop your overleaves. Both of your parents are highly emotional creative artisans who contibute to your passion and emotional centering from the beginning.

When you are two, a younger brother is born whom you greatly resent. When you are five and your brother is two, you lure him into the street to play and an automobile strikes him down him causing him extensive injuries and permanent brain damage [this also is a karmic repayment from a time when he caused a similar mishap to you]. You feel terribly guilty [emotional center] and responsible for him and your idealism calls for you to vow to take care of him from then on. For years you are intensely and passionately involved in caring for your brother [healer-healed monad] who eventually dies when you are twenty.

Freed from the heavy responsibilities of his care you rush into an early marriage [impatience] with an attractive man [priest] whom you find exciting and entirely different from you. You sense his compassion and believe [idealism] he will take care of you.

In the beginning all is well but a year into your relationship you discover that your husband is having affairs on his frequent business trips [major karmic relationship]. Although you are devastated by this your idealism causes you to think it will get better which it never does. You wonder why you stay in the relationship but even with marriage counseling the affairs continue and you find that you are strangely unable to divorce him.

After ten years you no longer care about his affairs and one day he tells you he is leaving you. You wonder why you feel so bad when you really don't care for him any more and he has caused you so much pain [karma].

During your marriage you give birth to two children [agreements] even though you used birth control and questioned having children with this man. You become closely attached with your daughter [mother-daughter monad] who also prefers you. Your son seems more remote from you and prefers to be with his father when he is around. When your daughter is three you discover that she has learning disabilities and you throw yourself into helping her to overcome them. Your daughter is the apple of your eye and you have a close and helping relationship with her throughout your life.

You are now in your early thirties and decide to enter counseling [counselor is healer in your support group] to better understand yourself. You begin to cast off much unwanted imprinting from your childhood and decide to go to college and get your own career going. Your experience with your brother and your daughter's disabilities causes you to turn to a career in education.

While at school you meet an entertaining male professor [your sage essence twin] whom you feel an amazing attraction for. He reciprocates and you have an intense fiery relationship that throws you into much confusion. He is tremendously helpful to you in getting your career as a school teacher going and paves the way for interviews that land you a good job [pivotal facilitator]. Although you love him you find you cannot live with him so you break off the sexual relationship with him and remain friends for many years.

Your energy and drive [overleaves] move you up the career ladder fast and soon you become a vice-principal of your school. You get along well with the principal and two other teachers who are interested in forming a private progressive school [quadrant showing up; includes two of your task companions]. You are successful in this endeavor and you act as the doer in this group [power position]. You only run into problems with them when you try to go too fast [impatience] and things seem to go wrong.

For many years you are occupied teaching, running, and operating the new school. When you are working with your task companions and your quadrant things seem to go well for the most part. Yet your life is not easy and has many ups and downs. You have an opportunity to complete much karma as you come into contact with the many students who attend your school as well as their parents and families. You are able to be a great help to the teachers who work for you and in this way not only do you repay old karma but actually create new karma of a positive nature.

You are known for your uncanny ability to know what your colleagues are feeling [mature soul] and you have a great talent for communicating with the children, especially the younger ones [emotional centering].

As you become older you spend more time studying esoteric spiritual traditions and try to incorporate these into your educational philosophy. You enjoy being an older person and eventually when you are well into your seventies you retire to pursue reading, study, and gardening. You have remained surprisingly healthy due to your rigorous fitness workouts [warrior] and you live until your mid-eighties when you die of complications stemming from medication mis-prescribed by a doctor. [This represented a karmic completion owed to the doctor]. You are able to fulfill several more karmic debts by leaving your estate to several grandchildren whom you owed from past lifetimes.

You look back on your life from an after-death perspective and are satisfied with the tremendous growth and accomplishments of this rigorous life. You smile at the intensity you felt about events during your life and you can see the maya that surrounded you. You are now able to begin planning your next life based on what you have accomplished and what is yet to be learned. First however you must integrate everything that has happened during this last lifetime. You may want to replay some scenarios to see how they might have turned out had you made a different choice. For example you might have married your essence twin instead of ending the sexual form of your relationship.

Meanwhile your essence twin, who died much earlier than you, has already been born again and you have agreed to act as his principal spirit guide for a while. You are planning to be born as his brother in about ten years so you have much preparation to do.

Here then has been a segment of the whole ongoing path of development and evolution. Your overleaves and imprinting affect your relationships and promote the ongoing cycle of karma.

The thick veil of maya is gradually thinned until eventually it is dissipated entirely. Look at your own life as you looked at the woman's life in the story. What is the larger context of your life? What are your overleaves and how were you imprinted? Who are your relationships in the big picture? Are they monads, entity fragments, agreements, old friends, support people, task companions, group members? Do you have an essence twin and who might it be? Which relationships are karmic and how can you stop resisting them? What is your self-karma and do you want to continue it? How do your overleaves, relationships and karma interact to weave the life that you know? And finally what is the maya that obscures your vision?

You are the author of your script and you are the context of your life as well. You can rewrite the script any time you wish. You can certainly perceive your experiences in a transformed way.

You are here to experience, to evolve and ultimately to be. You are here to know unconditional acceptance of yourself and others no matter what the scenario. Enjoy the ride, you are the pilot.

PERSONAL GROWTH

Your main vehicle for experiencing the physical plane lessons is your body. Your body, built for survival, is the source of false personality and it is the one that must experience the brunt of karma. Nevertheless your body is a highly complex receiving and generating station that stays in communication with essence through the seven chakras and your aura. Keeping your body healthy through exercise and diet can prove exceptionally helpful in maintaining this communication. Keeping your energy body clear through meditation and visualization is just as important if not more so.

Knowledge of your male and female energy balance and your frequency can offer you opportunities for accelerated growth and transformation. Knowledge of the principles of manifestation and prosperity make it possible for you to expand and evolve through the soul levels and stages to join with the Tao. Development of personal power and understanding how to use parallel universes can contribute to this overall path of evolution.

SPIRITUALITY

The spiritual person is an awake person, a risk-taking person who has manifested his true soul age and remembers the Tao of which he is part. Spirituality means desiring to live in the world with an unconditionally loving, disidentified perspective and achieving this some of the time. Most importantly spiritual growth comes from becoming unconditionally accepting of yourself. There are seven steps to help you move in this direction.

1. Trusting your perceptions.
2. Ruthless truthfulness with yourself.
3. Developing tolerance and recognizing the perfection of the Tao in all things.
4. Being appropriately powerful.
5. Erasing fear and your chief feature.
6. Surrendering to your essence and the Tao. Let them lead.
7. Being truly humble.

A higher degree of spiritual growth comes from balancing the intellectual, emotional, and moving centers. This comes from a powerful desire to know the truth, a willingness to be emotionally open to life, and a practiced ability to be balanced energetically. As you balance yourself you begin to achieve degrees of enlightenment. As you become more enlightened you begin to recognize the degrees of essence that connect you to all seven spiritual planes. You get more effective at piercing the maya or veil of illusion that keeps you asleep.

TOOLS OF THE TRADE

Your tools for cutting through maya are the ancient tried and true methods of realizing the higher centers. Meditation, concentration, study, singing, dancing, fasting, and service are all effective means of spiritual growth. Communicating with your guides and non-physical companions through channeling and meditation is also an ancient, extraordinary tool for spiritual transformation and acceleration. With so many tools available how can you not become spiritually aware?

The planet Earth itself offers you tools and assistance in your path toward oneness and wholeness. Each of the seven Earthly levels that you experienced on your way to your first infant soul life, serves you in your evolution toward realization of the Tao.

1. Oceanic/mineral level.
2. Plant level.
3. Insect level.
4. Fish and reptile level.
5. Bird level.
6. Lower mammals and birds of prey level.
7. Higher mammals level.

Gems, minerals, and metals all influence the frequency of your body to assist you in overcoming obstacles within your personality and with the challenging overleaves that you encounter in others. Your use of each overleaf can be influenced by the gemstones and metals you choose to wear on your person. Remember that they are most effective when you use them consciously.

The contributions of the plant kingdom are obvious with their healing properties, dietary influences, and gifts of building materials and energy resources. The insect kingdom offers assistance with plant cultivation, food chain maintenance, and countless resources as yet untapped.

The animal kingdoms contribute in obvious and hidden ways. First they provide companionship, labor, and food products. Secondly they provide guidance and instinctive wisdom in the art of survival. Your experience with them helped to form who you are. They remind you of what you once knew but have now forgotten. In live form and in metaphor they can influence your overleaves just as the mineral kingdom does.

COMPLETION

Now you have it. You have seen the entire panorama of the school of life on the physical plane. You have seen your arrival on the planet, your contributions to every level of consciousness on the earth, your preparations for sentience, your plans for each life, and the evolutionary steps within each lifetime. You have seen the structure of your relationships from life to life and have learned the importance of working through these relationships to completion. You have seen the opportunities for both personal and spiritual growth and have learned methods for evolving each lifetime. You have become acquainted with the various tools of the planet and you are aware that by using them for spiritual growth they advance as well. Finally you have reviewed the entire process described throughout this book.

Together with a knowledge of the overleaves and soul levels you have a fairly complete set of tools to transform your entire experience of living. You can get off your rusty old tricycle, hop on your smooth new ten-speed bike, and enjoy the ride.

Happy trails!

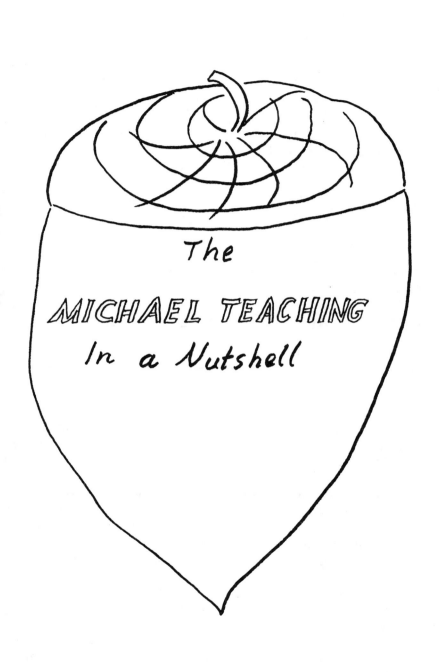

The

MICHAEL TEACHING

In a Nutshell

The Michael Teaching—A Summary

This section is a brief review of basic knowledge presented in The Michael Handbook *(formerly* Essence and Personality*). It is foundation material and will be most helpful in understanding the information in this book about relationships.*

Michael is a teacher from the causal plane who offers this body of knowledge freely and unconditionally in order to assist people to understand themselves and one another better. According to Michael this teaching is an ancient one that is occasionally updated to keep up with changes in language and culture.

Michael is a reunited entity who lived many lives on the earth before cycling off to other planes and experiences. Michael draws their name from the last life of their last fragment to live on the Earth. Michael's teaching has come through a variety of trance mediums and channels over the last twenty years and continues to do so.

Michael is available and willing to channel through anyone who is interested in this material. Michael suggests that all the information be self-validated and thrown out if it does not strike a chord with you.

This teaching represents an evolution of the works of Gurdjieff, Ouspensky, and Rodney Collin who began to bring forth this knowledge earlier this century.

According to the Michael entity, life is an exciting game of learning set up by the Tao (all that is) for purposes of creativity and pure expression. The physical plane, the seventh and most solid plane, is the dimension of forgetfulness and separation. Here the Tao is pretending not to know itself in a cosmic game of hide and seek. The goal is to find oneness and wholeness through a series of experiences and lifetimes where lessons are learned about unconditional acceptance of self and others.

Entities seeking to experience this grand adventure fragment themselves into hundreds of individuals who progress and develop through a series of lifetimes. Through their many chosen personalities these fragment essences gradually discover their essential oneness and eventually reunite with one another. They continue for further adventures in the six remaining planes enroute to final joyful unity with the Tao itself.

The fragment essences progress through seven distinct stages of development, each with seven levels apiece. Each stage is distinguished by a unique level of perception and by particular characteristics. Here then are the major soul ages passed through by each fragment.

Infant Soul

This is a beginning level of survival and an orientation to the physical human form. Infant souls are instinctively fearful and seek out extremes of experience in order to become acquainted with physical life. They experience life in a "me and not me" format and they approach their world superstitiously. Infant souls learn by rote and seek guidance from older, more experienced souls. They do not question nor philosophize, preferring to follow absolutely the authority of their leader. Infant souls are overwhelmed by complex urban society and prefer to learn basic rules of living in small tribal and out-of-the-way environments.

Baby Soul

The baby soul has become acquainted with the basics of living and now becomes focused on developing rules and structures for the building of society. As such, baby souls are oriented toward law and order, preferring to further develop their conscience through experiences that test the social rules they themselves have made.

Life for the baby soul is perceived in a "me and other me's" format. They seek and honor absolute higher authority to provide a meaningful context for living. Their religions are dogmatic and orthodox to the extreme. Tradition plays an important role in life of the baby soul and the breaking of tradition meets with dire consequences.

Khomeini of Iran is a Baby soul.

Young Soul

Young souls have become sophisticated and are highly enthusiastic about playing the material game. They seek power, notoriety, fame, fortune, and wealth. They aspire to the heights of human achievement in sports, campaigns, competitions, and academics. The perceptivity of the young soul is that of "me and you and I'm going to win." The young soul is predominantly focused on looking good and making it to the top of of the heap.

Young souls begin to reflect on their actions and question who they are in the final levels. However they are usually too focused on the maya of external events to achieve much self understanding. Alexander the Great was a young soul as was Cleopatra.

Mature Soul

The mature soul age is the adolescence of soul levels. Here dramatic changes occur in perception and overall awareness. The mature soul turns inward and reflects on his own awareness. Philosophy and the beginning of true spiritual awareness are the result. The perceptivity of the mature soul is "you and I are alike, I know how you feel inside." This represents the relaxing of psychic boundaries and at times the breakdown of personality. Highly emotional, the mature soul focuses on intensity and duration in relationship with others.

Mature souls seek peace and quiet and turn away from organized religion to find their guidance. Often feeling misunderstood and out of step with their cultures, they prefer to be with older souls for understanding and support. Even so they often make major contributions to human knowledge and understanding. Galileo was a mature soul as well as Fritz Perls.

Old Soul

The old soul is a contradiction in terms. Laid back, casual, and ofttimes lazy, the old soul accelerates the pace of spiritual search. You can imagine the intense inner activity of an older person who is no longer active in pursuing achievement but rather is focused on preparing for death.

Old souls are sensual, independent, and usually highly eccentric. They are capable and wise, often eschewing traditional forms of education in favor of their own form of study. They perceive the world as "you and I as part of something greater." John Muir was an old soul.

Transcendental Soul

When all the entity fragments have cycled off the physical plane at the end of their old soul cycle they reunite together again, enriched and expanded beyond measure. They may choose to incarnate in human form one more time as a group and not fragmented. This incarnation is called the transcendental soul or Bodhisattva, the helping soul who is recognized as a great spiritual teacher by older souls. Mohandas Ghandi was one.

Infinite Soul

The infinite soul is a representative of the Tao itself. The infinite soul takes human form very occasionally to provide leadership in times of chaos and distress. Buddha, Christ, Krishna, and Lao Tsu were the infinite soul manifested.

THE SEVEN LEVELS WITHIN EACH SOUL AGE

As mentioned, each soul age has seven levels of learning. These levels are progressive and and require at least one, if not several lifetimes to complete. The same set of seven applies to each soul age.

The Seven Levels within each Soul Age

1. Examine new soul age   —explore
2. Transition/creation   —self-karma: plunge in
3. Introspection   —adapt to change internally
4. Emotions   —exemplifies stage
5. New knowledge   —eccentricity
6. Karmic completion   —intense and busy life
7. Teaching   —share, consolidate, and prepare for next stage.

THE ESSENCE ROLE

Essence chooses one of seven roles to develop and master during its journey from infant soul to old soul perception. This role remains the same throughout the cycle of lifetimes and represents a particular approach to living that shall here be described. The seven roles are divided into four main categories or axes: inspiration, expression, action, and assimilation.

Servers and Priests

Under the inspiration classification is the ordinal role of server and the exalted role of priest. Servers comprise 30% of the population and derive profound satisfaction in being of service to others in a direct and immediate fashion. Priests on the other hand represent only 4% of the population and they seek to serve larger groups by providing spiritual guidance.

Artisans and Sages

The expression roles are the ordinal role of artisan, 20% of the population, and the exalted role of sage, 15% of the population. Artisans strive to express themselves through creativity of a direct and personal nature. Sages express themselves to larger groups through drama, communication and amusement.

Warriors and Kings

The action roles are the ordinal role of warrior, 20% of the population, and the exalted king role, only 1% of the population. Warriors are the most physical of the roles and enjoy lives of direct and confrontive experience in the physical world. They are productive and good at finding strategic ways of achieving their logically thought-out goals. Kings prefer to delegate the action to others and lead through their grandeur and sense of responsibility for the group.

Scholars

The scholar, 10% of the population, is the assimilative role and is primarily neutral. Scholars seek to experience life through the accumulation of knowledge and spend many lives researching and studying what is around them. They understand all the other roles and act as mediators between them.

OVERLEAVES

Essence has developed a personality, gradually formed over many lifetimes, and this larger personality expresses itself through the more limited personality adopted for each lifetime.

When essence takes physical form through birth in a human body, it chooses and develops this temporary personality by giving itself the proper life conditions to develop specific traits called overleaves. The negative expression of this limited and temporary personality is called the false personality. The task for each lifetime is to dissolve the false personality and express the true personality through the overleaves chosen.

Although the role remains the same throughout the cycle of lives, each lifetime the soul selects a new goal, attitude, chief feature, mode, center, and body type. This gives the individual a new personality to work with and provides a fresh and contrasting range of opportunities and challenges.

GOALS

The goal orients and motivates you to seek out certain life experiences. The seven goals available to choose from are re-evaluation, growth, discrimination, acceptance, submission, dominance, and stagnation.

Re-evaluation motivates you to take a closer look at yourself and is sometimes accompanied by a severe physical disability. Growth is the motivation to experience as much as possible in a given lifetime. These are usually full and busy lives. Discrimination leads you to reject all of the chaff in life and to retain only that which is considered best. Acceptance on the other hand leads you to accept life as it comes.

Submission teaches you to surrender to a teacher, cause, or a life's work. Dominance is the desire to lead and to command. Stagnation is the motivation to make life flow easily and is usually a lifetime for rest.

All goals are eventually chosen and mastered throughout the cycle of lives.

ATTITUDES

The attitude gives you a habitual point of view. There are seven attitudes to choose from: stoic, spiritualist, skeptic, idealist, cynic, realist, and pragmatist.

Stoics reserve judgment while spiritualists tend to see the overall picture about what can be.

Skeptics doubt and investigate and idealists strive for progress by seeing what should or ought to be.

Cynics readily see what won't work while realists see all the possibilities at once.

Pragmatists are efficient and want things to work.

All the attitudes are eventually selected and mastered.

CHIEF NEGATIVE OBSTACLE

In addition to the goal and attitude, each fragment selects from among seven chief negative obstacles. These act as impediments to be overcome and tend to neutralize efforts to attain the goal. The seven obstacles are self-deprecation, arrogance, self-destruction, greed, martyrdom, impatience, and stubborness.

Self-deprecation refers to a pervasive sense of low self-esteem, while arrogance hides an uncomfortable shyness resulting from a fear of vulnerability.

Self-destruction results in slow or rapid suicide. Greed comes from the fear that not enough of anything is available.

Martyrdom is feeling a victim of circumstances. Impatience is the fear of missing out.

Stubborness can impede through obstinacy and represents a fear of change.

MODE

The mode is the means of achieving the goal. The seven modes that can be chosen are reserve, passion, caution, power, perseverance, aggression, and observation.

Reserve appears restrained while passion is unbridled and expansive, identified with life's drama.

Caution appears tentative, while power mode appears authoritative and in control.

Perseverance makes one appear disciplined or repetitive.

Aggression leads one to impose oneself on the world.

Observation is a common mode and facilitates learning by careful watching.

All modes are eventually embraced and mastered.

CENTERS

Seven centers give a person even more alternatives to choose from each lifetime. The three centers that are predominantly chosen for everyday functioning are moving center, intellectual center, and emotional center.

These centers act as primary energizers and determine the way that a person generally responds to any stimuli.

A moving centered person will tend to be physically active and be fond of sports, travel, and action. An emotionally centered person will tend to be more perceptive and will experience situations in terms of likes and dislikes.

An intellectually centered person will tend to be more verbal and will enjoy philosophy and thinking for its own sake.

The instinctive center stores survival information and is operative in everyone all the time.

The higher centers—higher moving, higher intellectual, and higher emotional—are transformational states of awareness achieved during peak experiences or in meditation states. They are always available but seldom accessed by most people.

BODY TYPES

There are seven major bodytypes to choose from, determined by the configuration of planets at the time of your conception. These are Solar, Mars, Venus, Saturn, Lunar,

Mercury, and Jupiter. The planetary types influence physical characteristics as well as personality style. Most people are a combination of three planetary influences. Three additional planets, Uranus, Neptune, and Pluto, are more rare influences.

Solar is bright, elfish, and refined.
Mars is muscular, reddish, and vigorous.
Venus is voluptuous, warm, and passive.
Saturn is tall, rugged, and enduring.
Lunar is round, pale, and luminous.
Mercury is active, bright, and versatile.
Jupiter is grand, fleshy, and broad.
Uranus is eccentric.
Neptune is dreamy.
Pluto is far-reaching.

SUMMARY

This section has summarized the basics of the Michael teaching's perspective on life purpose and orientation. Here the focus has been on Michael's comprehensive system for understanding the fundamentals of personality and the uniqueness of each individual character structure. Accordingly, the uniqueness of a personality comes from the particular blend of traits chosen; the role, the stage of soul development, and the nature of accumulated past life experiences.

Remember that the fragment essence must pass through seven main stages of development, each with seven levels of growth. These stages and levels are specific, progressive, and characterized by particular lessons. Each lifetime a set of personality traits and a life purpose is selected for the role to master. Each of these traits or overleaves has a positive and a negative pole. Being in the negative pole creates disharmony and neurosis while being in the positive pole creates satisfaction and health. The older the soul, the greater facility in moving toward positive poles via understanding and self-awareness.

The overall goal is for each fragment to experience all of life and progress toward wholeness, integration, and balance through self-acceptance and agape.

A much more thorough and detailed presentation of soul ages, levels, and overleaves may be found in the book *A Michael Handbook* (formerly *Essence and Personality*) from Warwick Press, Orinda California, 1987.

Appendix B

Walk-ins

Who is a walk-in and exactly what does this mean? Are walk-ins common or rare? Are you a walk-in and how can you tell if you are?

A walk-in is a person whose essence has left and has been replaced by another essence. Although it happens rarely, this can be a frightening thought and is the source of confusion for many people. For if your essence has been totally changed, then who are you? Let us here attempt to answer these puzzling questions and shed some light on this option that is both efficient and creative.

First of all there are two ways that essence can select a body and live on the planet. The first and usual way is to be born into one. The second way occurs when the essence of a body vacates the body and another essence enters it. In this manner you can literally be born into a body that is fully grown. Not only that but essence can leave the body without enduring physical death.

The original essence may "check out" for a variety of reasons. Perhaps essence feels that it completed the karma that it set out to achieve that lifetime. Alternatively essence sometimes discovers that the task it had chosen on the astral plane to complete this lifetime is too difficult or has been blocked by unforeseen difficulties. So essence chooses to leave rather than endure what it perceives as an experiment that went awry.

> For example you may choose overleaves leading to a life of intense karma with your parents. Maybe they are both cynics in discrimination and you have chosen a goal of acceptance with a spiritualist attitude. You think that this will be a good challenge for you and that you will complete the karma. However, when you are actually living out the situation you find it unbearable. You become so angry with them for blocking you that you fear you might increase the karma by harming them. You are getting nowhere with your goal of acceptance and so you decide to opt out of this life without actually committing suicide. You are young and healthy and your body is in good shape. So, in order to leave, you arrange an accident where you become comatose. You give your body over to another essence providing the body is not too badly damaged.
>
> You decide to try to complete the karma in another lifetime with improved circumstances.

Sometimes, when essence decides to leave, you do physically experience death, for example in a car accident. If the body is still reparable another essence may assume it. This is often the case where someone is revived after being physically pronounced dead.

More often than not the actual transition does not happen easily. Sometimes the transfer occurs during an intense illness or emotional breakdown. The person often becomes disabled in some way that weakens the tie of the essence to the body. They can be laid up in bed for days, weeks, or months. In the meantime, the new essence hovers around the body, checking it out. Finally the switch is made. Occasionally however, the transition happens without fanfare in a night's sleep.

Now, for a walk-in to occur there must be agreement between the two essences for it to happen. Your essence cannot be snatched away in the night and replaced by another in a kind of cloak and dagger operation. All such rare transitions are chosen and planned fully.

The agreement to walk-in is made astrally, however, and the personality is usually not aware of it. From the viewpoint of the astral plane everything looks easy. Time doesn't exist, communication is instantaneous, and the essence is led to conclude that walking-in is easy. On arrival the truth is that it is a very difficult and strenuous task. The major difficulty is for the personality to adapt to the changes.

The choice of the new essence is constrained by such things as energetic compatibility (such as the male/female balance); the age and sex of the body; friends and relatives; imprinting; the original overleaves; and the location, race, and culture of the body. These variables must be in affinity with what the new essence wants to accomplish on the planet.

> _If the new essence has karma it wishes to complete in New York City that requires a male body with Western-style education, it will not walk-in to the body of a tribeswoman in Papua New Guinea._

When the original essence has left and the new essence enters the body it is in a similar position to a newborn baby. The new essence may not have been in a body for hundreds of years, so there is massive adaptation. The personality feels bewildered and confused in the extreme. There is a feeling of "I don't know what is the matter with me." As this often is concomitant with recovery from illness or accident, the disorientation is disguised by the person's extreme ill health.

To understand the confusion, let us look at the changes that must occur. First, the person is relieved of the previous occupant's overleaves and newly chosen overleaves gradually gain in influence. Secondly, the new essence is often a different role and that involves a fundamental personality change. Also the body type may or may not change.

> *For example the original essence may have been a server, comfortable with serving others on a small scale from behind the scenes. The walk-in essence might be a priest, a comfortable shift considering that both are inspiration roles. However the new personality will begin to pursue a more exalted course of action. The priest may prefer to deal with large groups of people in a highly visible manner. The body may actually grow taller and thinner or hair color might change as well as other features. Others will wonder at the sudden shift in style and presence.*

There is a complete shift in the person's astrology as they now have a new birth time. This creates new themes and patterns of behavior that become influential as the seasons change.

The memories remain intact, the old imprinting is selectively processed, and the desired aspects are retained. New imprinters are chosen—friends, job and so forth. The person may change their taste in clothes and decide to throw out all their previous clothes. They may no longer like some of their friends, desire entirely different foods, stay awake different hours and change sleep patterns. The person truly becomes a "new person."

> *Sometimes family and freinds are baffled at the radical changes in a person who has become a walk-in. They may get furious with them or worry about their strange behavior. They can be pleased at the changes,*

however, because the prior occupant may have been a difficult person, the new person a godsend.

As a baby a new essence has a host of supportive circumstances. It is fed, changed, nurtured and loved while it evolves gradually into an adult. The adult walk-in does not have that luxury. He or she often has a job, a spouse and perhaps a family. Yet the walk-in and all others involved have to work out afresh who they really are. Often the marriage doesn't survive. The aftermath of a walk-in can be traumatic for a while.

The shift from the old essence, personality, and imprinting to the new ones takes seven years to complete. This includes any change in body type. All bodily cells are gradually exchanged for ones that have a holistic memory of an entirely different history of lifetimes. So, you can see that although the transfer of essences may take place in a few seconds, the actual transformation takes much longer.

The new essence must gravitate to people and situations that will help to imprint the person with new desired personality traits. Typically an essence twin helps immensely with this task. Another common response is to enter psychotherapy in order to have a safe space to work out the transformation.

In terms of soul perceptivity, walk-ins are rarely younger than mid-cycle young, as younger soul levels find the notion of leaving the body too fearful. Walk-ins are the most common among old souls who have developed proficiency at such creative and complex arrangements.

One of the most common forms of walk-ins is the seventh level old soul who has completed karma but desires to return to the physical plane to help out friends or entity mates who are attempting to cycle off.

Occasionally, advanced level beings who wish to visit the earth to help out walk-in rather than suffer the inconvenience of being born and living through diapers and so forth.

It is important to realize that not everyone who undergoes a near death experience or a radical personality transformation is a walk-in. The manifestation of essence in mid-life can be equally transformative and dramatic as can other kinds of breakthroughs. Supposing one is a walk-in can be a convenient way to distance oneself from a former embarrassing lifestyle or series of perceived mistakes. A walk-in is a distinct event that happens occasionally and is marked by the characteristics described. In addition the walk-in, after an initial period of confusion, begins to know consciously that they are one. Therefore you need not fear that you are not the same person or that you are a walk-in and didn't want to be. Walk-ins chose to be here and have an awareness of what they have accomplished. A walk-in wants to be one, not out of convenience, but out of certainty.

Glossary

agape	Unconditional love.
agreement	An arrangement between two fragments.
aspect	A parallel self in a parallel universe.
astrology	Configuration of planets at birth influencing life plan.
attitude	Primary perspective.
audacity	Daring or bold move.
basic plan	General design for a lifetime.
being	Unit of intelligent consciousness sparked from the Tao.
belief	Trust without verification.
bird	Fifth major area of exploration for beings considering human form. Includes many simple mammals as well.
body type	Structure of body determined by astrological influences.

cadence	Set of seven fragments of which you are part. Your number within this group of seven influences.
cadre	Group of seven entities with whom you interact most lifetimes. There are about 7000 fragments in a cadre.
center	Overleaf that determines your primary reaction to any life situation. Vehicle of communication between essence and personality.
—higher center	Essence perception.
—lower center	Personality perception.
chakra	Vortex of energy principally located along the spinal column. Associated with the centers. Communication and energy distribution point.
channel	To receive and disseminate information and communication from non-physical planes.
chief feature	Principal obstacle to achieving your goal in a lifetime.
circuit	Completion of all seven roles in seven series of lifetimes.
coalescence	Coming together. Making possible.
coercion	The use of force to achieve an objective.
concentration	A form of spiritual practice that includes focusing the mind on specifics. Visualization and affirmations.
contingent	7000 cadres or 49 million fragments. One percent of the earth's population.
contradiction	To give opposing views or beliefs.
cord	Energetic connection between two people in order to communicate or draw energy. Specifically between their chakras.

cycle	A complete set of lifetimes from infant to old soul stages from the perspective of one role.
death	Seventh internal monad; facilitates much karma.
degree of essence	Level of knowing the Tao. There are seven degrees, ranging from limited to all-inclusive perception.
deva	Astral plane being that tends and assists oceans, minerals, plants, and animals. They gradually develop toward sentience.
ego	False personality. Dies with physical body.
energy	Action component of universe.
enlightenment	The experience of knowing the truth, love, and energy of the Tao.
entity	Your family of consciousness; oversoul; 800 to 1200 fragments. Comprised of several essences.
—fragment	A single member of an entity. Membership in an essence.
essence	Soul. Intermediary between the Tao and the fragment personality each lifetime. Comprised of a number of fragments. Several essences comprise an entity.
—twin	Soulmate. A fragment who parallels your lifetimes. An intense relationship with the fragment that understands you the most. You each reflect each other's overleaves and essence role.
—mate	Essence twin from a past cycle, a relationship of affinity.
exalted	Wide focus, visionary.

false personality	Behavior stemming from negative poles of overleaves, the chief feature, and imprinting.
frequency	Vibration rate of an essence or role.
gemstone	Minerals that intensify or reduce the effect of your overleaves when you wear them or are near them.
goal	Primary motivator each lifetime. Major overleaf.
God	Tao, Great Spirit, Atman, Supreme Being, All That Is.
Gurdjieff, G.	Armenian teacher who laid the foundations for the Michael teachings earlier in this century.
heart link	One with whom you have a special loving relationship resulting from many lifetimes of experience together.
identification	Loss of individuality without understanding. Taking on another's problems.
illusion	Maya, forgetfulness, belief in the physical plane appearance of things only.
imprinting	Conditioning, programming, hypnosis. Taking on another's way of seeing or doing things without conscious awareness.
insect	Third area of exploration for beings considering human form.
instinctive	Survival oriented reactions.
—center	Your memory banks of all past life and present life survival information.
—review	A look at recent past experience to help plan the next step.
integration	Putting together essence and personality for balance and harmony.

internal monad	There are seven. Rite of passage within a single lifetime that allows you to continue to the next level of growth. Includes birth, puberty, maturity, death.
karma	Universal law of consequences or balance; caused by interfering with or promoting another's free choice. Seen as positive or negative on the physical plane. Based on triadic processes.
ladder	See nontet.
love	Feeling or experience of oneness. First position of quadrant that gets ideas.
mammal	Sixth major area of exploration in devic form for beings considering sentience.
maya	Illusion, self deception, looking real but not so.
meditation	A form of spiritual exercise. Emptying the mind of all thought forms.
Michael	Causal plane reunited entity comprised of kings and warriors; non-physical author of this book.
mineral	First major area of exploration for a being coming to the planet. Includes all global experiences explored in devic form.
mode	Your primary method of doing things each lifetime; a major overleaf.
monad	A unit of life experience; must be experienced from both sides in order to complete the reincarnational cycle.
nontet	A group of nine, oriented to the success of a single goal.

octave	A stable group of eight made up of two quadrants. A complete cycle of learning that leads to the next level of growth.
order of casting	The position that you hold within your entity
ordinal	Narrowly focused; oriented toward immediacy and one-to-one interactions with others.
Ouspensky, P.D.	Student and essence twin of Gurdjieff. Put early versions of this teaching into writing.
overleaves	Specific traits and characteristics that make up personality each lifetime. Goal, mode, attitude, chief feature, centering, and body type.
pentangle	Unstable group of five. Usually dedicated to fulfillment of a spiritual task.
personality	Made up of overleaves and imprinting each lifetime; unique flavor or style of being.
—essence personality	Unique style of being, made up of role, cadence, casting number, entity membership, and experiences from accumulated lifetimes.
plane	Seven relative levels of experience created by the Tao for evolutionary purposes. Physical, Astral, Causal, Akashic, Mental, Messianic, Buddhaic.
—physical	Most solid, slow, forgetful of all planes offering the experience of separateness.
plant	Third area of exploration in devic form for a being considering human form.
pole	Extremes of overleaves, either positive or negative.
—positive	Essence oriented function of overleaf.

—negative   False personality function of overleaf.

power animal   Source of guidance and information. The sum total of all knowledge of one species of animal.

prosperity   Experience of abundance in health, spirituality, love, truth, etc.

quadrant   A stable group of four people, oriented toward fulfilling tasks.

reptile   Includes fish. Fourth major exploration area in devic form for beings considering sentience.

role   Primary beingness through which a fragment experiences all of life.

self-karma   Lessons that you give yourself that involve the extremes of an experience, such as rich-poor, happy-sad, healthy-sick. Also something that you either hate about yourself or are excessively vain about.

sentient   Ensouled; having intellectual part of intellectual center developed; having self-awareness.

septant   A group of seven people oriented toward visionary or special projects. An evolutionary growth pattern comprising seven steps. Leads to an octave.

service   A form of spiritual exercise that includes helping others.

sextant   A stable group of six people oriented toward the fulfillment of life tasks. Made up of two triads.

sexual   Combining male and female energies; can be physical or energetic as in the higher planes.

soul age	Development of perceptivity on a continuum from infant soul to old soul level.
—level	There are seven levels within each soul age. Each embodies a special set of lessons and experiences.
spirit	Essence and personality are contained within it.
spiritual	Awake and aware; state of remembering the Tao.
spirit guide	Assistant, healer, guide from a non-physical plane. Often a member of your own entity.
support circle	Twelve specific positions of assistance filled by family and friends.
Tao	All That Is, Great Spirit, God, Atman.
task companion	A special person chosen at the beginning of the cycle with whom you do life tasks.
teaching	A spiritual path that has the potential to guide you closer to the Tao.
triad	A group of three; also a process and unit of learning. Creates intensity and karma; sudivision of a septant; Law of Three.
truth	What is. Also relative to you, your perspective in the Tao.
universe	A sequence, complete in its entirety, of all the stars, planets, structures and beings of one of the Tao's creations. There are an infinite number of universes.
—parallel	A new universe created for every significant possible outcome of a given event.
wakefulness	Knowing or remembering the Tao; prerequisite to spiritual growth.

walk-in   One essence agrees to take over the body that
                          another essence is leaving without death
                          ensuing. Overleaves and role may completely
                          change. See Appendix B.

OVERLEAF CHART

	EXPRESSION		INSPIRATION		ACTION		ASSIMILATION
	Ordinal	Exalted	Ordinal	Exalted	Ordinal	Exalted	Neutral
ROLE	+Creation ARTISAN -Self-Deception	+Dissemination SAGE -Verbosity	+Service SERVER -Bondage	+Compassion PRIEST -Zeal	+Persuasion WARRIOR -Coercion	+Mastery KING -Tyranny	+Knowledge SCHOLAR -Theory
GOAL	+Sophistication DISCRIMINATION -Rejection	+Agape ACCEPTANCE -Ingratiation	+Simplicity RE-EVALUATION -Withdrawal	+Evolution GROWTH -Confusion	+Devotion SUBMISSION -Exploited	+Leadership DOMINANCE -Dictatorship	+Free-Flowing STAGNATION -Inertia
ATTITUDE	+Investigation SKEPTIC -Suspicion	+Coalescence IDEALIST -Naivety	+Tranquility STOIC -Resignation	+Verification SPIRITUALIST -Beliefs	+Contradiction CYNIC -Denigration	+Objective REALIST -Subjective	+Practical PRAGMATIST -Dogmatic
CHIEF FEATURE	+Sacrifice SELF-DESTRUCTION -Suicidal	+Appetite GREED -Voracity	+Humility SELF-DEPRECATION -Abasement	+Pride ARROGANCE -Vanity	+Selflessness MARTYRDOM -Victimization	+Daring IMPATIENCE -Intolerance	+Determination STUBBORNESS -Obstinacy
MODE	+Deliberation CAUTION -Phobia	+Authority POWER -Oppression	+Restraint RESERVED -Inhibition	+Self-Actualization PASSION -Identification	+Persistance PERSEVERANCE -Unchanging	+Dynamism AGGRESSION -Belligerence	+Clarity OBSERVATION -Surveillance
CENTER	+Insight INTELLECTUAL -Reasoning	+Truth HIGHER INTELLECTUAL -Telepathy	+Perception EMOTIONAL -Sentimentality	+Love HIGHER EMOTIONAL -Intuition	+Productive MOVING -Frenetic	+Integration HIGHER MOVING -Desire	+Aware INSTINCTIVE -Mechanical
BODY TYPES	+Grandeur JUPITER -Overwhelming	+Agile MERCURY -Nervous	+Luminous LUNAR -Pallid	+Rugged SATURN -Gaunt	+Voluptuous VENUS -Sloppy	+Wiry MARS -Impulsive	+Radiant SOLAR -Ethereal

New Michael Books

Available through your bookseller or from Pivot Press.

The Michael Handbook
formerly *Essence and Personality: The Michael Handbook*
by Jose Stevens, PhD, and Simon Warwick-Smith
This 350-page reference book entertains you while you learn. It covers the grand scheme, soul ages and levels, roles, overleaves, centering, body types, the planetary shift and more—in depth. Also, a guide to help you find your overleaves.
$12.95, Warwick Press.

Earth to Tao: Michael's Guide to Healing &Spiritual Awakening
by Jose Stevens, PhD
This guide continues where *Tao to Earth* leaves off. It covers spiritual practices, channeling, working with guides and power animals, healing methods and more.
$11.95, Affinity Press.

The Personality Puzzle: Solving the Mystery of Who You Are
by Jose Stevens, PhD, and J.P. Van Hulle
A questionnaire and a complete manual to discover your over-leaves, as well as those of your family and friends. Comprehensive lists of famous people by role and life histories of famous individuals such as Shakespeare, Anwar Sadat, Joan of Arc, and Galileo, with their overleaves. A must.

The World According to Michael: An Old Soul's Guide to the Universe
by Joya Pope
A delightful and succinct "sage's" romp through the basics of the Michael teaching—lots of information in a small, fun-to-read package. For friends who are curious, it's a starter book of choice.
$8.95, Sage Publications.

Michael: the Basic Teachings
by J. P. Van Hulle and M.C. Clark
Just what the title says, an overview of the basics; overleaves, relationships, etc.
$12.75, Affinity Press.

Michael's Gemstone Dictionary
by Judithann David, channeled by J.P. Van Hulle
Energies and uses of gems and minerals according to the Michael teaching. Hundreds of precious and semi-precious gems for memory, money, imagination, well being, etc. Find out why you're attracted to your favorite stones. Fascinating and useful.
$8.95, Affinity Press and the Michael Educational Foundation.

The Michael Game
by the Michael Digest Group
This collection of articles explores varying topics such as "Whales and Dolphins," and "101 Questions to Ask a Channel."
$8.95, Warwick Press.

By Jose and Lena Stevens

Secrets of Shamanism: Tapping the Spirit Power Within You
$3.95, Avon Books.

Resources

Reprints of the Essence and Personality Questionnaire from *The Personality Puzzle* can be obtained from Pivot Press, tel. (415) 845-5725 or The Michael Educational Foundation, tel. (415) 254-4730. $2.50 for one, $50 for 25, $175 for 100. Call or write for larger orders. Postage $0.50 for one, $1.00 for 50, $2.00 for 100. In California please add 6.5% tax.

Books may be ordered from Pivot Press, P.O. Box 5314, Berkeley, California, 94705. Add $1.00 per book for postage and handling. In California, please add 6.5% tax.

About the Author

Jose Stevens, PhD, is a writer and licensed psychotherapist in Berkeley, California. He obtained his masters degree at the University of California at Berkeley and his doctorate at the California Institute of Integral Studies in San Francisco. Currently he teaches in the Department for the Study of Consciousness at John F. Kennedy University and lectures widely on Essence and Personality, shamanism, and prosperity. He is the founder of Essence Psychology, a non-pathological perspective on personality. For information regarding workshops, consultation, channeling, and intuition trainings, write to him at P.O. Box 5314, Berkeley, California, 94705.

Keep In Contact
with
The Michael Community
Subscribe NOW to
THE MICHAEL CONNECTION

- Featuring all the latest information about the Michael Teaching
- Focusing each issue on the basics of the Michael Teaching
- Resource directory for Michael teachers in the Bay Area
- Periodic reports from the Michael Community nationwide
- Articles of general interest to Michael students and all others in the metaphysical community
- Pictures, poetry, gossip, personal ads and much, much more...

The Michael Connection exists to support those who wish to use
The Michael Teaching to become more effective players
in the game of life.

Join us and connect.

**Fill this out and mail to: The Michael Connection
P.O. Box 1873, Orinda, CA 94563**

- -

☐ **Subscription.** Mail the next 4 issues (1 year) to me at the address below for only $15. (Outside U.S. $20.00)

☐ **Back Issues.** Send me back issues featuring the following roles (Circle each you wish to have sent):
Warriors   Artisans   Servers   Scholars   Sages   Priests   Kings
I have enclosed $4 for each issue.*

☐ Send me information about other available back issues.

☐ **Advertising.** I'd love to enjoy patronage from the Michael community.

Name:_____ Phone:_____

Address: _____

City/State/Zip: _____

Please make checks payable to: The Michael Connection

*If an issue is sold out, a photocopy of the issue will be substituted. Please let us know if you prefer NOT to receive a photocopy